P9-DIY-734

ADVANCED
CONVERSATIONAL
SPANISH

THE LIVING LANGUAGE™ SERIES
BASIC COURSES ON CASSETTE

- *Spanish
- *French
- *German
- *Italian
- *Japanese
- *Portuguese (Continental)
- Portuguese (South American)
- Advanced Spanish
- Advanced French
- Children's Spanish
- Children's French
- Russian
- Hebrew
- English for Native Spanish Speakers
- English for Native French Speakers
- English for Native Italian Speakers
- English for Native German Speakers
- English for Native Chinese Speakers

*Also available on Compact Disc

LIVING LANGUAGE PLUS®

- Spanish
- French
- German
- Italian

LIVING LANGUAGE TRAVELTALK™

- Spanish
- French
- German
- Italian
- Russian

Living Language™

ADVANCED CONVERSATIONAL SPANISH

By Robert E. Hammarstrand, Ph.D.,

ASSISTANT PROFESSOR OF EDUCATION,
HUNTER COLLEGE
BASED ON THE METHOD DEVISED BY RALPH R.
WEIMAN, FORMER CHIEF OF LANGUAGE
SECTION, U.S. WAR DEPARTMENT

SPECIALLY PREPARED FOR USE WITH THE
LIVING LANGUAGE COURSE® IN ADVANCED
SPANISH

Crown Publishers, Inc., New York

This work was previously published under the title
Living Language Conversation Manual, Spanish Advanced Course.

Copyright © 1968, 1985 by Crown Publishers, Inc.

All rights reserved. No part of this book may be reproduced or
transmitted in any form or by any means, electronic or mechanical,
including photocopying, recording, or by any information storage and
retrievel system, without permission in writing from the publisher.

THE LIVING LANGUAGE COURSE is a registered trademark, and
CROWN, and LIVING LANGAGE and colophon are trademarks of
Crown Publishers, Inc., 201 East 50th Street, New York, N.Y. 10022.

Library of Congress Catalog Card Number: R68-3057

ISBN 0-517-55885-8

1985 Updated Edition

Manufactured in the United States of America

CONTENTS

vi

INTRODUCTION

Living Language™ Advanced Conversational Spanish is designed for students who have completed the 40 lessons of the basic *Living Spanish* course or for anyone with a sufficient grasp of the language who is ready for more sophisticated Spanish conversation and grammar. Although this book is intended for use with the *Advanced Living Spanish* cassette or record, it may be used alone as a textbook.

The material in the *Advanced Living Spanish* course is substantially more complex than that in the first 40 lessons of the basic *Living Spanish* course. These 20 units incorporate more advanced speech patterns and more intricate grammatical detail. Each unit is organized as follows:

Text. The recorded text (in boldface type) consists of dialogues between an American couple visiting Spain and their friends and business acquaintances in various situations travelers are likely to encounter in Spain. Latin American equivalents are given when necessary. The English translation appears directly beneath each line of Spanish. Spanish words in italics indicate dialogue that is not included in the recording.

Notes. The small circles in the body of the text refer to the notes which immediately follow the text. The notes contain grammatical details and comments on matter of general interest.

Grammatical Items for Special Study. This section treats carefully selected grammatical constructions in the lesson in thorough detail and supplements and enlarges upon the material already presented in the earlier lessons. All students should read over this material several times, and those who care to go more thoroughly into the language would do well to study the grammar intensively.

Drills and Exercises. The exercises furnish an overall review of the material in each unit. The answer key is in the back of the book. You will find it very useful to work through the complete advanced course and then do the translation sentences once again. This translation review will serve as a culmination of all your studies. When you have mastered the translation sentences, you have mastered the course.

You, will, of course, work through the course as fast or as slowly as is convenient, but we urge that you do a little work every day, if only for ten minutes.

Students will find it helpful to make up little dialogues with themselves, to keep a notebook of vocabulary words and phrases for frequent review, and to speak, read, and listen to Spanish as often as they can. Through this constant repetition and practice, the Spanish language—with all the pleasure and utility it affords—will become yours.

Course Material

The material of the *Advanced Living Spanish* course consists of the following:

1. *One hour-long cassette or 2 long-playing records*. The label on each face indicates clearly which lessons are contained on that side.

2. *Advanced Conversational Spanish book*. This book is designed for use with the recorded lesson, or it can be used alone. It contains the following sections:
   Advanced Spanish Vocabulary and Grammar
   Summary of Spanish Grammar
   Answers to the Drills and Exercises and Quizzes

3. *Spanish-English/English-Spanish Common Usage Dictionary.* A special kind of dictionary that gives literal translations of more than 20,000 Spanish words, plus idiomatic phrases and sentences to illustrate the everyday use of the more important vocabulary. One thousand essential words are highlighted for quick reference. The *Common Usage Dictionary* doubles as a phrasebook.

How to Use Advanced Conversational Spanish with the Living Language™ Cassette

The lessons, continuing from the basic *Living Spanish* course, are numbered from 41 through 60.

1. Look at page 1. Note the words in boldface type. These are the words you will hear on the cassette.

2. Now read Lesson 41. (The ▭ ▭ symbols indicate the beginning of the recorded material. In some advanced lessons, information and instructions precede the recording.) Note the points to look for when you play the cassette. Look at the first sentence, **Diga. ¿Quien habla?** and be prepared to follow the voice on the cassette.

3. Play the cassette, listen carefully, and watch for the points mentioned in Lesson 41. Then rewind, play the dialogue again, and this time say the words aloud. Keep repeating until you are sure you know the lesson. The more times you listen and repeat, the longer you will remember the material.

4. Now go on to the next lesson. It's always good to quickly review the previous lesson before starting a new one.

5. At the end of each section there are Grammatical Items for Special Study, Drills and Exercises, and a Quiz. Do these exercises faithfully, checking your answers at the back of the book, and if you make any mistakes, study the section again.

Living Language™

ADVANCED
CONVERSATIONAL
SPANISH

LESSON 41

LA CITA EN UN CAFE
APPOINTMENT AT A CAFE

A. *Se citan*   They make the date

1. Miguel: **Diga.° ¿Quién habla?**

   Hello. Who's speaking?

2. Carlos: **Soy Carlos Andrade, de México.**

   This is Carlos Andrade, from Mexico.

3. Miguel: **¡Qué gusto!° ¿Dónde está usted ahora?**

   What a pleasure! Where are you now?

4. Carlos: **En el Hotel Plaza. Acabamos de llegar,° la señora y yo.°**

   At the Hotel Plaza. My wife and I have just arrived.

5. Miguel: **¡Tengo ganas de verles lo más pronto posible! ¿Podemos vernos° esta tarde? ¿A las dos?**

   I'd like to see you as soon as possible! Can we meet this afternoon? At two o'clock?

6. Carlos: **Muy bien. ¿Dónde podemos encontrarnos?**

   Fine. Where can we meet?

7. Miguel: **En el Café Gijón,° en La Castellana cerca de Cibeles. Tome un taxi.**

   At the Café Gijón, on the Castellana near Cybele's Square. Take a taxi.

8. Carlos: **De acuerdo.°** ¿**Será posible encontrar una mesa a esa hora?**
All right. Can we get a table at that hour?

9. Miguel: **Sin duda, hombre. Hasta luego, entonces.**
No doubt about it. (Of course.) See you in a little while, then.

10. Carlos: **Entendido. Hasta luego.°**
Right. So long.

B. *Se encuentran en el café*   They meet at the café

11. Miguel: **Bien, Carlos, por fin está usted aquí. ¡Bienvenido a Madrid!**
Well, Charles, at last you're here. Welcome to Madrid!

12. Carlos: **Gracias, Miguel. Juana y yo estamos tan contentos de estar en Madrid.**
Thank you, Michael. Jane and I are so happy to be in Madrid.

13. Miguel: ¿**Prefiere sentarse° aquí adentro o afuera, al aire libre?**
Do you prefer to sit in here or outside?

14. Carlos: ¡**Al aire libre, claro!**
Outdoors, of course!

15. Miguel: ¡**Ah! Allí hay una mesa libre. Pero . . . ¿dónde está Juana?**
Ah! There's an empty table. But . . . Where's Jane?

16. Carlos: **Ella se quedó en el hotel para deshacer las maletas. Además, ha sido un viaje largo y cansado.**
She stayed at the hotel to unpack. Besides, it was a long and tiring trip.

17. Camarero: **¿Qué quieren tomar,° señores?**
    Waiter: What will you have, gentlemen?

18. Miguel: **Una limonada, por favor. ¡Hace tanto calor!°**
    A lemonade, please. It's so hot!

19. Carlos: **Y para mí, una cerveza.**
    And for me, a beer.

20. Camarero: **En seguida,° señores.**
    Right away, gentlemen.

21. Carlos: **¡Qué manera más agradable de empezar la estancia en Madrid! ¡Ah! Aquí está el camarero con las bebidas. ¡Salud!°**
    What a pleasant way to begin my stay in Madrid! Ah! Here's the waiter with our drinks. To your health!

22. Miguel: **¡Salud! ¡Y que ustedes lo pasen bien° en Madrid!**
    To yours! And I hope you have a good time in Madrid!

23. Carlos: **Se está° muy bien aquí. Tengo ganas de° quedarme aquí todo el día.°**
    It's really nice here. I feel like staying here all day.

24. Miguel: **Uno puede quedarse en el café toda la tarde, si quiere.**
    You can stay at the café all afternoon, if you wish.

25. Carlos: **¿Y jamás hacen marcharse a° los clientes?**
    Don't they ever ask the customers to leave?

26. Miguel: **¡Jamás! Y, si quiere, puede leer el periódico, escribir cartas, charlar con los amigos, o solamente observar a la gente que pasa.**

Never! And, if you wish, you can read the newspaper, write letters, chat with friends, or simply look at the people passing by.

27. Carlos: **En la vida de negocios, uno pierde fácilmente el arte de descansar.**

In a workaday world, one easily loses the art of relaxing.

28. Miguel: *Espero que hayan hecho° buen viaje. Ustedes vinieron en el Satrústegui ¿Verdad?*

I hope you had a good trip. You came on the Satrústegui, didn't you?

29. Carlos: *Sí. La travesía fue excelente. Los compañeros de viaje eran todos muy simpáticos y la vida a bordo° fue muy divertida.*

Yes. The crossing was excellent. Our traveling companions were very congenial and life on board was very amusing.

30. Miguel: *Bueno, si no tienen planes para mañana, tal vez podríamos pasear° un poco.*

Well, if you have no plans for tomorrow, perhaps we can take a little walk.

31. Carlos: *¡Qué buena idea!° Estoy seguro que Juana querrá acompañarnos. Gracias, amigo.*

What a good idea! I'm sure Jane will want to come with us. Thank you, my friend.

32. Miguel: *Camarero, la cuenta, por favor. Voy a pagar la cuenta, dejar una propina, y nos marchamos. . . . No, no, Carlos. Yo le invito para celebrar su llegada a Madrid.*

Waiter! The check, please. I'm going to pay the bill, leave a tip, and we'll go. . . . No, no, Charles. I'm treating you to celebrate your arrival in Madrid.

NOTES

1. *Diga.:* In Spain, *Diga* or *Dígame* (imperative form of *decir*) is used as the equivalent of the English "hello" in answering the telephone. There is considerable variety in other countries of the Spanish-speaking world: *Bueno* in Mexico, *A ver* in Colombia, *Oigo* or *¿Qué hay?* in Cuba, *Holá* in Argentina, and *Aló* in most other countries.

3. *¡Qué gusto!:* Note the use of *qué* before nouns to express "What a . . ." in exclamations.

4. *acabamos de llegar:* Note use of *acabar de* plus infinitive to express "to have just."
   la señora y yo: Note that in Spain the article is preferred to the possessive adjective. But in most Latin-American countries the possessive form is more commonly used: *mi señora (or mi mujer) y yo.*

5. *vernos:* Note the use of the reflexive pronoun to indicate mutual action: "to see each other" or "to meet one another." Compare *encontrarnos,* used later.

7. *Café Gijón:* Popular rendezvous for writers, directors, and actors on the long and beautiful, tree-lined boulevard, *Avenida de la Castellana,* near the lovely fountain and statue of *Cybele* in front of Madrid's main post office, *El Correo.*

8. *De acuerdo:* Agreed. O.K. *Muy bien, bien, entendido, perfectamente,* are all frequently used with this meaning of general assent or agreement in Spanish.

10. *Hasta luego:* Until then. *Hasta entonces, Hasta la vista, Hasta pronto, Hasta más ver,* are all frequently employed in the sense of "So long."

13. *sentarse:* to sit down. Note the use of the reflexive pronoun, here attached to the complementary infinitive, and in sentence 16 placed before the form of the main verb in *Ella se quedó.*

17. *tomar:* to take; used in the sense of "to eat" or "to drink."

18. *¡Hace tanto calor!:* The verb *hacer* is generally used with expressions concerning weather conditions. Compare *hace frío* (it's cold); *hace fresco* (it's cool); *hace buen tiempo* (the weather is fine); *hace viento* (it's windy).

20. *En seguida:* Right away. Equivalents: *inmediatamente, ahora mismo.*

21. *¡Salud!:* lit., "health." In toasting one another, Spanish-speaking people generally exchange this single word.

22. *Y que ustedes lo pasen bien:* In expressing a wish or desire, the verb "to hope" *(esperar)* is frequently omitted and the statement begins with the introductory *que*, with the following verb in the subjunctive. Equivalent to the English "May you have a good time." Compare *¡Que vivan mil años!* ("May they live a thousand years!") and *¡Que siga usted bien!* ("May you continue in good health!").

23. *se está:* Note the use of the reflexive here for the impersonal "one is."
    tengo ganas de; me gustaría: I feel like, I'd like to.
    todo el día: all day. Note the use of the article in such expressions as *todo el año* (all year), *toda la tarde* (all afternoon), *toda la semana* (all week), *todo el verano* (all summer), etc.

25. *hacen marcharse a:* lit., "make go away." Note the use of the personal *a* before *clientes.* Compare *observar a la gente* in sentence 26.

28. *hayan hecho:* Note the use of the subjunctive after the verb of emotion, "to hope."

29. *la vida a bordo:* shipboard life.

30. *pasear:* to stroll, to walk around. This verb can also be used with *pasear en coche* (to drive around in a car), *pasear a caballo* (to ride around on horseback).

31. *¡Qué buena idea!:* "What a good idea." See Note 3, above.

GRAMMATICAL ITEMS FOR SPECIAL STUDY

I. *acabar de:* to have just

Study:

	acabar	de	Infinitive
1.	Acabo	de	llegar
2. Juan	acaba	de	llamar

1. *I have just arrived.*
2. *John has just called.*

II. *tener ganas de:* to feel like

Study:

	tener	ganas	de	Infinitive	Comple-ment
1.	Tengo	ganas	de	comer	helado.
2. María	tiene	ganas	de	salir.	
3. Los niños	tendrán	ganas	de	acostarse.	

1. *I feel like eating ice cream.*
2. *Mary feels like leaving.*
3. *The children will feel like going to bed.*

Note: For forms of *tener,* see Summary of Grammar.

III. *poder* + infinitive + complement: to be able to

Study:

A.	poder	Infinitive	Complement
1.	Puedo	hacer	el trabajo.
2. Juan	puede	estudiar	la lección mañana.
3.	Podemos	pasar	las vacaciones allí.
4. Ellos	pueden	ver	a María la semana que viene.

1. *I can do the work.*
2. *John can study the lesson tomorrow.*
3. *We can spend our vacation there.*
4. *They can see Mary next week.*

Note: The *a* is used before nouns or pronouns referring to persons

Ex: He visto a papá.
   I have seen my father.

B. Study:

	poder	Infinitive	Object Pronoun
1. El	podía	hacerlo.	
2. Ellos	podrán	comerlo.	
3. Ella	puede	mandarlo.	

1. *He was able to do it.*
2. *They will be able to eat it.*
3. *She can send it.*

Note:

1. The object pronoun may precede the form of *poder*.
   1. *Lo podía hacer.*
   2. *Ellos lo podrán comer.*
   3. *Ella lo puede mandar.*

2. *Poder* generally implies physical ability to do something. When knowledge or learned skills are implied, *saber* is generally used.

   Compare:

   Puedo leerlo. ("I can read it" in the sense of having ability to read it; i.e., in spite of the darkness, fog, bad script, etc.)

   Sé leerlo. ("I can read it" in the sense of knowing how to, as a language, a code, etc.)

IV. Adjective + *de*

estar	Adjective	+ de	Infinitive and + Object
1. Estoy	contenta	de	saberlo.
2. Estaba	sorprendido	de	verme.
3. Estarán	encantados	de	recibirnos.

1. *I'm happy to know it.*

2. *He was surprised to see me.*

3. *They will be happy to receive us.*

Note:

1. Adjectives agree with preceding subject.

   María está conten*ta*.   *Mary is happy.*

2. Notice that subject pronouns are generally understood.

DRILLS AND EXERCISES

I. Substitute each of the words or expressions in parentheses for the italicized word(s) or expressions in the model sentence. Write each new sentence and say it aloud.

A. Juan acaba de *comer*. (estudiar, entrar, salir, acostarse, lavarse)

B. Los hombres acaban de *llegar*. (verlo, escucharlo, hablar, telefonear)

C. Tengo ganas de ir *al cine*. (al concierto, a la biblioteca, al museo, al parque, al banco)

D. Tienen ganas de *bailar*. (cantar, leer, mirar la televisión, escuchar la radio, ir al cine)

E. Puedo *hacer*lo. (comer, beber, comprar, estudiar, ganar, aprender)

F. *Los niños* están contentos de estar aquí. (Los padres, Los hombres, Juan y José, Los profesores, María y Rafael)

II. Convert these sentences to the plural. Write the
    complete sentence, and translate. Answers will be
    found at the back of the book.

   1. Acabo de llegar.

   2. El niño tiene ganas de comer.

   3. Usted puede hacerlo.

   4. La muchacha está contenta de verlos.

   5. Lo puedo hacer ahora.

III. Translate the following sentences into Spanish,
     then say them aloud. Answers will be found at
     the back of the book.

   1. He has just come in.

   2. She has just eaten.

   3. We feel like going to the movies.

   4. I feel like dancing.

   5. I can do it now.

   6. We can see him tomorrow.

   7. They'll be able to go there.

   8. I am happy to see you.

   9. We are surprised to hear it.

   10. They are pleased to know it.

QUIZ

From among the three choices given, choose the one
which correctly renders the English given at the
beginning of each sentence. Write the complete sentence, and translate.

1. *(Who)* _____ habla?
   - (a) Qué
   - (b) Cuál
   - (c) Quién

2. *(What a)* ¡ _____ gusto!
   - (a) Qué
   - (b) Cuál
   - (c) Cuál un

3. *(way)* ¡Qué _____ más agradable de empezar el día!
   - (a) vía
   - (b) manera
   - (c) camino

4. *(had)* Espero que hayan _____ buen viaje.
   - (a) habido
   - (b) tenido
   - (c) hecho

5. *(at)* Vimos a Miguel _____ el Café Gijón.
   - (a) al
   - (b) en
   - (c) entre

6. *(all)* Estábamos aquí _____ el día.
   - (a) todos
   - (b) toda
   - (c) todo

7. *(There are)* _____ muchos monumentos en Madrid.
   - (a) Están
   - (b) Allí son
   - (c) Hay

8. *(sit down)* ¿Quiere usted _____ aquí?
   (a) sentarte
   (b) sentarse
   (b) sentar

9. *(so much)* El señor tiene _____ dinero.
   (a) tan
   (b) tantas
   (c) tanto

10. *(arrived)* Acabamos de _____.
    (a) llegado
    (b) llegar
    (c) llegamos

Answers at back of book.

LESSON 42
EL KIOSCO DE REVISTAS°
THE NEWSSTAND

1. Carlos: *(Al vendedor de periódicos)* **Acabamos de llegar de México, señor, y no conozco° los periódicos de España. Podría usted ayudarme?**
   (To the news vendor) We've just arrived from Mexico, sir, and I'm not familiar with Spanish newspapers. Could you help me?

2. Vendedor: **Con mucho gusto, señor. Para información política y noticias en general, tenemos varios periódicos diarios en Madrid. Luego, hay publicaciones literarias también ... Indice,° Insula,° La estafeta literaria.°**
   With pleasure, sir. For politics and general news, we have several daily papers in Madrid. Then, there are also literary publications... *Indice, Insula, The Literary Post...*

3. Juana: **Esas son todas literarias, ¿verdad? ¿Hay una revista dedicada al teatro?**
Those are all literary, aren't they? Is there a magazine devoted to the theatre?

4. Vendedor: **Sí, señora. Hay una muy buena que se llama** *Primer acto.*
Yes, madam. There's a very good one called *First Act.*

5. Carlos: **Si no me equivoco, veo aquí unos siete u ocho° diarios.**
If I'm not mistaken, I see about seven or eight dailies here.

6. Juana: **¿Pero cuál de ellos es el mejor, el más leído? Si uno quiere llegar a conocer un país...**
But which one is best, the most read? If one wants to get to know a country...

7. Vendedor: **En cuanto a eso, señora, no es difícil decírselo.° Es el** *A B C,°* **sin duda alguna. Tenga, ¿quiere usted mirarlo?**
As to that, madam, it's not difficult to tell you. It's the *A B C,* without any doubt. Here, would you like to look at it?

8. Carlos: **Parece una revista. Con este grabado en la portada. Y luego un artículo sobre la novela del siglo diecinueve. No veo nada de política, ni de noticias en general.**
It looks like a magazine. With this picture on the cover. And then an article on the nineteenth-century novel. I don't see anything about politics or news in general.

9. Vendedor: **Pero, señor, allí dentro hay todo lo que le hace falta° en un periódico; noticias, teatro, programas de radio y televisión, modas, noticias de sociedad, deportes, hasta comentan las carreras de caballos y los toros.**

   But, sir, there is everything there that you need in a newspaper: news, theatre, radio and television programs, fashions, society news, sports . . . they even comment on horse racing and bullfights.

10. Carlos: **De todas formas, parece muy serio . . . casi no hay fotos. ¿No tendría usted° algún otro con más fotos, y un aspecto menos serio?**

    Still, it looks very serious . . . there are almost no pictures. Wouldn't you have another with more pictures, and a less forbidding appearance?

11. Vendedor: **Bueno, entonces lleve usted *Informaciones* o *Ya*.**

    Well, take *Information* or *Ya* then.

12. Carlos: **Bien, voy a empezar con *Informaciones*.**

    O.K. I will start with *Information*.

13. Juana: **Veo que usted tiene revistas de todo el mundo—francesas, italianas, alemanas, inglesas, americanas, ¡y hasta rusas!**

    I see you have magazines from all over the world—French, Italian, German, English, American, and even Russian!

14. Vendedor: **Sí, señora, y de todas clases. Hay revistas semanales y mensuales y hasta hay otras quincenales.**

    Yes, madam, and of all kinds. There are weekly and monthly magazines, and there are even some that come out every other week.

15. Juana: **Aquellas son de interés general, ¿verdad?** *Blanco y Negro* **y** *Gaceta Ilustrada.*
Those over there are of general interest, aren't they? *Blanco y Negro* and *Gaceta Ilustrada.*

16. Vendedor: **Eso es,°** **señora, y aquí en este lado tenemos todas las que pueden interesar a una mujer: revistas de modas, de cocina, y** *Hola* **y** *Arte y Hogar.* **. . .**
That's right, madam, and on this side we have all those that could interest a woman—fashion magazines, cooking, and *Hola* and *Arte y Hogar.* . . .

17. Juana: **¿Me permite hojear°** **un poco este número de** *Hola?*
May I look through this issue of *Hola* for a moment?

18. Vendedor: **Por supuesto, señora. Usted puede ver aquí en el sumario que hay secciones dedicadas a los libros, discos, televisión . . . y además, comentarios sobre el hogar, el jardín, la cocina, los niños, la belleza, la salud . . .**
Of course, madam. You see here in the table of contents, there are sections on books, records, television . . . and also comments on home-making, gardening, cooking, children, beauty, health . . .

19. Carlos: **¡Qué cansado!°**
What a bore!

20. Juana: **Cállate, querido, porque tú no entiendes nada de eso. Cuando yo haya terminado°** **de leerla, te daré todos los crucigramas.°**

Be quiet, dear, because you know nothing about it. When I finish reading it, I'll give you all the crossword puzzles.

21. Vendedor: **¿Me permiten recomendarles también esta pequeña revista, *La Semana en Madrid*? Les da información sobre todos los espectáculos.**
May I also recommend this little magazine, *La Semana en Madrid*? It gives you information about all the shows.

22. Carlos: **Es exactamente lo que nos hace falta, señor.** *¿Tendría usted también una guía urbana de Madrid que indique los monumentos y sitios de interés turístico?*
It's exactly what we need, sir. Would you also have a map of the city with all the monuments and places of interest marked?

23. Vendedor: *Claro. Esta° es muy buena.*
Of course. This one is very good.

24. Juana: *Tenemos una guía de toda España, pero nos hace falta un librito fácil de llevar.*
We have a guidebook of all of Spain, but what we need is a small book that will be easy to carry around.

25. Vendedor: *Este librito debe ser exactamente lo que quieren.*
This little book should be exactly what you want.

26. Carlos: *Usted ha sido tan amable, señor. ¿Podría decirnos si hay una tienda cerca de aquí donde vendan discos y cintas magnetofónicas?*
You have been so kind, sir. Could you tell us if there's a store near here where they sell records and tapes?

27. Vendedor: *Hay una a cuatro pasos de aquí, en la esquina de la calle. Adiós, señores, que les vaya bien.*
There's one very nearby, at the corner of the street. Good-bye, all the best.

NOTES

Title. *kiosco de revistas:* newsstand. There are *kioscos* on street corners in Madrid where one can buy newspapers, magazines, maps, guidebooks, etc.

1. *no conozco:* I don't know, in the sense "not to be familiar with" from *conocer.* See also sentence 6.

2. *Indice, Insula, La Estafeta Literaria:* literary magazines which include reviews of films, theater, art, television, as well as articles on political and economic topics.

5. *siete u ocho:* Note that *o* ("or") changes to *u* before a word beginning with *o.*

7. *decírselo:* Notice that "it" is expressed in Spanish even though it is frequently omitted in similar English expressions.
A B C: The best of Madrid's newspapers, which has the format of a magazine. The cover always has a large photograph or watercolor. The first article is usually a full-page discussion of some literary or cultural topic.

9. *lo que le hace falta:* from *hacer falta,* to be lacking (to someone). Compare *Me hace falta un libro:* I need a book. *Nos hace falta más dinero:* We need more money.

10. *no tendría usted:* The conditional is frequently used in polite expressions. See sentences 23, 27.

16. *Eso es.*: That's it. That's right. Frequently used to express agreement.

17. *hojear:* from *hoja* (leaf), lit., to "leaf through" or "glance over" the pages.

19. *¡Qué cansado!:* How tiresome! Note that *Qué* is used before adjectives to give the idea of the English "how" in an exclamation. *¡Qué bonito!* (How pretty!) *¡Qué difícil!* (How difficult!)

20. *Cuando yo haya terminado:* Note the use of the subjunctive following "when" referring to a future and indefinite time.
    los crucigramas: Note that it is <u>el crucigrama</u>, masculine. A number of words that end in *a* are masculine in Spanish. Compare *el programa, el dilema.* These words derive from Greek and retain the masculine of the original.

23. *Esta:* Note that there is no written accent on the capital letter.

GRAMMATICAL ITEMS FOR SPECIAL STUDY

I. *conocer:* to know, to be acquainted (familiar) with something or someone; to meet (a person)

saber: to know as a fact

Study:

conocer

1. Conozco a los señores Hernández.

2. No conocemos el norte de España.

3. Ellos conocen bien el sistema.

4. Conocí a María err Francia.

1. *I know Mr. and Mrs. Hernandez.*

2. *We do not know (are not familiar with) the north of Spain.*

3. *They know the system very well.*

4. *I met Mary in France. (i.e., we met for the first time, became acquainted)*

saber

1. Sé que están aquí los señores Hernández.

2. Todos sabemos la verdad.

3. Ella lo sabrá mañana.

1. *I know that Mr. and Mrs. Hernandez are here.*

2. *We all know the truth.*

3. *She will know it (i.e., some fact) tomorrow.*

II. **hay:** there is, there are

Study:

1. Hay muchos libros sobre la mesa.

2. Habrá un desfile mañana.

3. Había muchos amigos allí.

1. *There are many books on the table.*

2. *There will be a parade tomorrow.*

3. *There were many friends there.*

III. **¿Qué?:** What? **¿Cuál?:** Which? **¿Quién(es)?:** Who?

Study:

1. ¿Qué sabe usted de la familia?

2. ¿Cuál de los niños es amigo tuyo?

   3. ¿Quién es aquel niño?

   1. *What do you know about the family?*

   2. *Which of the children is a friend of yours?*

   3. *Who is that child?*

IV. *hacer falta:* to need (to lack)

Study:

Indirect object pronoun	hacer falta	Subject
1. Me	hace falta	más dinero.
2. Te	hacen falta	tres pesetas.
3. Le	hará falta	(a él) mucha experiencia.

1. *I need more money.*
2. *You need three pesetas.*
3. *He will need a lot of experience.*

DRILLS AND EXERCISES

I. Substitute each of the words or expressions in the parentheses for the italicized words or expressions in the model sentence. Write each new sentence and say it aloud.

   A. Acaba de conocer *a María.* (a tu hermano, a los señores La Torre, a la señora de Aguirre, a la señorita Domenech, a los amigos de mi padre)

   B. *Ellos* conocen a Juan. (María y yo, yo, Pepe, Francisco y Miguel, todo el mundo)

   C. Ellos deben saber *el número.* (la dirección, la verdad, el precio, la fecha, el nombre, la palabra)

   D. Hay *muchas personas* en el hotel. (una peluquería, varios salones, un comedor, algunas reuniones, un conserje)

E. Me hace(n) falta *un libro*. (unos discos, más información, un corte de pelo, más tiempo, los nombres)

F. ¿Quién(es) es (son) *aquel muchacho?* (tu amigo, María Velarde, estos señores, el professor, los alumnos)

II. Convert these sentences to the plural. Write the complete sentence and translate. Answers will be found at the back of the book.

1. El sabe bailar.

2. Usted conocerá a los señores Perez.

3. Hay una clase por la tarde.

4. Me hace falta una peseta.

5. ¿Quién es el médico?

III. Translate the following sentences into Spanish, then say them aloud. Answers will be found at the back of the book.

1. Do you know the number?

2. They know how to dance.

3. There were many parades.

4. Which of these books do you want?

5. Who are the men on the corner?

6. What do you need?

7. Do they know the address?

8. Who knows Mary?

9. They need many classes.

10. We need more time.

QUIZ

From among the three choices given, choose the one which correctly renders the English given at the beginning of each sentence. Write the complete sentence, and translate.

1. *(know)* Estoy seguro de que ellos _____ a María.
   - (a) sepan
   - (b) conocer
   - (c) conocen

2. *(knew)* Me dijeron que ellos _____ el título del libro.
   - (a) sabían
   - (b) conocerán
   - (c) conozco

3. *(need)* Me hace _____ un libro nuevo.
   - (a) necesito
   - (b) falta
   - (c) faltas

4. *(good)* Hay una revista muy _____ que sale el lunes.
   - (a) bueno
   - (b) buenas
   - (c) buena

5. *(which one)* No me dijo _____ de estas novelas es mejor.
   - (a) qué
   - (b) quién
   - (c) cuál

6. *(there are)* En este lado _____ muchos periódicos extranjeros.
   - (a) hay
   - (b) estarán
   - (c) habían

7. *(German)* Es interesante esta revista

   _____.
   (a) alemanes
   (b) alemana
   (c) alemán

8. *(must be)* Este librito _____ lo que
   quieren Vds.
   (a) debe ser
   (b) tiene que estar
   (c) son

9. *(feel like)* Ellos _____ de ir a la fiesta.
   (a) sienten como
   (b) tienen ganas
   (c) quieren

10. *(you)* Este libro _____ da a usted muchos
    informes.
    (a) le
    (b) os
    (c) les

Answers at back of book.

LESSON 43

AL TELEFONO
ON THE TELEPHONE

A. *Una Conferencia*   A long-distance call

(Carlos habla con una empleada cerca de las cabinas telefónicas en la Telefónica Central de Madrid.)

(Charles speaks to an employee near the telephone booths of the Main Telephone Building in Madrid.)

1. Carlos: **¿Puedo poner una conferencia° desde aquí, señorita?**
   May I make a long-distance call here, Miss?

2. Empleada: **¿Con qué ciudad, señor?**
   To what city, sir?

3. Carlos: **Con Barcelona, pero no sé el número.**
   Barcelona, but I don't know the number.

4. Empleada: **No hay problema, señor. Yo puedo conseguirlo del servicio de información.**
   That's no problem, sir. I can get it from Information.

5. Carlos: **No se moleste usted. Yo lo buscaré en la lista.°**
   Don't bother. I'll look it up in the telephone book.

6. Empleada: **Muy bien, señor. Usted encontrará la Guía allí, a la derecha.**
   Very well, sir. You'll find the directory over there, to the right.

7. Carlos: **Gracias, señorita. Vamos a ver... ¡Ah! Huerta, Felipe... cuarenta y ocho, sesenta y dos, cincuenta y siete.**
   Thank you, Miss. Let's see... Ah! Huerta, Philip... forty-eight, sixty-two, fifty-seven.

8. Empleada: **Veo que lo ha encontrado usted. Eso será veinticinco pesetas por tres minutos.°**
   I see you found it. That will be twenty-five pesetas for three minutes.

9. Carlos: **Y si es más de tres minutos, pago más, ¿verdad?**
   And if it's more than three minutes, I pay more, don't I?

10. Empleada: **Eso es, señor. ¿Quiere usted°
entrar en la cabina número ocho? Yo le haré
una señal en cuanto tenga su número.** *(Ella
llama a la telefonista.)*
That's right, sir. Please go into booth number
eight. I'll signal you as soon as I have your
number. *(She calls the operator.)*

11. Telefonista: **Número, por favor.**
Number, please.

12. Empleada: **Señorita, póngame con el cuarenta y ocho, sesenta y dos, cincuenta y
siete, en Barcelona, por favor.**
Operator, connect me with forty-eight, sixty-
two, fifty-seven in Barcelona, please.

13. Telefonista: **Espere usted. Aquí tiene usted
la comunicación.**
Wait. Here's your party.

14. Empleada: **Gracias, señorita.** *(Ella le hace
una señal a Carlos.)*
Thank you, operator. *(She motions to
Charles.)*

15. Carlos: *(En la cabina número ocho)* **Diga.
Quiero hablar con el Sr. Huerta, por favor.**
(In booth number eight) Hello. I'd like to speak
to Mr. Huerta, please.

16. Una criada: **¿De parte de quién, por favor?**
Who's calling, please?

17. Carlos: **Soy Carlos Andrade. Llamo desde
Madrid.**
This is Charles Andrade. I'm calling from
Madrid.

18. Una criada: **Voy a ver si el señor está.... No, señor, acaba de marcharse. ¿Quiere usted dejar un recado?**
I'll see if he's here.... No, sir, he's just left. Do you want to leave a message?

19. Carlos: **Dígale que volveré a llamarle esta noche, por favor.**
Please tell him that I'll call him again this evening.

20. Una criada: **Muy bien, señor. Yo le daré el recado.**
Very well, sir. I'll give him your message.

21. Carlos: **Gracias. Adiós.**
Thank you. Good-bye.

B. *Una llamada local*   A local call

22. Carlos: *(En la ventanilla°)* **Siento molestarla otra vez, señorita, pero...**
(At the service window) I'm sorry to bother you again, Miss, but...

23. Empleada: **No es molestia, señor, en absoluto.**
It's no trouble at all, sir.

24. Carlos: **No estoy acostumbrado todavía a los teléfonos automáticos de aquí, ¿comprende usted?**
I'm still not used to your dial phones, you know.

25. Empleada: **No es muy complicado, señor. ¿Sabe usted el número?**
It's not very complicated, sir. Do you know the number?

26. Carlos: **Sí, esta vez quiero hacer una lla-mada local, treinta y ocho, veinte y cinco, quince.**
Yes, this time I want to make a local call, thirty-eight, twenty-five, fifteen.

27. Empleada: **Le hace falta una ficha,° señor. Descuelgue usted, meta la ficha, espere la señal, y marque el número.**
You need a token, sir. Pick up the receiver, put your token in, wait for the dial tone, and dial your number.

28. Carlos: **Lo comprendo todo ... pero ¿qué son estos botones?**
I understand everything ... but what are these buttons?

29. Empleada: **Bueno, usted oirá la llamada, y cuando contesten, apriete el botón A.**
Well, you will hear the ring, and when they answer, press button A.

30. Carlos: **Pero, ¿si no contestan? ¿O si la línea está ocupada? ¿O si me equivoco de nú-mero?**
But what if they don't answer? Or if the line is busy? Or if I get a wrong number?

31. Empleada: **Pues entonces, cuelgue usted, simplemente. Espere un rato y vuelva a marcar.**
Well then, just hang up. Wait a while and dial again.

32. Carlos: **Muy amable, señorita. Gracias a usted estoy seguro de que todo irá bien.**
You are very kind, Miss. Thanks to you I'm sure that everything will go well.

NOTES

1. *conferencia:* long-distance call. *Larga distancia* is used in Mexico and other countries of Latin America.
   poner una conferencia: Make a long-distance call.

5. *la lista:* Frequently used for *Guía de teléfonos* (from English "listing").

8. Long-distance telephone calls are frequently paid in advance.

10. *¿Quiere usted?:* Frequently used in polite request, followed by the infinitive.

22. *ventanilla:* a small service-window such as is found in banks, post offices, and theatres.

27. *ficha:* a metal token, used in place of coins for telephones.

GRAMMATICAL ITEMS FOR SPECIAL STUDY

I. *ir a* + infinitive: going to + infinitive

Study:

1. *I'm going to study the lesson.*

2. *We're going to go to the store.*

3. *They're going to dance the twist.*

II. *más que (de):* more than

Study:

ir	a	Infinitive	Complement
1. Voy	a	estudiar	la lección.
2. Vamos	a	ir	a la tienda.
3. Van	a	bailar	el twist.

más que

1. Juan tiene más libros que María.
2. Yo estudio más que Juan.
3. Ellos viajan más que nadie.

1. *John has more books than Mary.*
2. *I study more than John.*
3. *They travel more than anyone.*

más de (used with numbers)

1. El vendió más de cien libros.
2. Ellos compraron más de cuatro casas.
3. Ustedes tienen más de tres horas.

1. *He sold more than a hundred books.*
2. *They bought more than four houses.*
3. *You have more than three hours.*

Note: In the negative, *no más que* usually means "only" and *que* is used even before numbers.

No tengo *más que* diez pesetas.
I have only (I have no more than) ten pesetas.

III. Command or Request forms:

Study:

POLITE FORMS

1. Ponga usted el libro allí.
2. Vengan ustedes mañana.
3. Vaya usted a verlo.
4. No fumen ustedes.
5. Entre usted.

6. No coman ustedes tanto.

1. *Put the book there.*

2. *Come tomorrow.*

3. *Go (sing.) to see it.*

4. *Don't smoke.*

5. *Come in (Enter).*

6. *Don't eat so much.*

Note: The polite forms are the third person singular (for **usted**) and the third person plural (for **ustedes**) of the present subjunctive.

FAMILIAR FORMS

1. Mira. No mires.

2. Escucha. No escuches.

3. Come el helado. No comas el helado.

4. Ven aquí en seguida. No vengas aquí.

5. Ponte el sombrero. No te pongas el sombrero.

6. Vete. No te vayas.

1. *Look. Don't look.*

2. *Listen. Don't listen.*

3. *Eat the ice cream. Don't eat the ice cream.*

4. *Come here at once. Don't come here.*

5. *Put on your hat. Don't put on your hat.*

6. *Go away. Don't go away.*

Note:

1. The familiar singular affirmative command (**tú**)

is usually the same as the third person present indicative. There are some irregular forms: *ten, pon, ven, ve, sal.*

2. The negative uses the second person singular of the present subjunctive.

3. The object pronouns *(direct, indirect,* and *reflexive)* are added to affirmative commands:

Démelo. *Give it to me.*
Póngaselo. *Put it on.*
Tráigamelo. *Bring it to me.*

   but not to *negative commands:*

No me lo dé usted. *Don't give it to me.*
No se lo ponga usted. *Don't put it on.*
No me lo traiga usted. *Don't bring it to me.*

FAMILIAR PLURAL (VOSOTROS)

1. Hablad más alto. No habléis más alto.

2. Escuchad. No escuchéis.

3. Venid. No vengáis.

4. Compradlo. No lo compréis.

5. Traédmelo. No me lo traigáis.

6. Dádnoslo. No nos lo déis.

1. *Speak louder. Don't speak louder.*

2. *Listen. Don't listen.*

3. *Come. Don't come.*

4. *Buy it. Don't buy it.*

5. *Bring it to me. Don't bring it to me.*

6. *Give it to us. Don't give it to us.*

Note: The affirmative familiar plural imperative is formed by changing the final *r* of the infinitive to *d*. The negative is the second person plural form of the present subjunctive. Note the position of pronouns.

IV. *querer* + infinitive: I want

Study:

1. Quiero llamarle ahora.

2. No queremos ir al cine.

3. Querían hablar con Pablo.

1. *I want to call him now.*

2. *We don't want to go to the movies.*

3. *They wanted to speak with Paul.*

DRILLS AND EXERCISES

I. Substitute each of the words or expressions in the parentheses for the italicized word or expression in the model sentence. Write each new sentence and say it aloud.

A. Van a comprar *la casa.* (los libros, el disco, un coche, dos entradas, el sombrero)

B. Voy a *estudiar* mañana. (escribir, comprarlo, salir, llamar, descansar)

C. Tengo más de tres *clases.* (libros, problemas, billetes, programas, pesetas)

D. Juan y María viajan más que *yo.* (el profesor, nadie, la Sra. Andrade, ella, nosotros)

E. No escuches *la radio.* (el programa, la música, las noticias, la broma, el cuento)

F. Ellos quieren *cantar.* (bailar, comer, comprarlo, irse, verlo)

II. Change these commands to the negative. Write the complete sentence and translate. Answers will be found at the back of the book.

Example: *Dámelo.—No me lo des.*

1. Dígamelo.

2. Vete.

3. Póngaselo.

4. Quítatelo.

5. Cómpramelo.

III. Translate the following sentences into Spanish, then say them aloud. Answers will be found at the back of the book.

1. I work more than John.

2. They will travel more than three hours today.

3. We have more than ten pages to read *(que leer).*

4. They are going to buy a new car.

5. He is going to rest tomorrow.

6. We were going to sell the house.

7. Do you want to see the doctor?

8. He wants to give me the book.

9. Don't send it to him.

10. They don't want to leave.

QUIZ

From among the three choices given, choose the one which correctly renders the English given at the beginning of each sentence. Write the complete sentence, and translate.

1. *(the telephone book)* Usted encontrará
   _____ allí.
   (a) el guía
   (b) el listín
   (c) la telefónica

2. *(than)* Tenemos más dinero _____ ellos.
   (a) de
   (b) que
   (c) el que

3. *(send to him)* Quieren _____ el libro.
   (a) mandarnos
   (b) mandarse
   (c) mandarle

4. *(go into)* Tenía que _____ la cabina.
   (a) ir a
   (b) entrar por
   (c) entrar en

5. *(Tell him)* _____ que estoy en Madrid.
   (a) Dale
   (b) Dígale
   (c) Dícele

6. *(make)* Puedo _____ una conferencia con Madrid.
   (a) dar
   (b) poner
   (c) hacer

7. *(know)* ¿_____ usted el número?
   (a) Sé
   (b) Sabe
   (c) Conozco

8. *Don't tell it to him.*
   (a) No dígaselo
   (b) No le lo diga
   (c) No se lo diga

9. *(it to us)* Mánde _____ usted mañana.
   (a) lonos
   (b) noslo
   (c) noslos

10. *(to send them)* Ellos quieren _____ en seguida.
    (a) mandarle
    (b) mandarlos
    (c) los mandar

Answers at back of book.

LESSON 44

TRANSPORTES URBANOS
CITY TRANSPORTATION

A. *El metro°*   The subway

1. Carlos: **Escucha, querida, tengo una idea maravillosa: Para volver al hotel, puesto que tenemos que hacer un recorrido tan largo, vamos a dividirlo en tres partes. Tomaremos el metro, luego el autobús, y finalmente, un taxi. ¿Quieres?**
   Listen, dear, I have a marvelous idea: To get back to the hotel, since we have such a long way to go, let's divide it into three parts. We'll take the subway, then a bus, and finally a taxi. Do you want to?

2. Juana: **¿Te has vuelto loco?° El taxi nos costará un ojo de la cara.°**
Have you gone crazy? The taxi will cost us a fortune.

3. Carlos: **¿Desde cuándo has empezado a pensar en hacer economías?**
When did you start thinking of economizing?

4. Juana: **Es que prefiero gastar el dinero en ir de compras,° querido.**
It's just that I prefer to spend the money going shopping, dear.

5. Carlos: **Bueno, ya habrá suficiente para eso. Pero yo creía que sería divertido. Y de ese modo conoceremos todos los medios de transporte.**
Well, there'll be enough for that. But I thought it would be amusing. And that way, we'd get to know all the means of transportation.

6. Juana: **Pero...¿Tenemos que hacerlo todo en un día? Bien, de acuerdo. Vamos a sacar los billetes.**
But...Do we have to do everything in one day? Well, agreed. Let's get our tickets.

7. Carlos: **¿Cómo hacemos para ir a Correos?°**
How do we get to Correos (the Post Office)?

8. Empleado: **Es muy fácil. Es la cuarta parada en esta misma línea.**
It's very easy. It's the fourth stop on this very line.

9. Carlos: **Ya ves, Juana. Es facilísimo. Y tan rápido. Estaremos allí en un momento.**
You see, Jane. It's very easy. And so fast. We'll be there in a few minutes.

10. Juana: **Sí, ya lo veo . . . pero hay tanta gente y con el calor que hace . . .**

Yes, I see . . . but there are so many people and with the heat . . .

11. Carlos: **Bueno. Piensa en el dinero que estamos ahorrando. Y podemos bajar° dentro de poco.**

Well, think of the money we're saving. And we can get off in a little while.

12. Juana: **Gracias a Dios. Espero que los autobuses no vayan° tan atestados.**

Thank God. I hope the buses aren't so crowded.

B. *El autobús*   The bus

13. Juana: *(En la parada del autobús)* **¡Mira la gente que hay!**

(At the bus stop) Look at all the people!

14. Carlos: **Sí, desgraciadamente es la hora en que salen todos del trabajo. Tendremos que hacer cola.**

Yes, unfortunately it's the hour when everyone gets out of work. We'll have to stand in line.

15. Juana: **¡Las ideas maravillosas que se te occuren!°** **¿Qué hacemos si no podemos subir?**

The marvelous ideas you get! What do we do if we can't get on?

16. Carlos: **Hay muchos que suben La Castellana. Nos hace falta un número veintidós.**

There are many that go up The Castellana. We need a number twenty-two (bus).

17. Juana: **Ya° viene uno. ¡Y está casi vacío! A ver si podemos subir.**

Here comes one already. And it's almost empty! Let's see if we can get on.

18. Carlos: **¿Estás contenta? Vamos sentados, cómodos, con una vista magnífica.**

Are you happy? We are seated, comfortable, and we have a magnificent view.

19. Juana: **Desde luego es muchísimo más cómodo que el metro, y La Castellana es preciosa... los árboles, la sombra. Me gusta ver a los niños jugando por aquí. Tan limpios y bien vestidos, y las niñeras y las mamás tan orgullosas de ellos.**

Of course, it's much more comfortable than the subway, and The Castellana is beautiful . . . the trees, the shade. I like to see the children playing along here. So clean and well dressed, and the nursemaids and mothers so proud of them.

20. Carlos: **Estamos casi en la parada de Colón. Vamos a bajar allí.**

We're almost at the Columbus Circle stop. Let's get off there.

21. Juana: **¡Ah! ¡Qué día más hermoso! ¿Jamás has visto un cielo tan azul y despejado? Vamos a sentarnos° aquí en la terraza, a la sombra, a tomar un refresco. ¡Qué contenta me siento!**

Ah! What a beautiful day! Have you ever seen a sky so blue and cloudless? Let's sit down here at the sidewalk café, in the shade, and have something to drink. How happy I feel!

22. Carlos: **Me alegro tanto, querida. Vamos a hacer lo que te da la gana. No tenemos prisa ninguna. Luego podemos tomar un taxi al hotel, echar una siesta...**

I'm glad you are, dear. We'll do whatever

you want. We are not in any hurry. Then we
can take a taxi to the hotel, take a nap . . .

23. Juana: **¡Ahora sí que has tenido° una idea
magnífica! Estoy un poco cansada.**
Now you have really had a wonderful idea! I'm
a little tired.

24. Carlos: **Bien, querida. ¡Camarero! Trái-
ganos un café helado y una limonada, por
favor.**
Fine, dear. Waiter! Bring us an iced coffee and
a lemonade, please.

25. Camarero: **En seguida, señores.**
Right away.

26. Juana: **¡Ah, qué delicia! ¿Verdad que es
agradable, Carlos?**
Ah, what a delight! Isn't it pleasant, Charles?

27. Carlos: **¡Ya lo creo! ¡Ojalá° todos los días
fueran así!**
It certainly is! I wish every day could be like
this!

C. *El taxi*   The taxi

28. Carlos: *¡Taxi! ¡Taxi!*
Taxi! Taxi!

29. Juana: *Ese debe estar ocupado. ¿Ves? La ban-
dera está bajada. Vamos al otro lado de la
calle, a la parada de taxis.*
That one must be taken. See? The flag is
down. Let's go to the other side of the street to
the taxi stand.

30. Carlos: *(En el taxi) ¿Cuánto es al Hotel Em-
peratriz?*
(In the taxi) How much is it to the Hotel
Emperatriz?

31. Taxista: **Lo que marca aquí, señor.** *(Señalando el taxímetro.) Debe ser unas cincuenta pesetas.*
Whatever it shows here, sir. *(Indicating the meter)* It should be about fifty pesetas.

32. Juana: *Mira, querido, el taxímetro se llama "Taxi-Baby." ¿No es divertido?*
Look, dear, the meter is called "Taxi-Baby." Isn't that amusing?

33. Carlos: *Ya estamos. Bueno, Juana, hemos descubierto que el taxi es la manera más agradable de viajar en la ciudad.*
We're here already. Well, Jane, we discovered that the taxi is the most pleasant way to travel in the city.

34. Juana: *Ya lo sabía, querido. ¿Por qué no me lo preguntaste, si tenías dudas? Podíamos habernos ahorrado muchas molestias.*
I already knew it dear. Why didn't you ask me if you were in doubt? We could have saved ourselves a lot of trouble.

35. Carlos: *¡Ya, ya! Vamos a descansar un rato, porque luego tenemos que arreglarnos para salir a cenar... y tal vez ir a una sala de fiestas° a bailar.*
O.K., O.K. Let's rest awhile, because then we have to get ready to go out to dinner... and perhaps go to a nightclub and dance.

NOTES

Title. *El metro:* Abbreviated form of *El metropolitano,* the name of the city subway system.

2. *¿Te has vuelto loco?: volverse loco* = to go crazy.

un ojo de la cara: a fortune (lit., "an eye from your face").

3. *¿Desde cuándo?:* lit., "since when." Notice *empezar a* and *pensar en*.

4. *ir de compras:* to go shopping.

7. *Correos:* The Post Office. The central post office in Madrid is sometimes affectionately called *Nuestra Señora de Correos* ("Our Lady of the Mail") because of its Gothic, churchlike architecture.

11. *podemos bajar:* we can get off. *Subir* and *bajar* are used to express the idea of "getting into" and "getting out of" any vehicle.

12. *no vayan:* Note the use of subjunctive after *esperar*, "to hope."

15. *que se te ocurren:* lit., "that occur themselves to you." *Ocurrírsele* is used very frequently in this sense. *Se me ocurre una idea.* = I have an idea; i.e., "It suddenly occurred to me." *Cuando se le ocurre una idea a Pepe...* "When Joe gets an idea..."

17. *ya:* already. Often used to preface an expression of pleasant surprise, the sense is often difficult to translate, as in *¡Ya lo creo!* ("I really *do* believe it!") Often equivalent to positive agreement: "You bet!"

21. Note the use of *sentarse* (to sit down) and *sentirse* (to feel).

23. *sí que has tenido:* you've *really* had. *Sí que* prefaces very definite agreement.

27. *ojalá:* Would to God that. Always followed by imperfect subjunctive in expressions of strong wish or desire.

35. *sala de fiestas:* nightclub, in Spain. This expression is not used in Latin America, where the equivalents are *cabaret, club nocturno* (lit., "nightclub"), the French word "boîte," or just the English "nightclub."

GRAMMATICAL ITEMS FOR SPECIAL STUDY

I. *Por:* in exchange for, in place of, per

Study:

1. El me dió diez dólares por el libro.

2. Ellos ganan treinta pesetas por hora.

3. Carlos vendió el coche por muy poco dinero.

1. *He gave me ten dollars for the book.*

2. *They earn thirty pesetas an hour.*

3. *Charles sold the car for very little money.*

II. *Para:* to, in order to, for (directed toward)

Study:

1. El me dió un libro para leer.

2. Trabajan mucho para ganarse la vida.

3. El regalo es para nuestro vecino.

4. Entraron aquí para buscar a Juan.

1. *He gave me a book to read.*

2. *They work hard in order to earn a living.*

3. *The gift is for our neighbor.*

4. *They entered here to look for John.*

III. *tener que* + infinitive: to have to

Study:

1. Tenemos que ir temprano.
2. Ellos tendrán que comprar el libro.
3. Tengo que quedarme aquí.

1. *We have to go early.*
2. *They'll have to buy the book.*
3. *I have to stay here.*

IV. *Estar* + present participle

Study:

1. Estoy ley*endo* ahora.
2. Estaban durmi*endo* cuando sonó el timbre.
3. Estamos aprendi*endo* mucho.

1. *I am reading now.*
2. *They were sleeping when the bell rang.*
3. *We are learning a lot.*

Note: *Estar* + *present participle* denotes action in progress.

DRILLS AND EXERCISES

I. Substitute each of the words or expressions in the parentheses for the italicized word or expression in the model sentence. Write each new sentence and say it aloud.

A. Juan lo compró por *cincuenta pesetas.* (poco dinero, diez dólares, más de cien pesetas, un precio muy bajo, mucho menos dinero)

B. Juan lo compró para *dárselo a su padre.* (regalar, enviar, despachar, mandar, enseñar)

  C. Tendremos que *estudiar* mucho. (aprender, trabajar, escribir, practicar, andar)

  D. Estarán *comiendo* cuando lleguemos. (bailando, estudiando, leyendo, durmiendo, hablando)

  E. Juan estaba leyendo *el periódico* cuando entré. (el libro, la lección, las noticias, la comedia, el primer acto)

  F. *María y Juana* tienen que hacer el trabajo. (Los chicos, José y su hermano, Ellas, Todos, Los alumnos)

II. Change these sentences to the plural. Write the complete sentence and translate it. Answers will be found at the back of the book.

1. El tiene que verlo mañana.

2. Yo tendré que levantarme temprano.

3. Ella está lavando los platos.

4. Tú tienes que leer la novela.

5. Usted me dió treinta pesetas por el libro.

III. Translate the following sentences into Spanish, then say them aloud. Answers will be found at the back of the book.

1. John bought the car for his wife.

2. They paid thirty pesetas for the tickets.

3. We have to leave at once.

4. They are writing letters now.

5. How much do you want for the suit?

6. You have to go through the park in order to get to the museum.

7. They gave him two hundred pesetas in order to pay (for) the trip.

8. They were listening to the radio when I arrived.

9. In order to see well, you have to be in the front row.

10. Michael has to buy a new book.

QUIZ

From among the three choices given, choose the one which correctly renders the English given at the beginning of each sentence. Write the complete sentence, and translate.

1. *(to)* Juan cree que tenemos _____ ir al banco.
   - (a) a
   - (b) que
   - (c) ----

2. *(for)* Paco pagó _____ el billete.
   - (a) ----
   - (b) por
   - (c) para

3. *(per)* Hace cuarenta kilómetros _____ hora.
   - (a) para
   - (b) por
   - (c) el

4. *(walking)* Los vimos _____ por la calle.
   - (a) andando
   - (b) andados
   - (c) andandos

5. *(sitting)* Nosotros estábamos _____ en la terraza.
   - (a) sentado
   - (b) sentando
   - (c) sentados

6. *(reading)* Juan está _____ el periódico.
   - (a) lee
   - (b) leyendo
   - (c) leído

7. *(for)* Esta propina es _____ el camarero.
   - (a) de
   - (b) para
   - (c) a

8. *(She has to)* _____ comprar el traje.
   - (a) Ella hay que
   - (b) Ella tiene que
   - (c) Ella ha que

9. *(they want)* No sé lo que _____.
   - (a) quieren
   - (b) querer
   - (c) queremos

10. *(we)* Ellos van a los mismos sitios que

    _____.
    - (a) nosotros
    - (b) ir
    - (c) van

Answers at back of book.

LESSON 45

VAMOS A DAR UN PASEO
LET'S TAKE A WALK

A. *Antes del paseo*   Before the walk

1. Juana: **¡Vamos a dar un paseo!°** **¿Qué te parece? Solamente los dos. Podíamos bajar La Castellana hasta el Museo del Prado.°** **¿No tienes ganas de verlo? Yo, sí.**
   Let's take a walk! What do you think (of that)? Just the two of us. We could walk down The Castellana to the Prado Museum. Don't you feel like seeing it? I do.

2. Carlos: **¿Dar un paseo los dos? ¿Y si nos perdemos? Hace tanto tiempo que no salgo solo en Madrid.**

Take a walk, the two of us? And what if we get lost? It's such a long time since I've been out in Madrid by myself.

3. Juana: **¡Estás bromeando! ¡No seas tonto! Además, podemos preguntar al conserje. El nos dirá cómo tenemos que ir. Y si nos perdemos, podemos volver aquí en taxi. ¡Es fácil!**

You're kidding! Don't be silly! Besides, we can ask the concierge. He will tell us how we can go. If we get lost we can get back by taxi. It's easy!

4. Carlos: **Todo te parece fácil. Bueno, ¡vámonos! Pero...como hace un día tan espléndido, vamos a visitar la Plaza Mayor° y la parte antigua de la ciudad. Y, desde luego, si nos cansamos, podemos volver en taxi.**

Everything seems easy to you. O.K., let's go! But...since it's such a beautiful day, let's visit the Plaza Mayor and the old part of the city. And, of course, if we get tired, we can come back in a taxi.

B. *En la recepción*   At the reception desk

5. Carlos: **Dígame, señor, ¿cómo se puede ir a la Plaza Mayor?**

Tell me, sir, how can one get to the Plaza Mayor?

6. Conserje: **Pues, ustedes pueden tomar aquí en la esquina el autobús número...**

Well, here on the corner you can get bus number...

7. Carlos: **No, perdone. Yo quería decir a pie.**
No, I'm sorry. I meant on foot (walking).

8. Conserje: **¡Ah! Bueno, pues, es bastante lejos para ir andando. Pero si ustedes quieren. Miren este plano de la ciudad. Nosotros estamos aquí, y ¿ven la Plaza Mayor, allí?**
Oh! Well, then, it's quite a distance to walk. But if you want to. Look at this map of the city. We are here, and . . . Do you see the Plaza Mayor there?

9. Juana: **Sí que es lejos. Pero tenemos muchas ganas de andar. Nos gusta tanto.**
It *is* a long way. But we feel like walking. We enjoy it so much.

10. Conserje: **Bueno . . . Ustedes tendrán que seguir La Castellana abajo, hasta llegar a Cibeles. ¿Se acuerdan? Es la fuente delante de Correos. ¿Sí? Bueno, allí, hay que volver a la derecha y subir por la calle de Alcalá. Sigan hasta la Puerta del Sol . . .**
Well, you'll have to walk down The Castellana, to Cibeles. You remember? It's the fountain in front of the Post Office. Yes? Well, there, you must turn right and go up Alcalá to the Puerta del Sol . . .

11. Juana: **Ah, sí, la Puerta del Sol. Me acuerdo de haber visto muchas fotos de ella.**
Oh yes, the Puerta del Sol. I remember having seen many pictures of it.

12. Conserje: **Sí, señora. ¡Es muy conocida! Bueno, como iba diciendo . . . Vuelvan a la izquierda allí y suban por la calle de Carretas. ¿La ven ustedes?** (*indicando el plano*) **Al ver el Teatro Calderón en la esquina,**

**vuelvan a la derecha otra vez y· verán los
arcos de la Plaza Mayor.**

Yes, Madam. It's very well known! Well, as I
was saying . . . Turn to the left there and go up
Carretas Street. Do you see it *(pointing to the
map)?* When you see the Calderon Theatre on
the corner, turn to the right again and you will
see the arches of the Plaza Mayor.

13. Carlos: **Gracias, señor. Parece muy claro y
bastante fácil.**

Thank you, sir. It seems very clear and quite
easy.

14. Conserje: **De nada, señores. Que lo pasen
bien.**

You're welcome. I hope you enjoy it.

15. Juana: **¿Ves? Ya te lo había dicho . . . Es
facilísimo.**

You see? I told you . . . it's very easy.

16. Carlos: **Pero, será una caminata de media
hora, por lo menos. ¿No te parece demasiado?**

But it will probably be a half-hour's walk, at
least. Don't you think it's too much?

17. Juana: **Claro que no, querido. Ya verás.
¡Qué gusto!**

Of course not, darling. You'll see. What a
pleasure!

C. *Un cuarto de hora más tarde*   Fifteen minutes
                                       later

18. Carlos: **Muy poco nos falta para llegar a
Cibeles. ¿No ves el Correo allá, con las
torres?**

We have just a little way to go to Cibeles.
Don't you see the Post Office there, with the
towers?

19. Juana: **Sí, ya lo veo. Es donde hay que volver a la derecha y subir por la calle de Alcalá, ¿verdad?**
Yes, I can see it. That's where we have to turn right and go up Alcalá, isn't it?

20. Carlos: **Eso es. Y si te parece, podemos sentarnos un rato en aquella terraza tan agradable y descansar un poco antes de seguir.**
That's right. And if you want to, we can sit down for a while at that pleasant sidewalk café and rest a bit before continuing.

21. Juana: **Sí, querido. Pero, me parece que eres tú el que quiere descansar. Te cansaste, ¿verdad?**
Yes, dear. But it seems to me that you're the one who wants to rest. You've got tired, haven't you?

22. Carlos: *(Después del descanso)* **Creo que nos hemos equivocado. ¿Será ésta la calle de Alcalá? ¿Tienes aquella guía de la ciudad?**
(After the rest) I think we've made a mistake. Can this be Alcalá? Do you have that map of the city?

23. Juana: **¡Ay! La dejé sobre la mesa en aquella terraza. ¡Qué lástima! No vale la pena volver a buscarla ahora. Pregunta a aquel señor si vamos bien.**
Oh! I left it on the table at the café. What a pity! It's not worth the trouble going back to look for it now. Ask that man if we're on the right track.

24. Carlos: **Perdone, señor. ¿Vamos bien para llegar a la Puerta del Sol?**
Pardon me, sir. Are we going the right way to the Puerta del Sol?

25. Un Señor: ¿A la Puerta del Sol? No, no. Esta es la Gran Vía,° que baja directamente a la Plaza de España. Ustedes tienen que volver atrás hasta el punto donde se separan la Gran Vía y la calle de Alcalá. Alcalá es la que sube a mano izquierda. No es muy lejos. ¿Ven aquel edificio grande, frente a la iglesia? Pues, es allí donde tienen que subir a la izquierda.

To the Puerta del Sol? No, no. This is the Gran Vía, that goes directly down to the Plaza de España. You have to go back to the point where the Gran Vía and Alcalá separate. Alcalá is the one that goes up to the left. It's not very far. Do you see that big building opposite the church? Well, that's where you have to go up to the left.

26. Carlos: **Muchísimas gracias, señor. Usted es muy amable. Vamos, Juana, o no llegamos nunca a la Plaza Mayor.**

Thank you very much, sir. You are very kind. Come on, Jane, or we'll never get to the Plaza Mayor.

27. Juana: **No me importa tanto. El paseo es agradable de todas maneras y estamos viendo cosas muy interesantes. Las tiendas por aquí son muy elegantes.**

It doesn't matter much to me. The walk is pleasant anyway and we're seeing interesting things. The shops along here are very elegant.

28. Carlos: **Ya sé que estás contenta si puedes mirar los escaparates llenos de joyas preciosas y trajes de alta costura.**

I know that you're happy if you can look at shop windows full of beautiful jewelry and high fashion suits.

29. Juana: **¡Qué simpático eres! Ya veremos la
     Plaza Mayor. Si no hoy, otro día será.**
     How sweet you are! We'll see the Plaza
     Mayor. If not today, another.

D. *De vuelta en el hotel*   Back at the hotel

30. Conserje: **Buenas tardes, señores. ¿Les ha
     gustado la Plaza Mayor?**
     Good afternoon. Did you like the Plaza
     Mayor?

31. Carlos: **Ni hemos llegado a verla. Nos hemos
     equivocado de camino varias veces y hemos
     perdido tanto tiempo con los escaparates de
     la Gran Vía que ya se hacía demasiado tarde
     para eso.**
     We didn't even get to see it. We lost our way
     several times and we wasted so much time with
     the shop windows of the Gran Vía that it was
     getting too late for that.

32. Juana: **Bueno, mañana iremos de compras
     por la mañana, y por la tarde iremos a la
     Plaza Mayor.**
     Well, tomorrow we'll go shopping in the
     morning, and in the afternoon we'll go to the
     Plaza Mayor.

NOTES

1. *dar un paseo:* to take a walk.

1. *Museo del Prado:* The famous Madrid museum that has one of the richest collections in
   the world.

4. *Plaza Mayor:* The old "Main Square" of Madrid. The center of the city's life in the sixteenth and seventeenth centuries.

25. *la Gran Vía:* The popular name for the Avenida de José Antonio Primo de Rivera, the main commercial artery in Madrid, which goes up from the Post Office to the Plaza de España.

GRAMMATICAL ITEMS FOR SPECIAL STUDY

I. *hacer* + time expression + *que:* for + time

Study:

1. Hace una semana que estoy aquí.

2. Hace dos horas que esperamos.

3. Hace un año que Juan estudia español.

1. *I have been here for a week.*

2. *We have been waiting for two hours.*

3. *John has been studying Spanish for a year.*

Note: (Lit., "It makes a week that I am here."—I have been here for a week.)

II. Personal *a* + singular masculine definite article: *al*

Study:

1. Vamos a preguntar al conserje.

2. Tengo que ver al dentista.

3. Ellos llamaron al médico.

but:

4. Hay que preguntar *a los* conserjes.

5. Tengo que ver *a la* costurera.

6. Veo *a* María.

1. *Let's ask the concierge.*

2. *I have to see the dentist.*

3. *They called the doctor.*

but:

4. *You must ask the concierges.*

5. *I have to see the dressmaker.*

6. *I see Mary.*

III. Impersonal *se*

Study:

1. ¿Se puede fumar?

2. Se tiene que ir de prisa.

3. Se come bien aquí.

1. *May one smoke? Is smoking permitted?*

2. *One has to go fast. You (impersonal) must go fast.*

3. *One eats well here. The food is good here.*

IV. *Acordarse de:* to remember

1. Me acuerdo muy bien de ella.

2. ¿Se acuerda usted del accidente?

3. Nos acordamos frecuentemente de aquel viaje.

1. *I remember her very well.*

2. *Do you remember the accident?*

3. *We frequently remember that trip.*

DRILLS AND EXERCISES

I. Substitute each of the words or expressions in parentheses for the italicized word or expression in the model sentence. Write each new sentence and say it aloud.

A. Hace *una semana* que vivo en Madrid. (un año, dos meses, mucho tiempo, varias semanas, muy poco [tiempo])

B. Hace tres horas que Juan *trabaja.* (viaja, estudia, duerme, escribe, lee)

C. Usted tiene que llamar *al médico.* (al dentista, al sereno, al oficial, al camarero, al agente)

D. Se *come* bien en Madrid. (duerme, bebe, está, habla, canta)

E. Nos acordamos mucho *de España.* (del viaje, de Madrid, de Teresa, de ustedes, del médico)

F. No me acuerdo de *nada.* (ella, María, Juan y Francisco, ellos, él)

II. Change these sentences to the negative. Write the complete sentence and translate. Answers will be found at the back of the book.

1. *Usted se acuerda de María.*

2. *Hace una semana que Juan está aquí.*

3. *Teresa tiene que llamar al médico.*

4. *Se come bien en este restaurante.*

5. *Ellos se acuerdan del viaje.*

III. Translate the following sentences into Spanish, then say them aloud. Answers will be found at the back of the book.

1. They've been here for a month.

2. You have to call the doctor.

3. I remember you very well.

4. I have been sleeping for two hours.

5. You eat well in this restaurant (i.e., the food is good).

6. I don't see Mary.

7. We can sit down to rest awhile.

8. We feel like walking.

9. You have to turn to the right.

10. Let's visit the museum.

QUIZ

From among the three choices given, choose the one which correctly renders the English given at the beginning of each sentence. Write the complete sentence, and translate.

1. (I have been) _____ aquí hace dos años.
   (a) Estuve
   (b) He estado
   (c) Estoy

2. (for three months) Ellos viven en Madrid
   _____.
   (a) en tres meses
   (b) hace tres meses
   (c) de tres meses

3. (have you been) ¿Hace cuánto tiempo
   _____ aquí?
   (a) ha usted estado
   (b) está usted
   (c) usted estuve

4. (is spoken) Aquí _____ ruso.
   (a) hablamos
   (b) se habla
   (c) está hablando

5. *(One finds)* _____ muchos anuncios en el periódico.
   (a) Se encuentran
   (b) Se encuentra
   (c) Encontrar

6. *(remember)* Creo que ellos _____ la fecha.
   (a) se acuerda
   (b) se acuerdan de
   (c) acordarse

7. *(one meets)* Esta es una fiesta en la que _____ a mucha gente simpática.
   (a) se conoce
   (b) se conocen
   (c) se encuentran

8. *(my friend)* ¿Conoce usted _____?
   (a) amigo mío
   (b) a mi amigo
   (c) mi amigo

9. *(they have been)* Hace tres años que _____ en Nueva York.
   (a) son
   (b) están
   (c) habían estado

10. *(for an hour)* Hace _____ que espero.
    (a) por una hora
    (b) una hora
    (c) un hora

Answers at back of book.

LESSON 46

EN UNA TIENDA
IN A STORE

A. *En la sección de guantes*   In the glove department

1. Vendedora: **¿Puedo servirle en algo, señora?**
   Saleslady: Can I help you with something, madam?

2. Juana: **Sí, por favor. Me gustaría ver unos guantes, para uso corriente, como los míos pero de piel.°**
   Yes, please. I'd like to see some gloves for every day; like mine, but in leather.

3. Vendedora: **Los tenemos de todas clases y de todos colores. Aquí tiene usted unos preciosos de ante.**
   We have all kinds and all colors. Here are some beautiful ones in suede.

4. Juana: **Sí, son muy bonitos. ¿Quiere usted enseñármelos en negro, por favor?**
   Yes, they're very pretty. Would you show them to me in black, please?

5. Vendedora: **¿Qué talla,° señora? Me parece que usted debe usar siete, ¿no?**
   What size, madam? I think you must wear a seven, don't you?

6. Juana: **Sí, generalmente, pero depende de los guantes. A veces uso seis y medio.**
   Yes, generally, but it depends on the glove. At times I wear a six and a half.

7. Vendedora: **Un momento, señora. Voy a buscárselos. Aquí los tiene usted. ¿Quiere probárselos?**
   One moment, madam. I'll get them for you. Here they are. Would you like to try them on?

8. Juana: **Me quedan perfectamente. ¿Cuánto es (¿Cuántos son?), por favor?**
   They fit me perfectly. How much [are they], please?

9. Vendedora: **Ochenta pesetas.°**
   Eighty pesetas.

10. Juana: **Está bien. ¿Quiere envolverlos, por favor?**
    That's fine. Will you wrap them, please?

11. Vendedora: **Con mucho gusto, señora. Aquí los tiene usted. Muchas gracias.**
    With pleasure, madam. Here you are. Thank you very much.

B. *En la sección de vestidos de señoras*
   In the ladies' dress department

12. Vendedora: **¿Quiere que le ayude, señora?**
    May I help you, madam?

13. Juana: **Sí, estoy buscando un vestido de seda, de un verde claro, con mangas cortas.**
    Yes, I'm looking for a light green silk dress, with short sleeves.

14. Vendedora: **Este vestido, señora, es de última moda, y una verdadera ganga a seiscientas pesetas.**
    This dress is the latest style, madam, and a real bargain at six hundred pesetas.

15. Juana: **¡Ah! Pero es demasiado. ¿No tendría usted otro, menos caro?**
Oh, but it's too expensive. Don't you have another, less expensive?

16. Vendedora: **Hay este otro a cuatrocientas cincuenta. Vea que es un corte muy elegante. ¿Qué talla lleva usted, señora?**
There's this one at four hundred fifty pesetas. Notice that it's a very elegant cut. What size do you wear, madam?

17. Juana: **Creo que treinta y seis.**
I think a thirty-six.

18. Vendedora: **Este vestido le va divinamente, señora. Vamos aquí adentro a probarlo.**
This dress is perfect for you, madam. Let's go in here and try it on.

19. Juana: **Yo lo encuentro un poco ancho de espalda, y demasiado largo.**
I find it a little wide in the shoulders and too long.

20. Vendedora: **Desde luego, lo es. Vamos a probar una talla más pequeña entonces. ¡Ah! Eso ya es otra cosa. Le sienta a maravilla, señora. ¿Qué le parece?**
Of course it is. Let's try a smaller size, then. Ah! That's something else! It fits you marvelously, madam. What do you think?

21. Juana: **Me gusta muchísimo, y es la última moda. Espero que le guste a mi marido.**
I like it very much, and it is the latest style. I hope my husband likes it.

22. Vendedora: **Estoy segura que sí, señora. Es una prenda preciosa. Venga por aquí. La acompaño a la caja.**
I'm sure he will, madam. It's a beautiful garment. Come this way. I'll accompany you to the cashier's desk.

23. Juana: *(En la caja)* **¿Aceptan vds. cheques de viajero?**
(At the cashier's desk) Do you accept traveler's checks?

24. Cajera: **Claro que sí, señora. ¿Quiere Vd. llevar el paquete? Podemos mandárselo, si usted prefiere.**
Certainly, madam. Do you want to carry the package? We can deliver it, if you prefer.

25. Juana: **Sí, sería mejor. Aquí tiene mi tarjeta. Mándelo al Hotel Emperatriz, por favor. Esta tarde, si es posible.**
Yes, that would be better. Here's my card. Send it to the Hotel Emperatriz, please. This afternoon, if possible.

26. Vendedora: **No se preocupe, señora. Llegará esta misma tarde, sin falta.**
Don't worry, madam. It will arrive this very afternoon without fail.

C. *En el mostrador de pañuelos*
At the handkerchief counter

27. Vendedor: *¿Puedo ayudarle en algo, señora?*
May I help you with something, madam?

28. Juana: *Sí, por favor. Busco unos pañuelos para mi marido.*

Yes, please. I'm looking for some handkerchiefs for my husband.

29. Vendedor: *Estoy seguro de que le gustarán éstos. Son de algodón, a sesenta pesetas la docena.*
I'm sure he'll like these. They're cotton, and are sixty pesetas a dozen.

30. Juana: *¿No tiene algunos de mejor calidad? A él le gustan los pañuelos muy finos.*
Don't you have some of better quality? He likes very fine handkerchiefs.

31. Vendedor: *Por supuesto. Estos son de lino, hechos a mano. Se venden a quince pesetas cada uno.*
Of course. These arc linen, handmade. They sell at fifteen pesetas each.

32. Juana: *Sí, éstos me gustan más. ¿Quiere darme media docena, por favor?*
Yes, I like these better. Will you give me half a dozen, please?

33. Vendedor: *Muy bien, señora . . . Aquí tiene su cambio. Se los envolveré.*
Very good, madam . . . here's your change. I'll wrap them for you.

34. Juana: *Muchas gracias, señor.*
Thank you very much, sir.

35. Vendedor: *Para servirle, señora.*
At your service, madam.

NOTES

2. *piel:* (lit., "skin") used for all kinds of cured and worked light leathers such as would be used in gloves, handbags, etc.

cuero is the word used for heavier varieties of leather.

5. *talla, tamaño:* used to refer to sizes of articles of clothing. *Talla* is generally used for suits and dresses (cf. *talle:* waist measurement).
Número ("number") is frequently used for articles that are sized according to number. *¿Qué número lleva usted?* will be heard in reference to gloves and shoes.

9. There are at present approximately 175 pesetas to the dollar.

GRAMMATICAL ITEMS FOR SPECIAL STUDY

I. Indirect and Direct object pronouns may be

A. Attached to the complementary infinitive

Study:

	Infinitive	Indirect/Direct Object pronoun
1. Juan quiere	dárselo a él.	
2. María va a	mandármelo.	
3. Ellos tienen que	pagárnoslo.	

B. Or placed before the main verb:

1. Juan se lo quiere dar a él.

2. María me lo va a mandar.

3. Ellos nos lo tienen que pagar.

1. *John wants to give it to him.*

2. *Mary is going to send it to me.*

3. *They have to pay us for it.*

Note: Indirect *le* and *les* change to *se* before the direct object pronouns.

II. *Aquí* + direct-object pronoun + tener

Study:

1. ¿El libro? Aquí lo tiene usted.

2. ¿Los libros? Aquí los tiene usted.

3. ¿La novela? Aquí la tiene usted.

4. ¿Las novelas? Aquí las tiene usted.

1. *The book? Here it is. (Lit.: "Here you have it.")*

2. *The books? Here they are.*

3. *The novel? Here it is.*

4. *The novels? Here they are.*

III. The use of the verb *gustar*—to be pleasing

Study:

Indirect object	*gusta(n)*	Subject
1. Me	gusta	el vestido.
2. Me	gustan	los vestidos.
3. Nos	gusta	el hotel.
4. Nos	gustan	los hoteles.

1. *I like the dress.*

2. *I like the dresses.*

3. *We like the hotel.*

4. *We like the hotels.*

DRILLS AND EXERCISES

I. Substitute each of the words or expressions in the parentheses for the italicized word or expression in the model sentence. Write each new sentence and say it aloud.

A. Mi padre quiere *dár*selo a él. (regalar, mandar, vender, pendir, preguntar)

Note: Indirect *le* and *les* change to *se* before the direct-object pronoun.

B. Ellos me lo *quieren* comprar. (pueden, van a, desean, tienen que, podrán)

C. Me gusta *comer*. (bailar, cantar, beber, dormir, trabajar)

D. *Nos* gustan los viajes. (Te, Me, Le, Os, Les)

E. Le gustan a él *los vestidos*. (los trajes, los libros, las películas, los barcos, los coches)

F. Aquí lo *tiene usted*. (tienes, tienen, tenéis, tenemos, tengo)

II. Change the nouns to pronouns. Write the complete sentence and translate. Answers will be found at the back of the book.

1. María va a comprar el libro para Juan.

2. Ellos quieren mandarle el coche al señor Hernández.

3. Nosotros podemos regalarle los vestidos a tu madre.

4. Tú prefieres pedirle el dinero a su padre.

5. Tenéis que enviarles el paquete a mis padres.

III. Translate the following sentences into Spanish, then say them aloud. Answers will be found at the back of the book.

1. They want to give it *(el ragalo)* to me.

2. You will have to ask him for it.

3. We want to send it to them.

4. He will have to put it on.

5. We like to travel in Spain.

6. Here they (the books) are.

7. You (familiar singular) like ice cream.

8. I'm going to look for it (the hat) for you.

9. Do you want to carry the package?

10. We can send it to you, if you prefer.

QUIZ

From among the three choices given, choose the one which correctly renders the English given at the beginning of each sentence. Write the complete sentence, and translate.

1. *(they are)* Aquí _____ usted.
   (a) lo tiene
   (b) los tiene
   (c) la tiene

2. *(them to me)* Quiere dár _____ ahora.
   (a) -losme
   (b) -melos
   (c) ellos me

3. *(Give it* [el libro] *to me.)*
   (a) Dámelo
   (b) Me lo das
   (c) Dámela

4. *(We have them)* [guantes] _____ de todas clases.
   (a) Tenémoslas
   (b) Los tenemos
   (c) Ellos tenemos

5. *(it)* [el pasaporte] Aquí _____ tiene usted.
   - (a) los
   - (b) lo
   - (c) el

6. *(for you)* Voy a buscar _____ el paquete.
   - (a) le
   - (b) se
   - (c) los

7. *(silk dress)* Quiero comprar un _____.
   - (a) vestido seda
   - (b) seda vestido
   - (c) vestido de seda

8. *(it is)* ¿Es demasiado caro? Creo que
   _____.
   - (a) está
   - (b) lo es
   - (c) el es

9. *(Here it is—Here you are.)* _____
   - (a) Aquí lo tiene usted.
   - (b) Aquí lo está.
   - (c) Aquí estamos.

10. *(send them* [las cartas] *to me)* ¿Quiere usted
    _____?
    - (a) mandárlasme
    - (b) me las mandar
    - (c) mandármelas

Answers at back of book.

LESSON 47

UN CORTE DE PELO
A HAIRCUT

A. *En la peluquería*   In the barbershop

1. Peluquero: **Buenos días, señor. ¿En qué puedo servirle?**
   Barber: Good morning, sir. What can I do for you?

2. Carlos: **Un corte de pelo, para empezar. Me parece que el pelo me crece como nunca en estos días.**
   A haircut, to begin with. It seems to me that my hair is growing more than ever these days.

3. Peluquero: **Será la buena vida que lleva usted, señor. ¿Se lo corto como siempre?**
   It must be the good life you live, sir. Shall I cut it as usual?

4. Carlos: **Sí, por favor. Pero déjelo bastante llenito a los lados y detrás. Cuidado con la maquinilla. No quiero verme "pelado."**
   Yes, please. But leave the sides and back fairly full. Careful with the clippers. I don't want to look "skinned."

5. Peluquero: **Muy bien, señor. Tendré mucho cuidado en hacérselo tal como usted desea . . . ¡Ya está hecho! ¿Qué le parece, señor?**
   Very well, sir. I'll be very careful to do it just as you wish. . . . It's done. What do you think of it, sir?

6. Carlos: **Muy bien. ¿Me permite usted el peine, un momento? ¡Eso es!**

Very good. Will you let me use the comb a
minute? There, that's it!

7. Peluquero: **¿Desea alguna otra cosa, señor?**
Do you want anything else, sir?

8. Carlos: **Vamos a ver... La señora está aquí
al lado, en la peluquería° de señoras. Mientras yo la espero...**
Let's see... My wife is right next door, at the
beauty shop. While I'm waiting for her...

9. Peluquero: **Tendrá usted que esperar bastante, si yo conozco bien a las mujeres.**
You'll have a long wait, if I know women.

10. Carlos: **Tiene usted razón. Bueno, una
afeitada, entonces. Pero cuidado, porque
tengo la barba bastante dura.**
You're right. Well, a shave then. But be careful because my beard is rather tough.

11. Peluquero: **No se preocupe, señor.**
Don't worry, sir.

12. Carlos: **¡Qué lujo! Es muy agradable hacerse
afeitar de vez en cuando. El masaje me
gusta muchísimo.**
What a luxury! It's a pleasure to get a shave
from time to time. I like a massage very much.

13. Peluquero; **Bien, señor. ¿Le veremos la semana que viene?**
O.K., sir. Will we see you next week?

14. Carlos: **Sí. Yo llamaré para fijar la hora.**
Yes. I'll call to make an appointment.

15. Peluquero: **Usted lo puede hacer al pagar la
cuenta, señor.**
You can do it when you pay the bill, sir.

16. Carlos: **Muy bien. Muchas gracias. Tome usted** (*dándole una propina*).
Very well. Thank you. Here (*giving him a tip*).

17. Peluquero: **Gracias, señor. Hasta la semana que viene.**
Thank *you,* sir. Until next week.

B. *En la calle*   In the street

18. Carlos: **¡Hola! ¡Ya estás!° Iba a buscarte.**
Hi! You're ready. I was going to get you.

19. Juana: **Sí, querido, ¡ya estoy! Parece que tú has tardado tanto como yo esta vez.**
Yes, dear, I'm ready! It seems you took as long as I did this time.

20. Carlos: **¡Claro que tú has empezado una hora antes que yo!**
Of course you began an hour before I did!

21. Juana: **Pero, ¡qué guapo estás! ¡Te hacía falta un corte de pelo! Y ¡qué bien afeitado vas!**
But how handsome you look! You needed a haircut. And how well shaved you are!

22. Carlos: **Y tú. ¿Qué te has hecho? Estás más bonita que nunca.**
And you. What have you done? You're prettier than ever.

23. Juana: **Un champú,° y un peinado nuevo. Es un poco más corto que de costumbre.**
A shampoo, and a new hairdo. It's a little shorter than usual.

24. Carlos: **¡Vamos! Hay algo más. No me lo has contado todo.**
Come on! There's something else. You haven't told me everything.

25. Juana: **Bueno, si insistes. Me he hecho aclarar un poco el pelo. ¿No te gusta?**
Well, if you insist. I had my hair lightened a little. Don't you like it?

26. Carlos: **¡Claro que sí! Es precioso. ¿Y la manicura?**
Of course! It's beautiful. And the manicure?

27. Juana: **Por supuesto. Me han barnizado las uñas. ¿Te gusta el color? Va con el lápiz de labios.**
Of course. I had my nails done. Do you like the color? It goes with my lipstick.

28. Carlos: **¡Una maravilla! ¿Qué? ¿Nos queda todavía un poco de dinero?**
Marvelous! What do you say? Do we still have a little money left?

29. Juana: **¡Claro que sí, querido! Tú sabes cuanto he ahorrado con las compras de ayer.**
Of course, darling. You know how much I saved with my shopping yesterday.

30. Carlos: **¡Ah! Ya me había olvidado de las economías de ayer.**
Oh! I had already forgotten about yesterday's savings!

31. Juana: **¿Te das cuenta ahora de que siempre pienso en ahorrarte dinero?**
Do you realize now that I'm always thinking of saving you money?

32. Carlos: **Sí, sí, querida. Vamos a cenar esta noche en el Pabellón.° Quiero que todo el mundo admire a mi mujer.**

Yes, yes, dear. Let's dine at the Pabellón tonight. I want everyone to admire my wife.

NOTES

8. *peluquería:* from *peluca* ("wig"). *Peluquería de hombres* = Barbershop. *Peluquería de señoras* = Beauty shop.

18. *¡Ya estás!:* A word such as *listo, lista* ("ready"), is understood in these expressions. See *¡Ya estoy!* in sentence 19.

23. *Un champú:* from the English "shampoo." One can also say *lavarse el pelo* ("to wash one's hair.") *Me he hecho lavar el pelo.* = I had my hair washed.

32. *el Pabellón:* A supper club for dinner and dancing in Madrid.

GRAMMATICAL ITEMS FOR SPECIAL STUDY
I. Future of probability

Study:

1. ¿Quién será?

2. Ellos habrán ido al cine.

3. Estarán aquí en alguna parte.

1. *Who can it be?*

2. *They must have gone (they probably went) to the movies.*

3. *They must be (they probably are) here somewhere.*

II. *tener razón:* to be right

Study:

1. Usted tiene razón.

2. Ellos siempre creen tener razón.

3. Tenemos razón como siempre.

1. *You're right.*

2. *They always think they are right.*

3. *We are right, as usual.*

III. Present tense with future meaning

Study:

1. ¿Se lo corto como siempre?

2. ¿Qué hago ahora?

3. Vuelvo en seguida.

1. *Shall I cut it in the usual way?*

2. *What shall I do now?*

3. *I'll come back right away.*

IV. *al* + (infinitive): on, upon, or when (doing something)

Study:

1. Usted lo puede hacer al pagar la cuenta.

2. Al volver a casa, te llamo.

3. Me saludó al entrar.

1. *You can do it when you pay (on paying) the bill.*

2. *Upon returning home (when I return home), I'll call you.*

3. *He greeted me on entering (when he entered).*

DRILLS AND EXERCISES

I. Substitute each of the words or expressions in the parentheses for the italicized word or expression in the model sentence. Write each new sentence and say it aloud.

    A. ¿Dónde estará *el libro*? (el lápiz, la novela, Miguel, el profesor, el lápiz de labios)

    B. ¿Qué le habrá pasado *a Teresa*? (al Señor Andrade, a Miguel, al libro, a mis amigos, al profesor)

    C. *Los libros* estarán en alguna parte. (Los señores, Juan y José, María y Juana, Ellas, Los jóvenes)

    D. ¿Se lo *hago* mañana? (digo, pregunto, pido, mando, pago)

    E. *Los chicos* siempre tienen razón. (Las chicas, Los profesores, Juan y Francisco, Mis padres, Las hermanas)

    F. Puedes hacerlo al *entrar*. (salir, pagar, acostarte, llegar, despertarte)

II. Change these sentences to the present tense. Write the complete sentence and translate. Answers will be found at the back of the book.

    1. Se lo diré al volver.

    2. Juan me lo dará.

    3. Usted tendrá razón.

    4. Vendré por la mañana.

    5. Ellos podrán dártelo.

III. Translate the following sentences into Spanish, then say them aloud. Answers will be found at the back of the book.

1. Where can the tickets be (future of probability)?

2. They must have gone home.

3. When he came in, he greeted us.

4. You can pay it when you leave.

5. I think he's right.

6. I'll give it (the book) to you tomorrow.

7. How handsome you are!

8. You need a haircut.

9. You're prettier than ever.

10. Do you like the color?

QUIZ

From among the three choices given, choose the one which correctly renders the English given at the beginning of each sentence. Write the complete sentence, and translate.

1. *(It will be)* _____ difícil.
   - (a) Será
   - (b) Es
   - (c) Sería

2. *(when you leave)* Usted puede dármelo
   _____.
   - (a) cuando salir
   - (b) al salir
   - (c) en salir

3. *(you are right)* Creo que siempre _____.
   - (a) está derecho
   - (b) tienes razón
   - (c) es razón

4. *(can it be)* ¿Quién _____?
   - (a) lo puede ser
   - (b) será
   - (c) sea

5. *(next door)* La señora está aquí _____ en la peluquería.
   - (a) próxima puerta
   - (b) lado
   - (c) al lado

6. *(I'm going)* Creo que _____ mañana.
   - (a) va
   - (b) voy
   - (c) estoy yendo

7. *(before)* Claro que usted empezó una hora _____ yo.
   - (a) antes que
   - (b) antes de
   - (c) delante

8. *(be right)* Le gusta _____ siempre.
   - (a) ser derecho
   - (b) tener razón
   - (c) estar razón

9. *(upon arriving)* Nos saludamos _____ al hotel.
   - (a) al llegar
   - (b) en llegando
   - (c) sobre llegar

10. *(else)* Hay algo _____.
    - (a) otro
    - (b) demás
    - (c) más

Answers at back of book.

LESSON 48

EN EL TEATRO
AT THE THEATRE

A. *En la taquilla*   At the ticket window

1. Carlos: **¿Tiene usted cuatro entradas para esta noche? Prefiero butacas° de patio, si es posible.**
   Do you have four seats for this evening? I prefer orchestra seats, if it's possible.

2. Empleado: **Vamos a ver... Podría darle unas localidades muy buenas, pero separadas. Me quedan cuatro juntas pero se encuentran bastante al lado. Tengo cuatro localidades excelentes en el centro de la primera fila de balcón, si le interesan.**
   Let's see... I could give you some very good seats, but they're separated. I still have four together but they are rather far over to the side. I have four excellent seats in the center of the first row balcony, if you're interested.

3. Carlos: **Está bien. Démelas, por favor.**
   Fine. Give them to me, please.

4. Empleado: **Son doscientas cuarenta pesetas, señor.**
   That's two hundred forty pesetas, sir.

5. Carlos: **¿A qué hora empieza la función, por favor?**
   At what time does the performance begin, please?

6. Empleado: **A las once,° señor.**
   At eleven o'clock, sir.

B. *En el Teatro Español*   In the Teatro Español

7. Carlos: **Mira, allí están Teresa y Miguel. Teresa, Miguel, ¡qué gusto de verles otra vez!**
Look, there are Theresa and Michael. Theresa, Michael, what a pleasure to see you again!

8. Miguel: **Ustedes han sido tan amables de invitarnos esta noche. Es un verdadero placer para nosotros. Salimos al teatro muy de vez en cuando, y es agradable....**
You have been so kind to invite us this evening. It's a real pleasure for us. We go out to the theater very rarely, and it's very pleasant. . . .

9. Teresa: **¡Qué vestido más elegante, Juana! Ese color te va divinamente.**
What an elegant dress, Jane! That color is very becoming to you.

10. Juana: **Eres muy amable. Acabo de comprarlo. Aquí en Madrid, naturalmente. A Carlos le gusta también y estoy tan contenta de que le agrade...**
You're very kind. I just bought it. Here in Madrid, of course. Carlos likes it too and I'm so happy that it pleases him . . .

11. Miguel: **Bueno, vamos ya que sube el telón dentro de muy poco.**
O.K., let's go, for the curtain is going up in a little while.

12. Vendedor de programas: **¿Programas? ¿Programas, señores?**
Programs? Programs, ladies and gentlemen?

13. Miguel: **Permíteme, Carlos. Dos programas, por favor.**
Permit me, Charles. Two programs, please.

14. Juana: **Me gusta tener estos programas especiales. Tienen tantas fotografías y los guardo como recuerdo de la noche.**
I like to have these special programs. They have so many photographs and I keep them as a souvenir of the evening.

15. Acomodador: **Las entradas, señores. Por aquí, por favor. Primera fila, las cuatro primeras butacas.**
Usher: Tickets, please. This way, please. First row, the first four seats.

16. Miguel: **¡Estas localidades son excelentes! Has tenido suerte, Carlos, porque al entrar esta noche, noté que habían puesto el anuncio "No hay localidades."**
These seats are excellent! You were lucky, Charles, because on entering this evening, I noticed that they had put up the sign "No seats available."

17. Teresa: **¡Qué lleno está! ¡No veo ni un sitio vacío!**
How full it is! I don't see a single empty seat!

18. Miguel: **Bajan las luces. Va a empezar.**
The lights are going down. It's going to begin.

C. *Durante el descanso°*   During intermission

19. Teresa: **Por los aplausos, parece ser un gran éxito. A mí me ha gustado enormemente. ¡Qué buena compañía tiene siempre El Español! Son todos tan buenos actores. ¿No les parece?**
Judging by the applause, it seems to be a great success. I liked it very much. What a fine company the Español always has! They are all such good actors. Don't you think so?

20. Juana: **Es una comedia muy entretenida y tiene unos efectos escenográficos muy bien logrados.**
It's a very amusing comedy and it has some very successful scenic effects.

21. Carlos: **La interpretación es estupenda. Se nota que la dirección ha sido muy cuidada.**
The acting is terrific. You can see that the direction was very painstaking.

22. Miguel: **No hay nadie como Luca de Tena° para estas comedias clásicas.**
There's no one like Luca de Tena for these classic comedies.

23. Teresa: **Los decorados están muy bien hechos además, y las luces, y el vestuario...**
The sets are very well done besides, and the lights and the costumes...

24. Carlos: **Ya veo que te gusta todo. Y ¿qué dices de la sala? Hay un público muy elegante, ¿verdad? ¡Verdadero público de estreno!**
I can see you like everything. And what do you say about the theatre? It's a very elegant audience, isn't it? A real first-night audience!

25. Teresa: **Sí, es verdad. ¿Te has fijado, Juana, en las joyas que lleva aquella señora del palco? Ya sabes la que digo. Las esmeraldas más grandes que he visto en la vida.**
Yes, it's true. Jane, did you notice the jewelry that the woman in the box is wearing? You know the one I mean. The biggest emeralds I've ever seen in my life!

26. Juana: **Sí, querida. ¿No te parecen demasiado grandes? Si yo tuviese...**
Yes, dear. Don't you think they're too large? If I had ...

27. Carlos: **Bueno, ¿es que vienen a ver la comedia o a comentar lo que lleva la gente?**
Well, do you come to see the comedy or to comment on what people are wearing?

28. Juana: **Perdona, querido, pero tienes que permitirnos un poco de chismorreo.**
Sorry, darling, but you must let us have a little gossip.

29. Miguel: *Hablando de comedias, Carlos, ¿viste aquella tan divertida que pusieron la otra noche en televisión?*
Speaking of comedies, Charles, did you see that funny one they put on television the other night?

30. Carlos: *¿Cuál? Vi una el miércoles pasado, una película vieja, pero bastante divertida. Creo que se llamaba. No hay burlas con el amor° o algo parecido.*
Which one? I saw one last Wednesday, an old movie, but quite amusing. I think it was called *Love Isn't a Joking Matter* or something like that.

31. Juana: *¡Ay, qué tonto eres, Carlitos! ¡Así se llama la comedia de esta noche!*
Oh! What a fool you are, Charlie! That's the name of tonight's comedy!

32. Carlos: *¡Ah, sí que es verdad! Perdona, es que siempre se me confunden estos títulos. Se parecen tanto ¿verdad?*

Oh yes, that's right! Sorry, it's just that these titles always confuse me. They're so much alike, aren't they?

33. Juana: *Para ti, sí. La película se llamaba Los secretos de Susana. ¡Verdad que se parecen muchísimo!*
For you, yes. The movie was called *Susan's Secrets*. It's true that they're very much alike!

34. Carlos: *¡No me tomes el pelo, querida! Tú sabes lo despistado que me encuentro con esas cosas.*
Don't pull my leg, dear. You know how confused I am about those things.

35. Miguel: *¿Les gusta la zarzuela?° Dicen que hay una obra buenísima ahora en el Teatro de la Zarzuela. No me acuerdo ahora del título, pero ha tenido muy buena crítica.*
Do you like the zarzuela? They say that there's a very good one now at the Teatro de la Zarzuela. I can't remember the title now, but it's had very good reviews.

36. Juana: *Es La Verbena de la Paloma. Y sí que es preciosa. Una amiga mía fué a verla la semana pasada, y dice que la impresionó mucho. Tenemos que ir a verla.*
It's *La Verbena de la Paloma*. And it *is* beautiful. A friend of mine went to see it last week, and she says that it impressed her very much.

37. Carlos: *Suenan los timbres. Va a empezar de nuevo. Entremos antes que bajen las luces.*
The bells are ringing. It's going to begin again. Let's go in before they lower the lights.

NOTES

1. *butaca:* lit., "armchair." *Butaca de patio* = Orchestra seat.

6. *A las once:* Spanish theater begins late by American standards. There is a "matinée" that begins at 7:30 P.M. and the evening performance begins at 10:45 P.M. or 11 P.M. The early show is called the *función de tarde* and the later one the *función de noche.*

Title C. *descanso:* intermission. In Latin America it is more common to say *intermedio.*

22. *Cayetano Luca de Tena:* Playwright and director who has presented some of the finest productions of Spanish Classic Theater.

30. *No hay burlas con el amor:* One of the comedies of the famous Golden Age playwright Pedro Calderón de la Barca. Best known for his drama *La vida es sueño.*

35. *Zarzuela:* A kind of short musical comedy, similar to the operetta, cultivated preeminently in the nineteenth century. The name comes from the Palace of the Zarzuela near Madrid, where these works were first performed. *La Verbena de la Paloma* (1893) by Tomás Bretón is one of the most beautiful and popular. The earliest varieties of the genre were written by the Golden Age playwrights Lope de Vega and Calderón de la Barca.

GRAMMATICAL ITEMS FOR SPECIAL STUDY

I. A. *por:* along, through, during (approximate time)

1. Le encontré andando por el parque.

2. Vengan ustedes por aquí.

3. Espero verle por la mañana.

4. Nos gusta andar por las calles céntricas.

1. *I met him walking through the park.*

2. *Come this way (along here).*

3. *I hope to see him in the morning (anytime during the morning).*

4. *We like to walk along the downtown streets.*

B. *para:* by (a certain time limit)
    for (a definite purpose)

1. Usted lo tendrá para las ocho sin falta.

2. Lo necesito para las once.

3. ¿Para qué necesita usted el dinero? Para pagar la cuenta.

1. *You'll have it by eight o'clock without fail.*

2. *I need it by eleven o'clock.*

3. *For what do you need the money? To pay the bill.*

II. Verbs: *o* ↘→ *ue*   *e* ↘→ *ie*

Study:

A. 1. No encuentro el número.

2. A ver si lo encuentras aquí.

3. Ella siempre lo encuentra.

4. Ellos lo encuentran fácilmente.

5. No lo encontramos nunca.

6. Vosotros lo encontráis allí.

1. *I can't find the number.*

2. *Let's see if you (familiar singular) find it here.*

3. *She always finds it.*

4. *They find it easily.*

5. *We never find it.*

6. *You (fam. pl.) find it there.*

Note: When the stress falls on the second syllable, the *o* of the stem breaks down to *ue* (that is, in the first, second, third persons singular and third person plural). (Similar verbs *o* ↘→ *ue* are: *poder, mover, contar, acostar, costar, acordar, probar, almorzar)*

B. 1. Lo entiendo todo.

2. ¿Lo entiendes tú?

3. Ella lo entiende.

4. Ellos lo entienden.

5. Nosotros lo entendemos.

6. Vosotros lo entendéis.

1. *I understand everything.*

2. *You (familiar singular) understand everything?*

3. *She understands everything.*

4. *They understand everything.*

5. *We understand everything.*

6. *You (fam. pl.) understand everything.*

As with the change from *o* to *ue* (above), the same thing happens here. The *e* of the stem breaks down to *ie* under stress, i.e., in the first, second, and third persons singular, and third person plural. These changes occur in the present indicative and the present subjunctive. Like *entender* in this respect are: *sentar,* cerrar, comenzar, despertar, empezar, pensar, perder, defender.

III. *¡Qué* + Noun! = What a _____!
   ¡Qué + Adjective! = How _____!

   Study:

1. ¡Qué día!	*What a day!*
2. ¡Qué mujer!	*What a woman!*
3. ¡Qué gusto!	*What a pleasure!*

1. ¡Qué bonito!	*How pretty!*
2. ¡Qué difícil!	*How difficult!*
3. ¡Qué tonto!	*How silly!*

Note: Some words may be used as either noun or adjective:

¡Qué tonto eres!	*What a fool you are!*
¡Qué tonto estás!	*How silly you are!*

IV. *Ser:* to be (permanent, fixed state existence) WITH NOUNS

   Estar: to be (in a place, in a transitory or varying state) WITH ADJECTIVES

   Study:

1. Soy profesor.	*I am a teacher.*
2. Juan es estudiante.	*John is a student.*
3. La puerta es grande.	*The door is large.*

1. Estoy en la clase.	*I am in the class.*
2. Juan está cansado.	*John is tired.*
3. La puerta está abierta.	*The door is open.*

Note: Some adjectives may be used with *ser* to denote a permanent, unchanging state or condition.

Es viejo. *He's old (i.e., an old man).*
Es aburrido. *He's dull (i.e., tiresome, a bore).*
Es joven. *He's young.*

contrasted with:

Está viejo. *He looks old. (He may not really be old.)*
Está cansado. *He's tired.*
Está joven. *He looks young. (He could actually be old.)*

DRILLS AND EXERCISES

I. Substitute each of the words or expressions in parentheses for the italicized words or expressions in the model sentence. Write the new sentence and say it aloud.

   A. Le ví andando por *la calle.* (el centro, el parque, el pasillo, el campo, la carretera)

   B. No tengo nada que hacer por *la mañana.* (la tarde, la noche, el día, esta semana, el verano)

   C. Me lo tiene que entregar para *las ocho.* (el fin de semana, esta noche, esta tarde, mediodía, la semana que viene)

   D. ¡Qué *hermosa está* tu hermana hoy! (cansada, vieja, fea, bonita, ocupada)

   E. ¡Qué *placer!* (gusto, pena, lástima, problema, palabra)

   F. ¿Cómo *va* tu hermano? (está, se siente, se encuentra)

II. Change these sentences to the plural. Write the complete sentence and translate. Answers will be found in the back of the book.

   1. Yo soy actor.
   2. El está en los Estados Unidos.
   3. Usted es de México.
   4. Tú estás cansado.
   5. Ella está en la sala.

III. Translate the following sentences into Spanish, then say them aloud. Answers will be found at the back of the book.

1. At what time does the performance begin?
2. What a pleasure to see you again!
3. I just bought this dress.
4. It's a very amusing comedy.
5. I saw a movie last Wednesday.
6. I don't remember the title.
7. It's going to begin again.
8. A friend of mine went to see the comedy.
9. She liked it.
10. Let's go in right away.

QUIZ

From among the three choices given, choose the one which correctly renders the English given at the beginning of each sentence. Write the complete sentence, and translate it.

1. *(How)* ¡_____ hermosa es la vida!
   (a) Cómo
   (b) Qué
   (c) Como

2. *(find)* Usted lo _____ siempre.
   (a) encontra
   (b) encuentras
   (c) encuentra

3. *(can)* Ellos dicen que _____ ir mañana.
   (a) pueden
   (b) poden
   (c) puden

4. *(What a)* ¡_____ día más agradable!
   (a) Qué un
   (b) Cómo
   (c) Qué

5. *(is)* Parece que él _____ un hombre muy importante.
   - (a) es
   - (b) está
   - (c) ser

6. *(understand)* Yo lo _____ todo.
   - (a) compriendo
   - (b) entiendo
   - (c) entendo

7. *(tells)* Juana les _____ una historia todos los días.
   - (a) conta
   - (b) cuentas
   - (c) cuenta

8. *(can _____ be)* ¿Dónde _____ el libro?
   - (a) puede ser
   - (b) estará
   - (c) estar

9. *(was)* El hermano de Juan _____ el héroe.
   - (a) estuvo
   - (b) estaba
   - (c) era

10. *(What a)* ¡_____ placer me da verles aquí!
    - (a) Qué
    - (b) Que un
    - (c) Cómo

Answers at back of book.

LESSON 49

EN EL MUSEO DEL PRADO
IN THE PRADO MUSEUM

1. Empleado: **Quince pesetas, por favor.**
   Fifteen pesetas, please.

2. Carlos: **Aquí tiene usted. Treinta por dos
   entradas.** *(A Juana)* **Debiéramos haber
   venido el domingo. No cobran entrada.**
   Here you are. Thirty for two tickets. *(To Jane)*
   We should have come on Sunday. There's no
   entrance charge.

3. Juana: **Sí; pero hay tanta gente, y tantos
   niños que no se puede ver nada.**
   Yes, but there are so many people and so many
   children that you can't see anything.

4. Carlos: **Tienes razón, como siempre. Quiero
   verlo todo detenidamente. Es una de las
   colecciones más fabulosas del mundo.**
   You're right, as usual. I want to see it all,
   taking my time. It's one of the most fabulous
   collections in the world.

5. Guía: **¿Quieren un guía, señores? Yo les
   puedo dar informes y detalles sobre todas
   las obras, y ayudarles a encontrar las que les
   interesan sin perder tiempo.**
   Guide: Do you want a guide? I can give you
   information and details about all the works,
   and help you find the ones that interest you
   without wasting time.

6. Juana: **A mí me gustaría tener un guía. Mi
   marido entiende mucho pero...**

I'd like to have a guide. My husband knows a
great deal but . . .

7. Carlos: **No soy más que un aficionado. Me
gusta pintar un poco los fines de semana.**
I'm just an amateur. I like to paint a little on
weekends.

8. Guía: **Usted encontrará inspiración aquí.
Hay obras de todas las épocas, de todos los
estilos, de antiguos a modernos.**
You'll find inspiration here. There are works
from every period, of every style, from ancient
to modern.

9. Juana: **¿Dónde está la Dama de Elche?°
Primero quiero verla a ella. Se dice que es
preciosa. Un amigo mío me ha dicho que
siempre va a saludarla al entrar en el Prado.**
Where is the Dama de Elche? First I want to
see her. They say she's beautiful. A friend of
mine told me he always goes to greet her when
he enters the Prado.

10. Guía: **El hermoso busto de la Dama de Elche
se encuentra aquí en este piso, señora. Allí
al final, en un nicho a la derecha.**
The beautiful bust of the Dama de Elche is
right here on this floor, madam. There at the
end, in a niche to the right.

11. Carlos: **Gracias, señor. Tenemos un plano
del museo y sabemos lo que queremos ver
hoy. Así que me parece que no nos hace falta
su ayuda.**
Thank you, sir. We have a plan of the museum
and we know what we want to see today. So I
don't think we need your help.

12. Juana: **Vamos, Carlos. Y luego podemos dar
una vuelta rápida a la sala de las estatuas
grecorromanas que se encuentra detrás del
nicho de la Dama.**
Come on, Charles. And then we can take a
quick walk around the room of Greco-Roman
statues that's right behind the niche of the
Dama.

13. Carlos: **Bien. ¿Qué maravilla es esta Dama
de Elche! La comparan con La Nefertiti en
hermosura. ¿Verdad que es una belleza clá-
sica?**
O.K. What a marvel this Dama de Elche is!
They compare her with Nefertiti in beauty.
Isn't it a classic beauty?

14. Juana: **¡Me encanta! ¡Qué peinado° más
original!**
She's enchanting! What an unusual hairdo!

15. Carlos: **Vamos a subir aquí por esta escalera
a los salones de la pintura española. Es lo
que me interesa más.**
Let's go up this stairway here to the rooms of
Spanish painting. That's what interests me
most.

16. Juana: **¡Ah! Aquí están las obras maestras de
El Greco,° Velázquez,° Murillo,° Goya°
. . . Quiero ver "Las Meninas," y "Las Lan-
zas," y "Los Borrachos" y . . .**
Oh! Here are the masterworks of El Greco,
Velázquez, Murillo, Goya . . . I want to see
"The Meninas," "The Lances," "The Drunk-
ards" and . . .

17. Carlos: **¡Despacio! Espera un momento,
querida. No podemos verlo todo de un**

golpe. Vamos a empezar con este salón de las pinturas de El Greco.

Slow down! Wait a minute, dear. We can't see everything all at once. Let's begin with this room of paintings by El Greco.

18. Juana: **¡Ay sí! Mira, allí delante está "La Adoración de los Pastores." ¡Qué hermosa es la figura de la Virgen! ¿Verdad que es luminoso y espiritual todo en este cuadro?**

Oh, yes! Look, there in front of us is "The Adoration of the Shepherds." How beautiful the figure of the Virgin is! Isn't everything luminous and spiritual in this picture?

19. Carlos: **Fíjate qué alargadas parecen todas las figuras. Es como si se las mirase desde abajo. Todo tiende a subir.**

Notice how elongated the figures look. It's as if we were looking at them from below. Everything seems to be rising.

20. Juana: **¡Es verdaderamente una maravilla! Quiero ver el famoso cuadro "El Entierro del Conde Orgaz." ¿Dónde está? No lo veo por ninguna parte.**

It's really marvelous! I want to see the famous painting "The Burial of Count Orgaz." Where is it? I don't see it around here anywhere.

21. Carlos: **Es que no está aquí, Juana. Para eso, tendremos que hacer un viaje a Toledo. Se encuentra en la Iglesia de Santo Tomé.**

That's because it's not here, Jane. For that, we'll have to take a trip to Toledo. It's in the Iglesia de Santo Tomé.

22. Juana: *¡Ah, sí! Es verdad. Debiéramos ir a Toledo a verlo. Todos me dicen que es una*

*ciudad encantadora. Allí podemos visitar el
museo de El Greco. Es la casa en que vivió el
pintor. Está restaurada y se encuentra ahora
en las mismas condiciones del siglo diecisiete.
¿Cuándo podremos hacerlo? ¡Me entusiasma
la idea!*

Oh, yes! That's true. We should go to Toledo
to see it. Everyone tells me that it's a charming
city. We can visit the El Greco Museum there.
It's the house in which the painter lived. It's
restored and is in the same condition as in the
seventeenth century. When can we do it? I'm
enthusiastic about the idea!

23. Carlos: *Seguramente tendremos tiempo de ha-
    cerlo. A mí también me gusta la idea. Mirare-
    mos nuestros planes para la semana que viene
    a ver si podemos arreglarlo algún día.*

    We'll surely have time to do it. *I* like the idea
    too. We'll look at our plans for next week to
    see if we can arrange it some day.

24. Juana: *¡Qué bien! Pero ahora vamos a pasar a
    ver los cuadros de Velázquez. Quiero ver los
    famosos retratos del rey Felipe Cuarto y el del
    príncipe Don Baltasar Carlos.*

    How wonderful! But now let's go to see the
    paintings of Velázquez. I want to see the fa-
    mous portraits of King Philip IV and the one of
    Prince Baltasar Carlos.

25. Carlos: *Mira, querida, allí está "Las
    Meninas" con el famoso autorretrato. ¿Ves
    que el pintor está allí, a la izquierda, con el
    pincel en la mano como si estuviese pintando
    lo que tiene delante? Fíjate en la inocencia y
    belleza del retrato de la princesita.*

Look, darling, there's "The Meninas" with
the famous self-portrait. Do you see that the
painter is there, on the left, with his brush in
his hand as if he were painting what is before
him? Notice the innocence and beauty of the
portrait of the little princess.

26. Juana: *¡Qué perfección! Se ve que Velázquez
    era un maestro prodigioso. ¡Qué variedad de
    temas y estilos! No sé cual de estos pintores me
    gusta más. Todos me gustan tanto.*
    What perfection! One can see that Velázquez
    was a prodigious master. What a variety of
    themes and styles. I don't know which of these
    painters I like best. I like all of them so much.

27. Carlos: *Veo que tendremos que volver para ver
    lo demás. Es casi la hora de cerrar el museo, y
    todavía no hemos visto nada de Zurbarán,° ni
    de Murillo, ni de Goya que te interesaba tanto.
    Las tres horas han pasado volando.*
    I see that we'll have to come back to see the
    rest. It's almost time to close the museum, and
    we still haven't seen anything of Zurbarán, or
    Murillo, or Goya, that interested you so much.
    The three hours have flown by.

28. Juana: *¡Qué lástima! ¡Cuando uno está pasán-
    dolo bien el tiempo sí que vuela!*
    What a pity! When you're having a good time,
    the time really flies!

NOTES

9. *la Dama de Elche:* A polichrome bust of an
   idol or goddess, so-called because it was found
   in Elche, a small town on the Mediterranean
   coast south of Alicante. It dates from the fifth

century B.C. and is considered one of the most important, as well as the most beautiful, of early Iberian artworks.

14. *¡Qué peinado...!* What here is referred to as the "hairdo" of the Dama de Elche is actually an elaborate and ornate headdress that consists of two impressive round wheel-like pieces framing the severe beauty of the face.

16. *El Greco:* Domenico Theotocopoulis, born in Crete, lived in Spain from approximately 1577 until his death in 1614. He is generally known by the name *El Greco* ("The Greek").

16. Velázquez: Painter, born in Seville in 1599; court painter for Philip IV. He has left a rich gallery of portraits of the royal family and retainers, as well as a justly famed variety of paintings of mythological and historical subjects.

16. Murillo: Painter, also from Seville (1617–1682), known as "the Spanish Correggio."

16. Goya: Born in a small town in Aragón, Fuendetodos, in 1746; died in Bordeaux in 1828. One of the giants of Spanish art, his influence is felt to the present day. He is considered a precursor of Expressionism.

27. Zurbarán: Born in Fuentes de Cantos, Extremadura, in 1598. Studied and painted in Seville. Known for his monochromatic portraits of monks and nuns, he was a master of perspective and effects of light.

GRAMMATICAL ITEMS FOR SPECIAL STUDY

I. **Deber** + infinitive: must, should, ought to

Study:

1. Juan debe tener las entradas.

2. Deben estar por aquí.

3. Debes estudiar la lección.

1. *John must have the tickets.*

2. *They must be around here.*

3. *You ought to study the lesson.*

II. **Tanto** + noun: so much (sing.), so many (pl.)

Study:

A. 1. Hay tanta gente en el teatro.

2. Nunca he visto tantas joyas.

3. No sabía que tenía tanto dinero.

1. *There are so many people in the theatre.*

2. *I have never seen so many jewels.*

3. *I didn't know that he had so much money.*

B. **tan** + adjective (or adverb): so _____

Study:

1. Teresa está tan ocupada.

2. Estaban tan enfermos que no podían ir.

3. Me parece tan fácil.

1. *Theresa is so busy.*

2. *They were so sick they couldn't go.*

3. *It seems so easy to me.*

C. 1. Me habló tan lentamente que lo entendí todo.

 2. Ella lo explicó tan claramente que todos lo entendieron.

 3. No debes hacerlo tan de prisa.

 1. *He spoke to me so slowly that I understood everything.*

 2. *She explained it so clearly that everyone understood it.*

 3. *You shouldn't do it so rapidly.*

D. *Tanto* is used by itself adverbially.

 Study:

 1. ¡Las obras de Velázquez me gustan tanto!

 2. ¡Todo me interesa tanto!

 3. ¡He comido tanto!

 1. *I like the works of Velázquez so (very) much!*

 2. *Everything interests me so (very) much!*

 3. *I ate so much!*

III. *No, nunca, nadie, ninguno:* Double and triple negatives to reinforce a negative idea.

 Study:

 1. *No* veo a *nadie.*

 2. *No* veo *nunca* a *nadie.*

 3. *No* voy *nunca* a *ninguna* parte.

 1. I don't see anyone.

 2. I never see anyone.

 3. I never go anywhere.

A negative word may be placed before the verb, replacing "no." Compare:

1. No veo nunca a nadie. Nunca veo a nadie.

2. No me habla nadie. Nadie me habla.

3. No voy nunca a ninguna parte. Nunca voy a ninguna parte.

1. I never see anyone.

2. No one speaks to me.

3. I never go anywhere.

DRILLS AND EXERCISES

I. Substitute each of the words or expressions in parentheses for the italicized word or expression in the model sentence. Write each new sentence and say it aloud.

A. Juan debe estar en *la biblioteca*. (el banco, la casa, la sala de estar, el parque, el centro)

B. Ellos deben haber *estudiado*. (descansado, comido, ido, salido, terminado)

C. Juana y yo debemos *empezar*. (terminar, leer, practicar, hablar, salir)

D. Hay *tanta gente* en el museo. (tantos cuadros, tantas pinturas, tanto ruido, tantos niños, tantas señoras)

E. El lo hizo tan *claramente*. (lentamente, rápidamente, de prisa, fácilmente, bien)

F. Nunca he estado tan *ocupado*. (cansado, enfermo, perezoso, contento, equivocado)

II. Rephrase the following sentences, placing *no* before the verb. Write the complete sentence and translate. Answers will be found in the back of the book.

1. Nunca escribo a nadie.

2. Nadie me escribe.

3. Nunca compramos nada.

4. Juan y José nunca van a ninguna parte.

5. Nunca he visto a tanta gente en el museo.

III. Translate the following sentences into Spanish, then say them aloud. Answers will be found at the back of the book.

1. There are so many people here.

2. He explained it so clearly that I understood everything.

3. I have never been so busy.

4. You must be tired.

5. John and Mary ought to study more.

6. I never want to see her.

7. How elongated all the figures look!

8. We have to take a trip to Toledo.

9. When can we do it?

10. I want to see the famous painting.

QUIZ

From among the three choices given, choose the one which correctly renders the English given at the beginning of each sentence. Write the complete sentence, and translate.

1. *(so)* Es _____ difícil comprenderlo.
   (a) tanto
   (b) tanta
   (c) tan

2. *(ever)* No le veo _____.
   - (a) nunca
   - (b) algo
   - (c) algunas veces

3. *(everything that)* Creo _____ me dice
   Juan.
   - (a) todo lo que
   - (b) todos que
   - (c) todas las

4. *(all the _____)* Juan ha comprado
   _____ libros que quería.
   - (a) todos
   - (b) todo el
   - (c) todos los

5. *(so much)* ¡Roberto tiene _____ tiempo
   libre!
   - (a) tan mucho
   - (b) tanto
   - (c) tanto que

6. *(anything)* No quiero _____ ahora.
   - (a) alguna cosa
   - (b) nada
   - (c) algo

7. *(ought to)* Me parece que yo _____
   levantarme ahora.
   - (a) debo
   - (b) tengo que
   - (c) hay que

8. *(so many)* No he tenido nunca _____
   problemas.
   - (a) tan muchos
   - (b) tantos
   - (c) tantas

9. *(anything)* No le debo _____.
   - (a) algo
   - (b) alguna cosa
   - (c) nada

10. *(such)* Nunca ha leído libros _____
    difíciles.
    - (a) tan
    - (b) tanto
    - (c) tantos

Answers at back of book.

LESSON 50

LA ARTESANIA ESPAÑOLA
SPANISH HANDICRAFTS

A. *Una visita al Rastro de Madrid*
   A visit to the Rastro (Flea Market) in Madrid.

1. Juana: **Nos han hablado° tanto del Rastro
   que debiéramos ir a verlo. Tiene que ser
   interesante. No sé exactamente lo que es.**
   People have talked to us so much about the
   Flea Market, we should go to see it. It must be
   interesting. I don't know exactly what it is.

2. Carlos: **Seguramente debe ser interesante.
   Es una sección de calles donde hay muchas
   tiendas de antigüedades, y además vende-
   dores de toda clase de cosas que tienen su
   mercancía al aire libre. A veces los artículos
   están tendidos en el suelo.**
   It must be interesting. It's a section of streets
   where there are many antique shops and, besides, vendors of all kinds of things who have
   their merchandise in the open air. At times the
   articles are spread out on the ground.

3. Juana: **Se dice que es más divertido los domingos° por la mañana.**
They say it's more amusing on Sunday mornings.

4. Carlos: **Sí. Es cuando todo el mundo va. ¿Quieres ir hoy, cuando hay menos gente?**
Yes. It's when everyone goes. Do you want to go today, when there are fewer people?

5. Juana: **Sí, vamos. Miguel y Teresa me dijeron que querían ir también. Vamos a ver si pueden acompañarnos hoy. Puesto que ellos lo conocen ya, pueden ayudarnos un poco.**
Yes, let's go. Michael and Theresa told me that they wanted to go too. Let's see if they can go with us today. Since they know it already, they can help us a little.

6. Carlos: *(al teléfono)* **¿Miguel? Hola, ¿cómo está usted? Bien, bien, me alegro. Juana y yo estábamos hablando, y pensábamos ir al Rastro esta mañana. Como Juana me ha dicho que ustedes habían hablado de ir, llamo a ver si pueden hacerlo hoy. Nos gustaría muchísimo. ¡Ah, sí! ¡Estupendo! Entonces, pasaremos a buscarles,° ya que están en el camino. ¿Cuánto tiempo necesitan? ¿Una hora? Bien, Miguel, estaremos dentro de una hora. ¡Hasta pronto!**
(on the telephone) Michael? Hello, how are you? Fine, fine, I'm glad. Jane and I were talking, and we were thinking of going to the Flea Market this morning. Since Jane told me that you had spoken of going, I'm calling to

find out if you can do it today. We would like
that very much. Oh, yes! Terrific! Then, we'll
come by to pick you up, it's on the way. How
much time do you need? An hour? O.K.,
Michael, we'll be there in an hour. See you
soon!

7. Juana: **¡Qué bien! Ellos van con nosotros.
Me alegro tanto. Teresa dice que hay que
saber regatear, y ella ha prometido enseñarme la manera de hacerlo.**
How nice! They're going with us. I'm so
pleased. Theresa says that you have to know
how to bargain, and she promised to show me
the way to do it.

8. Carlos: **Eso es, hay que saber regatear. Y no
debes dar la impresión de ser muy rica. No
lleves todas las joyas que te he dado.**
That's right, you have to know how to bargain.
And you shouldn't give the impression of being very rich. Don't wear all the jewelry I've
given you.

9. Juana: **¡Qué bromista! ¿Tú crees que con las
joyas que tengo me van a tomar por rica?**
What a joker! Do you think that with the jewels
I have, they're going to think I'm rich?

B. *En el Rastro*   At the Flea Market

10. Carlos: **Vamos a entrar en esta tienda. ¡Hay
tantos artículos de loza! Vean aquellos platos y tazas. ¡El diseño y los colores son
hermosos! Dígame, señor, ¿dónde hacen
esos platos?**
Let's go into this store. There is so much
china! Look at those plates and cups. Both the
design and colors are beautiful! Tell me, sir,
where are those plates made?

11. Vendedor: **Son de Valencia, señor, de una de las fábricas más conocidas. Se puede reconocer la producción de esa fábrica por la extraordinaria finura de todo el trabajo. Estos platos son todos del siglo pasado.**
They're from Valencia, sir, from one of the best-known factories. You can recognize the products of that factory by the extraordinary quality of the work. These plates are of the last (past) century.

12. Juana: **Son preciosos. Me imagino que serán carísimos, ¿verdad? Me gustaría tener algunos de los más grandes para colgar en la pared del comedor.**
They're beautiful. I imagine they must be very expensive, aren't they? I would like to have some of the larger ones to hang on the wall in the dining room.

13. Carlos: **¿Cuánto valen los grandes, señor? Especialmente estos en azul y amarillo, con el diseño de pájaros.**
How much are the large ones, sir? Especially these in blue and yellow, with the design of birds.

14. Vendedor: **Esos son precisamente los más caros. Están pintados a mano y son de un estilo que no se encuentra muy a menudo.**
Those are precisely the most expensive. They're hand painted and in a style that isn't very often found.

15. Carlos: **Bueno, de acuerdo. Pero, ¿cuánto valen?**
Well, agreed. But how much do they cost?

16. Vendedor: **¿Cuántos quieren ustedes? Se los puedo dejar a muy buen precio.**

How many do you want? I could make a very
good price for you.

17. Carlos: **Depende de lo que quiere decir
"muy buen precio." Queremos cuatro o
cinco, ¿no te parece, Juana?**
That depends on what "a very good price"
means. We want four or five, don't you think,
Jane?

18. Juana: **Sí. Y éstos son los que me gustan
más. ¿Cuánto quiere usted por ellos?**
Yes. And these are the ones that I like best.
How much do you want for them?

19. Vendedor: **Bueno, para ustedes, y como precio especial, se los dejo los cinco en quinien-
tas pesetas.**
Well, for you, and as a very special price, I'll
let you have the five of them for five hundred
pesetas.

20. Carlos: **Es demasiado. Por cuatrocientas, me
los llevo.**
It's too much. At four hundred, I'll take them.

21. Vendedor: **Lo siento. Ya les he dado el mejor
precio posible.**
I'm sorry. I've already given you the best
possible price.

22. Juana: **¡Ay, y me gustan tanto! ¿Qué le
parece cuatrocientas cincuenta?**
Oh, and I like them so much! What do you
think of four hundred and fifty?

23. Vendedor: **Bueno, como ustedes me son muy
simpáticos, se los dejo en cuatrocientas cincuenta.**
Well, since I like you, I'll let you have them
for four hundred fifty.

24. Carlos: **Bien, tome usted. Envuélvalos con cuidado y volveremos a buscarlos dentro de poco.**
O.K. Here you are. Wrap them carefully and we'll come back for them in a little while.

25. Teresa: *Vamos a aquella tienda de muebles antiguos. Tienen tantos arcones de madera labrada.*
Let's go to that store of antique furniture. They have so many chests of carved wood.

26. Juana: *¡Qué comedor! Mira aquellos sillones tan regios. ¿No lo encuentras estupendo, Carlos?*
What a dining room set! Look at those big regal-looking chairs. Don't you think it's terrific, Charles?

27. Carlos: *Desde luego. Pero ten en cuenta que no podemos cargar con cosas tan pesadas. Costaría una fortuna embalarlos y mandarlos.*
Of course. But bear in mind that we can't load ourselves down with such heavy things. It would cost a fortune to pack and send them.

28. Juana: *Tienes razón. Yo no estaba pensando en comprarlo, solamente quería admirarlo.*
You're right. I wasn't thinking of buying it, I only wanted to admire it.

29. Teresa: *¿Qué les parece la idea de tomar algún refresco? Me cansa un poco tanto andar y mirar.°*
What do you think of the idea of having something to drink. So much walking and looking tires me a little.

30. Carlos: *¡Claro que sí! ¿Por qué no se sientan ustedes en aquella terraza de allí enfrente? Yo*

volveré a buscar los platos. Los debe tener envueltos ya. °
By all means. Why don't you sit down in that sidewalk café across the street? I'll go back to get the plates. He ought to have them wrapped by now.

31. Juana: *¿Qué quieres tomar, Carlos? Te lo pido mientras tanto.*
What are you having, Charles? I'll order it meanwhile.

32. Carlos: *Me gustaría una cerveza bien fría. Tengo mucha sed.*
I feel like having a cold beer. I'm very thirsty.

NOTES

1. *nos han hablado:* Note the third person plural (they) used impersonally.

3. *los domingos:* The article is used with days of the week, "on Sundays."

6. *buscarles: buscar,* to look for. This may also be used in the sense of "to stop by for someone," "to pick them up." See also sentence 24, *volveremos a buscarlos.*

29. *tanto andar y mirar:* Notice the use of the infinitives as nouns here.

30. *ya:* Here, "already," has the idea of "by now" or "by this time." In this final position *ya* often gives the sense.

GRAMMATICAL ITEMS FOR SPECIAL STUDY
I. A. *Todos (as)* + article: every, all

Study:

1. Tenemos todos los estilos.

2. Hay pinturas de todas las épocas.

3. Quiero ver todos los muebles.

1. *We have every style (all the styles).*

2. *There are paintings from every period (all the periods).*

3. *I want to see all the furniture.*

  B. **Todo (a)** + article: the whole, the entire

    Study:

1. Me gusta toda la ciudad.

2. El ha viajado por todo el país.

3. Todo el mundo estaba allí.

1. *I like the whole city.*

2. *He has traveled through the entire country.*

3. *The whole world (everybody) was there.*

Note: *Todo el día*—all day (the entire day)
     Todos los días—every day (all the days)

II. A. **Todo lo que:** everything (that)

    Study:

1. Ella quiere comprar todo lo que ve.

2. Todo lo que hemos visto nos ha gustado.

3. Juan comió todo lo que le pusieron delante.

1. *She wants to buy everything (that) she sees.*

2. *We like everything (that) we saw.*

3. *John ate everything (that) they put in front of him.*

B. *Lo + todo:* everything

Study:

1. Quiero verlo todo.

2. Me lo explicó todo.

3. Ellos querían comprarlo todo.

1. *I want to see everything.*

2. *He explained everything to me.*

3. *They wanted to buy everything.*

III. *El* and *Los* + days of the week

Study:

1. Estoy menos ocupado los sábados.

2. Voy a verle el lunes.

3. Hay corridas los domingos por la tarde.

1. *I am less busy (not so busy) on Saturdays.*

2. *I am going to see him on Monday.*

3. *There are bullfights on Sundays in the afternoon.*

IV. *Pensar + en:* think "of" or "about"

Study:

1. ¿En qué piensa usted?

2. Estaba pensando en todo lo que tengo que hacer.

3. Ellos piensan en las dificultades que tienen.

1. *What are you thinking about?*

2. *I was thinking about everything I have to do.*

3. *They think about the difficulties they have.*

DRILLS AND EXERCISES

I. Substitute each of the words or expressions in the parentheses for the italicized word or expression in the model sentence. Write each new sentence and say it aloud.

  A. Juan quiere comprar todos los *muebles.* (libros, zapatos, coches, cuadros, ceniceros)

  B. Ella ha visto todas las *pinturas.* (blusas, casas, obras de teatro, bolsas, medias)

  C. Ellos han visto todo el *país.* (museo, pueblo, centro, mercado, teatro)

  D. Lo *vieron* el martes. (compraron, vendieron, visitaron, hicieron, terminaron)

  E. Me gusta *descansar* los domingos. (pasear, ir al cine, leer, dormir hasta tarde, jugar)

  F. Estaba pensando en *el trabajo.* (el viaje, el tiempo, la comedia, el museo, la música)

II. Change these sentences to the negative. Write the complete sentence and translate. Answers will be found in the back of the book.

  1. Siempre pienso en el viaje.

  2. Vamos al museo el lunes.

  3. Le gusta comprar todo lo que ve.

  4. Los niños comieron todo el helado.

  5. Es difícil comprenderlo.

III. Translate the following sentences into Spanish, then say them aloud. Answers will be found at the back of the book.

  1. They have told us so much about the museum.

  2. It is said *(se dice)* that it's more amusing on Sundays.

3. We can go with you tomorrow.

4. You have to know how to bargain.

5. You shouldn't give the impression of being rich.

6. One can recognize all of the work of that factory by the style.

7. I can let you have it all at a very good price.

8. That depends on what you mean.

9. All the pictures are expensive.

10. He ought to have them (the plates) wrapped now.

QUIZ

From among the three choices given, choose the one which correctly renders the English given at the beginning of each sentence. Write the complete sentence, and translate.

1. *(Every)* Le veo _____ martes.
   (a) todas las
   (b) todo el
   (c) todos los

2. *(all _____)* He pasado _____ tarde en la piscina.
   (a) todo el
   (b) toda la
   (c) toda

3. *(all day)* Juan estaba leyendo _____.
   (a) todo el día
   (b) todo día
   (c) toda la día

4. *(on)* Voy a verle _____ domingo.
   (a) en
   (b) el
   (c) por

5. *(everything)* Usted cree _____ él le dice.
   (a) todos los que
   (b) todo el que
   (c) todo lo que

6. *(every)* Normalmente voy a visitarle
   _____ sábados.
   (a) cada
   (b) todos los
   (c) algunos

7. *(on)* _____ miércoles, vamos a ir de
   compras.
   (a) En
   (b) El
   (c) La

8. *(about her)* Nunca pienso _____ ahora.
   (a) en ella
   (b) sobre ella
   (c) de ellas

9. *(all the news)* Siempre oigo _____ por
   radio.
   (a) todo la noticia
   (b) todas las noticias
   (c) todas noticias

10. *(of)* Yo no estaba pensando _____
    comprarlo.
    (a) en
    (b) sobre
    (c) a

Answers at back of book.

LESSON 51

SACAMOS FOTOGRAFIAS
WE TAKE PICTURES

A. *En el hotel*   At the hotel

1. Carlos: **¿Recuerdas que hoy habíamos decidido volver a algunos de los sitios que nos gustan más a sacar fotos?**
   Remember that today we had decided to go back to some of the places we like best to take pictures?

2. Juana: **Claro que sí. ¿Has comprado película° para los aparatos?°**
   Of course. Did you buy film for the cameras?

3. Carlos: **Sí. Tengo dos rollos para cada una, pero me gustaría ir a una tienda fotográfica a comprar más, y a hacer unas preguntas.**
   Yes. I have two rolls for each one, but I'd like to go to a photography shop to buy more and to ask some questions.

4. Juana: **Recuerda que queremos hacer algunas transparencias° y que nos hace falta película para la máquina° de filmar.**
   Remember that we want to make some slides and that we need film for the movie camera.

5. Carlos: **¿Prefieres las películas en color o en blanco y negro? ¡Las de color son tan caras!**
   Do you prefer color film or black and white? Color film is so expensive!

6. Juana: **Debiéramos comprar por lo menos dos en color. Con el cielo tan claro que tenemos en Madrid estos días, las fotos en color deben salir preciosas.**

We ought to buy at least two in color. With the
clear skies that we have in Madrid these days,
the color photos ought to turn out beautiful.

7. Carlos: **Tienes razón. Quiero recordar siempre estos cielos azules y todo el colorido de
algunos barrios de Madrid.**
You're right. I always want to remember the
blue skies and all the color of some districts of
Madrid.

8. Juana: **Y a mí me gustaría tener algunas
películas y diapositivas de las plazas más
hermosas, del Palacio Nacional y de muchos
otros sitios.**
And *I* would like to have some movies and
slides of the prettiest squares, of the National
Palace and of many other places.

B. *En la tienda*   In the shop

9. Carlos: **¿Tiene usted película para esta máquina, por favor?**
Do you have film for this camera, please?

10. Empleado: **Permítame verla, por favor. ¿En
blanco y negro o en color?**
Let me see it, please. In black and white or in
color?

11. Carlos: **Dos rollos de cada clase, por favor.**
Two rolls of each, please.

12. Empleado: **Aquí los tiene. Esa que tiene
usted es una máquina muy buena.**
Here you are. That's a very good camera that
you have.

13. Carlos: **Gracias. He tenido bastante suerte
con ella, aunque no soy experto. ¿Quiere
usted darme dos rollos para este otro
aparato, por favor?**

Thanks. I have had rather good luck with it although I'm no expert. Will you give me two rolls for this other camera, please?

14. Empleado: **¿De veinte o de treinta y seis?**
Twenty or thirty-six?

15. Carlos: **De treinta y seis, por favor. ¿Quiere usted revisar este aparato alemán, por favor? Hay algo que no funciona bien.**
Thirty-six, please. Do you want to take a look at this German camera? There's something that's not working well.

16. Empleado: **¿Qué es lo que no funciona?**
What is it that isn't working?

17. Carlos: **A veces, cuando aprieto este botón, se queda enganchado.**
Sometimes, when I press this button, it sticks.

18. Empleado: **Conozco bien este modelo. Hay que apretarlo rápidamente, sin dejarlo demasiado tiempo. Una presión rápida y ligera, leventando el dedo en seguida.**
I know this model well. You must press it rapidly, without leaving it too long. A rapid and light pressure, lifting the finger immediately.

19. Carlos: **Muchas gracias. Quiero también una docena de bombillas de flash.**
Thank you very much. I also want a dozen flashbulbs.

20. Empleado: **Muy bien, señor. ¿Desean ustedes algo más? ¿No? Entonces voy a envolver todo esto. Buena suerte.**
Very well, sir. Do you want anything else? No? Then I'll wrap all this. Good luck!

C. *En la Plaza de España*   At the Plaza de España

21. Juana: **Aquí estamos en la Plaza de España.°**
    Me gustaría tener una vista panorámica de
    toda la Plaza. No te olvides de quitar la tapa
    del lente.
    Here we are at the Plaza de España. I'd like to
    have a panoramic view of the square. Don't
    forget to take the cover off the lens.

22. Carlos: **No te preocupes. Ponte delante de la**
    estatua de Don Quijote. Así estarás en la
    foto.
    Don't worry. Stand in front of the statue of
    Don Quixote. That way you'll be in the pic-
    ture.

23. Juana: **Pero si vas a sacarla de tan lejos,**
    nadie podrá reconocerme.
    But if you're going to take it from such a
    distance, no one will be able to recognize me.

24. Carlos: **Pero nosotros sabremos que estás**
    allí, y se lo podremos decir a todos: "¿No
    ves aquel puntito azul a pie de la estatua de
    Don Quijote? Pues, ese puntito es Juana."
    But we'll know that you're there, and we can
    tell everyone: "Don't you see that little blue
    spot at the foot of the statue of Don Quixote?
    Well, that little spot is Jane."

25. Juana: **¡Qué tonto eres! ¿No quieres tomar**
    otra vista de la Torre de Madrid y del
    Edificio España?
    How silly you are! Don't you want to take
    another view of the Tower of Madrid and the
    España Building?

26. Carlos: **Sí, y luego vamos al otro lado de la**
    plaza para sacar algunas de La Gran Vía.°

A esta hora de la tarde es impresionante con todos los coches, el bullicio de la gente, las terrazas llenas y la luz tan fuerte.

Yes, and then let's go to the other side of the square to take in some of La Gran Vía. At this time of the afternoon it's impressive with all the cars, the hubbub of people, the crowded sidewalk cafés and such strong light.

27. Juana: **Quiero sacarte una foto, sentado en nuestra terraza preferida.**

I want to take a picture of you, seated at our favorite café.

D. *En la Plaza de Neptuno°*   At Neptune Square

28. Carlos: *Desde aquí podemos sacar unas fotos magníficas de la fuente con el Museo del Prado al fondo.*

From here we can take some magnificent shots of the fountain with the Prado Museum in the background.

29. Juana: *Y debiéramos tener algunas mirando a la Castellana, con los árboles.*

And we should have some looking up the Castellana, with the trees.

30. Carlos: *Espero que todas salgan bien. Tendremos una colección de fotos muy bonitas como recuerdo de nuestra visita a Madrid.*

I hope they all turn out well. We'll have a collection of very pretty pictures as a souvenir of our visit to Madrid.

31. Juana: *Debiéramos sacar unas de la Puerta de Alcalá° y del Retiro,° donde hay tantos rincones preciosos.*

We ought to take some of the Gate of Alcalá and of Retiro Park, where there are so many beautiful spots.

32. Carlos: *Claro que sí. Vamos allá ahora y podemos sentarnos un rato a la sombra, cerca del estanque.*
Of course. Let's go there now and we can sit down for a while in the shade, near the pool.

33. Juana: *Tendremos que sacar copias de las mejores para mandar a nuestros amigos.*
We'll have to make copies of the best ones to send to our friends.

34. Carlos: *Si es que algunas verdaderamente salen bien. Espero que no se haya estropeado ninguna.*
If some really turn out well. I hope that none of them is spoiled.

35. Juana: *Tú sabes que eres buen fotógrafo. Siempre te salen bien.*
You know you're a good photographer. They always turn out well for you.

NOTES

2. *película:* film. This word is also used for "movie" or "motion picture." *Lo que el viento se llevó* es una gran película: "*Gone with the Wind* is a great motion picture."

4. *máquina:* machine. Used in such combinations as: *máquina de escribir* (typewriter), *máquina de coser* (sewing machine). *Aparato* (apparatus) is also used in reference to mechanical things.
transparencia: slide. Notice in sentence 8 that *diapositiva* is another Spanish word for the same.

21. *Plaza de España:* This square, at the foot of the Gran Vía, has statues of Don Quixote and Sancho Panza in the center. Madrid's "skyscrapers," the Tower of Madrid and the España Building, are also there.

26. *La Gran Vía:* Officially, the Avenida de José Antonio Primo de Rivera, but known to everyone as "The Great Way." It is a broad and beautiful commercial street in the center of Madrid that curves up from the post office and ends at the Plaza de España. Many of Madrid's most elegant shops, movie theatres and restaurants are found here.

Title D: *La Plaza de Neptuno:* Neptune Square, on the Castellana, has a beautiful fountain of Neptune. It is between two of Madrid's finest hotels, The Ritz and the Palace.

31. *Puerta de Alcalá:* One of the beautiful baroque entrance gates to the city, just above the Post Office, on Alcalá Avenue.
El Retiro: Parque del Buen Retiro, the large and beautiful Central Park of Madrid.

GRAMMATICAL ITEMS FOR SPECIAL STUDY

I. The demonstrative adjectives *este, ese, aquel* in their various forms have a written accent to denote their use as pronouns.

Study:

A. *éste:* this (near the speaker)

1. ¿El libro? Este (que tengo) es muy interesante.

2. ¿Los cuadros? Me gustan éstos.

3. ¿La máquina fotográfica? Quiero ver ésta.

4. ¿Las pinturas? Podía venderle éstas.

1. *The book? This one (that I have) is very interesting.*

2. *The pictures? I like these.*

3. *The camera? I want to see this one.*

4. *The paintings? I could sell you these.*

B. *ése:* that (near the person spoken to)

1. Me gusta este libro pero no me gusta ése que estás leyendo.

2. Voy a llevar estos paquetes, y usted puede mandar ésos al hotel.

3. Esta foto es preciosa pero ésa que miras no salió bien.

4. Estas blusas son preciosas pero ésas no me gustan.

1. *I like this book but I don't like that one you're reading.*

2. *I'm going to carry these packages and you can send those to the hotel.*

3. *This photograph is beautiful but that one you're looking at didn't turn out well.*

4. *These blouses are pretty but I don't like those.*

C. *aquél:* that (removed from both speaker and person spoken to)

1. Ese disco (que tiene usted en la mano) es muy caro, pero es mejor que aquél que escuchamos ayer.

2. Esos cuadernos son muy buenos, pero no tan buenos como aquéllos de la otra tienda.

3. Esa mesa es demasiado grande, pero aquélla en el rincón es demasiado pequeña.

4. Esas lámparas son muy prácticas pero aquéllas que vimos en Segovia son más bonitas.

1. *That record (you have in your hand) is very expensive but it's better than that one we listened to yesterday.*

2. *Those notebooks are very good, but they're not as good as those in the other store.*

3. *That table is too large but that one in the corner is too small.*

4. *Those lamps are very practical but those that we saw in Segovia are prettier.*

Note: The written accent is not usually found on capital letters.

II. Special forms of the personal pronoun with prepositions for emphasis or clarification.

Study:

1. A mí me gusta este helado. ¿Y a tí?

2. A mí también me gusta.

3. A él no le gusta. ¿Y a ella?

4. A ella le gusta mucho.

1. *I like this ice cream. Do you?* ("to me is pleasing. This ice cream. And to you?")

2. *I like it too.*

3. *He doesn't like it. Does she?*

4. *She likes it very much.*

Note: These forms are used with all prepositions with the exception of the forms *conmigo* and *contigo*.

Study:

1. Este regalo es para mí.

2. Pablo lo ha hecho para tí.

3. ¿Quieres venir conmigo?

4. Juan hablará contigo mañana.

5. Dice que estaba pensando en mí.

6. Siempre pienso en tí.

But *entre tú y yo:* between you and me

1. *This gift is for me.*

2. *Paul did it for you.*

3. *Do you want to come with me?*

4. *John will speak with you tomorrow.*

5. *She says she was thinking of me.*

6. *I always think of you.*

III. *hay que:* one must, you must (impersonal)

Study:

1. Al llegar a la esquina hay que volver a la derecha.

2. Hay que estudiar mucho para comprenderlo.

3. Hay que comprar las entradas en la taquilla.

1. *When you reach the corner, you must turn to the right.*

2. *One must study a lot to understand it.*

3. *You must buy the tickets at the box office.*

IV. *Hay* + noun and *que* + infinitive: There are
_____ to _____.

Study:

1. Hay muchos libros que leer.

2. Hay unas películas interesantes que ver.

3. Hay muchas cosas que comprar.

1. *There are many books to read.*

2. *There are some interesting movies to see.*

3. *There are many things to buy.*

Compare
Hay que comprar muchas cosas.
(One) You must buy many things.
and
Hay muchas cosas que comprar.
There are many things to buy.

DRILLS AND EXERCISES

I. Substitute each of the words or expressions in
parentheses for the italicized word or expression in
the model sentence. Write each new sentence and
say it aloud.

A. Este *cuadro* es muy bonito pero no me gusta
aquél. (edificio, mueble, libro, color, cenicero)

B. Aquellas *pinturas* que vimos ayer me gustaron.
(obras, blusas, lámparas, mesas, camisas)

C. ¿Dónde compraste esa *camisa*? (máquina,
pluma, silla, papelera, chaqueta)

D. Hay que *comprar* el libro. (vender, leer, escribir, mandar, estudiar)

E. Se dice que hay *muchas cosas* que ver. (muchos
cuadros, muchas estatuas, muchas fuentes,
muchos monumentos, muchas pinturas)

F. *Juan* lo ha escrito para tí. (El poeta, El Señor Hernández, María, Mi amigo, Aquel señor)

II. Change these sentences to the present tense. Write the complete sentence and translate. Answers will be found in the back of the book.

1. Lo compraste para él.

2. Los señores Andrade hicieron el viaje conmigo.

3. No le he visto jamás contigo.

4. Ellos me lo regalaron a mí.

5. El cuadro era para usted.

III. Translate the following sentences into Spanish, then say them aloud. Answers will be found at the back of the book.

1. I prefer to buy that camera in the other shop.

2. We ought to buy at least two rolls of color film.

3. We can take some wonderful pictures of that park.

4. Do you like the view with that building in the background?

5. They want to take a picture of you.

6. Don't forget to take the cover off the lens.

7. We have to make copies for our friends.

8. They wanted to go to that museum on Sunday.

9. We have to buy more black-and-white film.

10. Do you think he likes that suit?

QUIZ

From among the three choices given, choose the one which correctly renders the English given at the beginning of each sentence. Write the complete sentence, and translate.

1. *(with me)* Van a ir _____.
   - (a) con mí
   - (b) conmigo
   - (c) con me

2. *(to him)* Déselo _____.
   - (a) a ella
   - (b) a él
   - (c) a ello

3. *(these)* No me gustan aquellas lámparas. Dame dos de _____.
   - (a) éstos
   - (b) éstas
   - (c) estos

4. *(that one)* La novela que más me gusta es _____ que tienes en la mano.
   - (a) eso
   - (b) esa
   - (c) ésa

5. *(that one)* Esta alfombra es muy bonita pero recuerdas _____ que vimos ayer.
   - (a) aquel
   - (b) aquélla
   - (c) ésa

6. *(one must)* Dicen que _____ estudiar mucho.
   - (a) debes
   - (b) hay que
   - (c) uno tiene

7. *(all these)* Tenemos que llevar _____ papeles a casa.
   (a) estos todos
   (b) todos estos
   (c) todo esto

8. *(all that)* La historia es muy interesante. Pablo no me contó _____.
   (a) todo eso
   (b) todos esos
   (c) toda esa

9. *(many things)* Hay _____ leer.
   (a) muchas cosas
   (b) muchas cosas que
   (c) mucha cosa

10. *(the whole)* Juan no me explicó _____ problema.
    (a) toda la
    (b) todo el
    (c) el todo

Answers at back of book.

LESSON 52

LA AGENCIA DE VIAJES
THE TRAVEL AGENCY

A. *En la Agencia*   In the agency

1. Empleado: **Buenos días. ¿En qué puedo servirles?**
   Good morning. How can I help you?

2. Carlos: **Nos gustaría viajar un poco por
España. Por los alrededores de Madrid. ¿Podría usted sugerirnos algunos itinerarios?**
We would like to take some trips in Spain, to the
area around Madrid. Could you suggest some
itineraries?

3. Empleado: **Desde luego. Tenemos muchos viajes de un día a los sitios de interés cerca de
Madrid. A Toledo, al Escorial,° al Valle de
los Caídos,° a Segovia° y muchos otros lu-
gares de gran interés turístico. Los viajes son
en autobús de lujo, con guía, a un precio fijo
con todos los gastos incluídos.**
Of course. We have many one-day trips to
places of interest near Madrid. To Toledo, to the
Escorial, to the Valley of the Fallen, to Segovia
and many other places of great interest to tourists. The trips are by bus, with a guide, at a set
price with all costs included.

4. Carlos: **Queremos ver tantas cosas. ¿Qué
piensa usted de la idea de alquilar un coche?**
We want to see so many things. What do you
think of the idea of renting a car?

5. Empleado: **El coche les permite mucho más
libertad de movimiento. Los tenemos con o
sin chófer. Este folleto les da detalles sobre
gastos y servicios.**
The car permits you much greater freedom of
movement. We have them with or without
chauffeur. This pamphlet gives you details of
costs and services.

6. Carlos: **¿A qué hora salen los autocares para
Toledo?**
What time do the buses leave for Toledo?

7. Empleado: **Hay varias salidas todos los días. A las ocho, a las diez, y a la una.**
There are several departures every day. At eight, at ten, and at one o'clock.

8. Juana: **Carlos, ¿Qué te parece la idea de ir mañana a Toledo? Tengo tantas ganas de verlo. Ya que hemos visto algunas obras del Greco, quiero ver donde vivía y trabajaba.**
Charles, what do you think of the idea of going to Toledo tomorrow? I want to see it so much. Now that we've seen some of the works of El Greco, I want to see where he lived and worked.

9. Empleado: **Yo podría arreglárselo todo ahora, si quieren ustedes. Reservarles asientos en el autocar de las nueve.¹ Claro que la comida en Toledo va incluída en el precio.**
I could arrange it all for you now, if you wish. Reserve seats for you in the nine o'clock bus. Of course, dinner in Toledo is included in the price.

10. Carlos: **Bien. Eso es lo que haremos mañana. Ahora nos interesan también algunos informes sobre el sur de España. Queremos ir a Sevilla,° a Córdoba,° a Jerez de la Frontera,° y tal vez podríamos hacer una breve visita a Gibraltar.**
Fine. That's what we'll do tomorrow. Now we're also interested in some information on the south of Spain. We want to go to Seville, Cordoba, Jerez de la Frontera, and perhaps we could make a brief visit to Gibraltar.

---

¹The agent should have said *echo* ("eight o'clock").

11. Empleado: **Todo eso es muy fácil de arreglar. Si quieren, les doy ahora varios folletos, mapas, horarios de tren y de autocares, y algunas sugerencias sobre posibles itinerarios.**
All of that is very easy to arrange. If you wish, I can give you now several pamphlets, maps, train and bus timetables, and some suggestions on possible itineraries.

12. Carlos: **Perfecto. Así podremos estudiarlo un poco esta noche y darle nuestra decisión mañana.**
Perfect. That way we can study it a little tonight and give you our decision tomorrow.

13. Empleado: **Muy bien. Ahora les voy a preparar una lista de todo lo que necesitan, para que puedan estudiarla detenidamente. Permítanme recomendarles el alquiler de un coche para visitar los sitios cerca de Madrid antes de hacer el viaje por el sur.**
Very well. Now I'm going to prepare a list of everything you need so that you can study it carefully. Permit me to recommend the rental of a car to visit the places near Madrid before you make the trip through the south.

14. Carlos: **Me parece muy buena idea. Mañana podremos arreglarlo todo. ¿A qué hora ha dicho usted que sale el autocar para Toledo?**
It sounds like a very good idea to me. Tomorrow we can arrange everything. At what time did you say the bus leaves for Toledo?

15. Empleado: **A las nueve en punto, señores. La agencia estará abierta a las ocho y media.**
At nine o'clock sharp. The agency will be open at eight thirty.

16. Carlos: **Bien. Así vendremos un poco antes
de la hora de salida para hablar de nuestros
planes.**
Fine. So we'll come a little before the depar-
ture time to talk to you about our plans.

B. *Al día siguiente*   The following day

17. Empleado: **Muy buenos días, señores. ¿Qué
han decidido ustedes?**
Good morning. What have you decided?

18. Carlos: **Pensamos ir a Segovia mañana y
queremos ir en tren. Nos han dicho que es
un viaje muy agradable. Así podemos ver el
acueducto y el Alcázar.**
We intend to go to Segovia tomorrow and we
want to go by train. They have told us it is a
very pleasant trip. That way we can see the
aqueduct and the Alcazar.

19. Empleado: **Muy bien. Yo les conseguiré los
billetes y los tendrán ustedes aquí al volver
de Toledo esta tarde. Y les recomiendo que
coman en El Mesón de Cándido, el Segoviano. Es famoso por el "tostón," el
cochinillo asado, y tendrán a la vista
el acueducto mientras están comiendo.
¿Quieren que llame para reservales una
mesa? Siempre está lleno.**
Very well. I'll get the tickets for you and you
will have them here on returning from Toledo
this afternoon. And I recommend that you eat
at the Mesón de Cándido, el Segoviano. It's
famous for its roast suckling pig, and you will
have a view of the aqueduct while you're
eating. Do you want me to call and reserve a
table for you? It's always full.

20. Juana: **Sí, por favor. Y queremos un coche para el día siguiente, ¿no es verdad, Carlos?**
Yes, please. And we want a car for the following day, don't we, Charles?

21. Carlos: **Sí. Se lo agradecería si pudiera arreglarlo para las ocho de la mañana. ¿Se puede pedir que nos lo entreguen en el hotel? Vamos a pasar dos o tres días visitando el Escorial, Salamanca° y Avila.°**
Yes. I would be grateful if you could arrange it for eight in the morning. May we ask that it be delivered to the hotel? We're going to spend two or three days visiting the Escorial, Salamanca and Avila.

22. Empleado: **Se lo puedo arreglar con mucho gusto, señor. Al volver de Toledo, tendré preparados los papeles necesarios. Los puede firmar usted entonces y tendrán el coche a las ocho de la mañana, pasado mañana.**
I can arrange it for you with great pleasure, sir. When you return from Toledo, I'll have the necessary papers ready. You can sign them then and you'll have the car at eight in the morning the day after tomorrow.

23. Juana: *¡Qué bien! Estoy segura que vamos a pasar un día espléndido en Toledo hoy. ¡Con el tiempo que hace! Y luego tendremos que hablar de hoteles y otros detalles del viaje por el sur.*
How wonderful! I'm sure we're going to have a marvelous day in Toledo today. With this weather! And then we'll have to talk about hotels and other details of our trip through the south.

24. Empleado: *Desde luego. Habrá bastante que hacer. ¿Han decidido ustedes si quieren ir en tren, en autocar o en coche?*
Of course. There'll be a lot to do. Have you decided yet whether you want to go by train, by bus, or by car?

25. Carlos: *Por el momento habíamos pensado hacer el viaje de Madrid a Sevilla en tren, y luego ir en autocar de allí a Córdoba y a Jerez de la Frontera.*
For the moment we had thought of making the trip from Madrid to Seville by train, and then to go by bus from there to Cordoba and Jerez de la Frontera.

26. Empleado: *Está bien. ¿Y luego?*
That's fine. And then?

27. Carlos: *Queríamos saber si no sería posible alquilar un coche en Cádiz° para seguir el viaje por la costa a Málaga° y luego, en Motril,° tomar la carretera que va a Granada.°*
We wanted to know if it wouldn't be possible to rent a car in Cadiz in order to continue the trip along the coast to Malaga and then, in Motril, take the highway that goes to Granada.

28. Empleado: *Sería ideal. Nuestra sucursal en Cádiz puede arreglar lo del coche. Luego tenemos que fijar las fechas en cada sitio para la reserva de habitaciones. Me imagino que querrán pasar unos días en Marbella° y Torremolinos° también, ¿no?*
That would be ideal. Our branch in Cadiz can arrange the matter of the car. Then we have to fix the dates in each place for the reservation of rooms. I imagine that you'll want to spend

some days in Marbella and Torremolinos too,
won't you?

29. Carlos: *¡Claro que sí! Se dice que esa parte de
la costa es muy bonita. Y nos gustaría reservar
habitaciones que dan a la playa en esos
pueblos de la costa.*
By all means! They say that that part of the
coast is very pretty. And we would like to
reserve rooms that open on the beach in those
towns of the coast.

30. Empleado: *Estoy seguro que podemos arreglarlo todo a su gusto. Tendremos mucho que
hablar cuando vuelvan esta tarde.*
I'm sure we can arrange it all to your pleasure.
We'll have a great deal to talk about when you
return this afternoon.

NOTES

3. *El Escorial:* Palace-pantheon-monastery built
   by order of Philip II in El Escorial, north of
   Madrid. It is the masterwork of the architect
   Juan de Herrera, begun in 1563 and finished in
   1584. It is an important treasury of art and
   incunabula.
   Valle de los Caídos: Grandiose and impressive
   monument to the dead in the Spanish Civil War
   in the Guadarrama Mountains, north of Madrid. It was also designated the burial place of
   the Spanish Chief of State, Francisco Franco.
   Segovia: Capital of the province of Segovia,
   famed for its impressive Alcázar, one of the
   most beautiful of all of Spain's many castles,
   and the remains of a Roman aqueduct.

10. *Sevilla:* Heart of southern Spain's Andalusia.
    Its cathedral with the Moorish tower of La
    Giralda, its Alcázar, and many treasures of art

and architecture, its parks and statues, its Spring Fair *(La Feria de Sevilla)* and its famed Holy Week processions make it justly popular as a tourist center.

Córdoba: Another of the gems of Andalusia, capital of the province of the same name, it was the seat of a powerful Arabic Caliphate and has the beautiful *Mezquita* (Mosque) and other architectural souvenirs of the period of Arabic occupation of Spain.

Jerez de la Frontera: Capital of the province, the heart of Spanish wine and olive country. From the earlier pronunciation of the name Jerez we get the English word "sherry."

21. *Salamanca:* Capital of the province, the seat of Spain's oldest university, one of the most important centers of learning in the Middle Ages.

Avila: Famed walled city, capital of the province of Avila, birthplace of Santa Teresa de Jesús, who, along with St. John of the Cross, represents the peak of Spanish mysticism. Avila is known as the *ciudad de los santos* ("city of saints").

27. *Cádiz:* Seaport on the southern coast, known as the *taza de plata* ("the silver cup").

Málaga: Another of southern Spain's beautiful Mediterranean ports, north on the coast from Cádiz.

Motril: A small coastal town, sometimes called *la playa de Granada* ("the beach of Granada"). It is on the coast due east of that mountain-locked city.

Granada: the capital city of the province. The famed Moorish palace, the Alhambra, is here, along with other artistic and historic monuments.

28. *Marbella:* Another town, similar to Torremolinos, on Spain's *Costa del Sol*—Sunny Coast—which attracts wealthy international residents and tourists.
Torremolinos: A new resort town on the coast, south of Malaga, it has now grown from a small fishing village to an international tourist center, with enormous luxury hotels.

GRAMMATICAL ITEMS FOR SPECIAL STUDY

I. Certain adjectives with a shortened form before a masculine singular noun: *buen, mal, primer, tercer, ningún, algún.*

Study:

1. Hace muy buen tiempo.

2. Hace mal tiempo.

3. Es el primer libro.

4. Es el tercer capítulo.

5. Ningún libro lo dice.

6. Algún amigo me lo ha dicho.

1. *It's nice weather.*

2. *It's bad weather.*

3. *It's the first book.*

4. *It's the third chapter.*

5. *No book says it.*

6. *Some friend told it to me.*

In other positions these adjectives agree in the regular way.

Study:

1. Es un buen hombre. Es un hombre muy bueno.
2. Es un mal hombre. Es un hombre muy malo.
3. Es una buena película.
4. Las buenas novelas son pocas.
5. La primera novela que leí fue muy mala.

1. *He's a good man. He's a very good man.*
2. *He's a bad man. He's a very bad man.*
3. *It's a good movie.*
4. *The good novels are very few.*
5. *The first novel I read was very bad.*

II. *gran* and *cualquier* are used before either a masculine or a feminine singular noun.

Study:

1. Se me ha ocurrido una gran idea.
2. Es un gran hombre.
3. Cualquier libro es bueno.
4. En cualquier tienda se encuentra eso.

1. *I've had a great idea.*
2. *He's a great man.*
3. *Any book is good.*
4. *In any store you find that.*

Note: *gran* before the noun usually has the figurative meaning of "great." After the noun, it has its literal meaning of "large."

Compare:

Es un gran hombre.	*He's a great man.*
Es un hombre muy grande.	*He's a very large man.*

cualquier (used before either masculine or feminine singular nouns) has the forms *cualquiera* and *cualesquiera* used elsewhere.

Study:

1. No es un hombre cualquiera.

2. No son señoras cualesquiera.

3. No son películas cualesquiera.

1. *He's not just any man. (whatever)*

2. *They are not just any ladies.*

3. *They're not just any movies.*

III. The subjunctive mood following verbs of emotion (when there is a change of subject).

Study:

1. Espero que ustedes hayan hecho buen viaje.

2. Temo que se hayan equivocado.

3. Me alegro de que te guste la habitación.

1. *I hope you have had a good trip.*

2. *I'm afraid you've made a mistake.*

3. *I'm happy that you like the room.*

IV. Verbs of volition with the subjunctive.

1. Quieren que lo hagamos ahora.

2. Juan prefiere que no lo leamos.

3. El recomienda que vayamos hoy al museo.

1. *They want us to do it now. ("They want that we do it now.")*

2. *John prefers that we don't read it.*

3. *He recommends that we go to the museum today.*

DRILLS AND EXERCISES

I. Substitute each of the words or expressions in parentheses for the italicized words or expressions in the model sentence. Write each new sentence and say it aloud.

A. Es un buen *libro.* (cuadro, hotel, hombre, parque, restáurante)

B. No me ha dado ningún *regalo.* (número, problema, horario, periódico, billete)

C. Me dijeron que es un(a) gran *hombre.* (poeta, idea, escritor, amigo, novela)

D. Espero que ellos *estudien.* (escriban, vengan, salgan, coman, lleguen)

E. Se alegran de que hayamos *comido* bien. (dormido, llegado, estudiado, oído, estado)

F. Los señores Fernández quieren que *estudiemos.* (descansemos, comamos, bebamos, nos vistamos, entremos)

II. Change the sentences to the plural. Write each complete sentence and translate. Answers will be found at the back of the book.

1. El no quiere ningún coche.

2. Ella no ha comprado ningún regalo.

3. Espero que Juan llegue a tiempo.

4. Ella quiere que Teresa estudie esta noche.

5. Yo prefiero que usted se vaya.

III. Translate the following sentences into Spanish, then say them aloud. Answers will be found at the back of the book.

1. They want us to see the movie.

2. We hope you have a good trip.

3. John wants you to buy color film.

4. There isn't any money in this jacket.

5. It is said that it's a great hotel.

6. He was a great poet.

7. Don't give me just any book.

8. Do you want them to do it?

9. He was a great friend.

10. I'm afraid you can't go now.

QUIZ

From among the three choices given, choose the one which correctly renders the English given at the beginning of each sentence. Write the complete sentence, and translate.

1. *(nice)* Me alegro de que haga tan _____ tiempo.
   (a) bueno
   (b) buen
   (c) buena

2. *(the first)* ¿Ha terminado usted _____ capítulo?
   (a) la primera
   (b) el primer
   (c) los primeros

3. *(some)* Espero que nos veamos _____ día.
   - (a) algún
   - (b) alguna
   - (c) algo

4. *(any)* Juan no tiene _____ dinero.
   - (a) ninguno
   - (b) ninguna
   - (c) ningún

5. *(good)* Es un hombre muy _____.
   - (a) bueno
   - (b) buen
   - (c) buenamente

6. *(any)* No me dé usted un libro _____.
   - (a) cualquier
   - (b) cualquiera
   - (c) cualesquiera

7. *(great)* Es una _____ idea.
   - (a) grande
   - (b) gran
   - (c) grandes

8. *(like)* Espero que te _____ las habitaciones.
   - (a) gusta
   - (b) gusten
   - (c) guste

9. *(do)* Prefieren que nosotros lo _____ ahora.
   - (a) hacemos
   - (b) hagamos
   - (c) hacen

10. *(us to go)* Juan quiere _____.
    - (a) que vayamos
    - (b) que vamos
    - (c) para nosotros ir

Answers at back of book.

LESSON 53

COCHES—DE ALQUILER O EN VENTA
CARS—RENTAL OR BUYING

A. *Alquilamos un coche*   We rent a car

1. Empleado: **Buenos días, señores. ¿Qué quieren ustedes?**
Good morning. May I help you?

2. Carlos: **Estábamos pensando en alquilar un coche. ¿Quiere usted decirme los precios y gastos? Me imagino que varían bastante, ¿verdad?**
We were thinking of renting a car. Will you explain the prices and costs? I imagine that they vary a good deal.

3. Emplcado: **Así es, señor. Depende del modelo que escojan. ¿Es para ustedes dos?**
That's right, sir. It depends on the model that you choose. Is it for the two of you?

4. Carlos: **Sí, pero tenemos bastante equipaje también.**
Yes, but we have quite a lot of baggage too.

5. Empleado: **Me parece que el Seat Mil Quinientos° sería ideal para ustedes. Hay sitio para cuatro cómodamente, y tiene cuatro puertas.**
I think the Seat 1500 would be ideal for you. There's room for four comfortably and it has four doors.

6. Carlos: **¿Se puede incluir un porta-equipajes sin cobrar más?**
Can a luggage-rack be included without charging extra?

7. Empleado: **Por supuesto, señor, si les hace falta. Y en cuanto al alquiler, se puede pagar por hora, por día, o por semana.**
Of course, sir, if you need it. And, as to the rates, you can pay by the hour, or daily or weekly.

8. Juana: **¿Qué se incluye en el precio?**
What's included in the price?

9. Empleado: **El aceite y el engrase, naturalmente, y los gastos normales. Los seguros y los impuestos también.**
The oil and the lubrication, naturally, and the normal expenses. Insurance and taxes too.

10. Carlos: **¿La gasolina y el kilometraje° no están incluídos?**
Gas and mileage are not included?

11. Empleado: **No hay límite en el kilometraje, señor. En cuanto a la gasolina, la Super sólo cuesta quince pesetas el litro.°**
There's no limit on mileage, sir. As for gas, Super only costs fifteen pesetas a liter.

12. Juana: **¿Y cuántos kilómetros da este coche por litro?**
And how many kilometers will this car go on a liter?

13. Empleado: **Veinte, por lo menos, señora. Como ve, este coche es económico.**
At least twenty, madam. As you see, this car is economical.

14. Carlos: **Pagamos al devolver el coche, ¿verdad?**
We pay when we return the car, don't we?

15. Empleado: **No, señor. Se paga al llevarse el coche, y hay además una fianza de doce mil pesetas que se le devuelven al entregarlo.**
No, sir. You pay when you take the car, and there is besides a deposit of twelve thousand pesetas that is returned to you when you bring the car back.

16. Carlos: **¿Cobran algo por entregar y recoger el coche?**
Do you charge something to deliver and pick up the car?

17. Empleado: **No, señor, si es aquí en Madrid, se lo podemos entregar en el hotel y mandar a alguien a buscarlo si ustedes nos llaman al volver.**
No, sir, if it is here in Madrid we can deliver it to your hotel and send someone to pick it up if you call us when you return.

18. Carlos: **Pero ¿qué pasa si decidimos dejarlo en otro sitio, por ejemplo en Málaga?**
But what happens if we decide to leave it somewhere else, for example in Málaga?

19. Empleado: **Si deciden ustedes dejarlo en una ciudad donde tengamos sucursal, se lo pueden entregar a la sucursal sin pagar más. En cambio, si quieren dejarlo en algún sitio donde no haya sucursal, tendrán que pagar los gastos de ir a buscarlo.**
If you decide to leave it in a city where we have a branch, you can deliver it to the branch office without paying anything extra. On the other hand, if you want to leave it in some place where there is no branch office, you will have to pay the expenses of going to pick it up.

20. Carlos: **¿Qué documentos necesitamos?**
What papers do we need?

21. Empleado: **Solamente un carnet de conductor. Y tendremos que ver los pasaportes. Nosotros les daremos todos los documentos del coche.**
Only a driver's license. And we'll have to see your passports. We will give you the papers for the car.

B. *La compra de un automóvil* Buying a car

22. Juana: **Estábamos pensando en comprar un coche en Europa.**
We were thinking of buying a car in Europe.

23. Empleado: **Creo que sería buena idea, señora. Dicen que, aun teniendo en cuenta los gastos de transporte y aduana, resulta mucho menos caro.**
I think that would be a good idea, madam. They say that even counting the cost of shipping and the customs charge it comes out to be much less expensive.

24. Carlos: **¿No hay impuestos sobre los precios de fábrica, verdad?**
There are no taxes on the factory prices, are there?

25. Empleado: **Hay enormes ventajas, señor. Pero les recomiendo que vayan a buscar el coche directamente a la fábrica. Cuando hayan escogido el modelo que quieren, resulta más económico y más rápido hacerlo en esa forma.**
There are great advantages, sir. But I recommend that you go directly to the factory to pick up your car. When you have chosen the model that you want, it's cheaper and faster to do it in that way.

26. Carlos: **No estoy seguro todavía. Hay una agencia de Citroën aquí en Madrid, ¿verdad?**
I'm not sure yet. There's a Citroën agency in Madrid, isn't there?

27. Empleado: **Sí. Hay agencias de todas las marcas conocidas, francesas, alemanas e italianas.**
Yes. There are agencies for all the well-known brands, French, German and Italian.

28. Carlos: **¿Sabe usted si hay que pagar al contado?**
Do you know if you have to pay cash?

29. Empleado: **Me parece que en ciertos casos se puede arreglar el pago a plazos.**
I believe that in certain cases time payments can be arranged.

30. Carlos: **Veo que tienen aquí algunos folletos anunciando los últimos modelos. ¿Me permite usted?**
I see that you have some pamphlets announcing the latest models here. May I?

31. Empleado: **No faltaba más, señor. Llévese cuantos quiera.**
Of course, sir. Take as many as you want.

32. Juana: **Mira, Carlos, este descapotable es precioso. Y fíjate en la tapicería tan elegante que tiene. Es una joya.**
Look, Charles, this convertible is beautiful. And notice the elegant upholstery it has. It's a jewel.

33. Carlos: **Sí, estoy de acuerdo. Es muy bonito. Pero, más importantes son las preguntas: ¿Es práctico? ¿Tiene cambio de velocidades automático? ¿Tiene...**

Yes, I agree. It's very pretty. But more important are the questions: Is it practical? Does it
have automatic transmission? Does it have . . .

34. Juana: *(Interrumpiéndole)* **Sí, sí, ya sé que son
más importantes los asuntos prácticos, pero
hay que buscar la belleza también.**
(Interrupting him) Yes, yes, I know that the
practical matters are more important, but you
have to look for beauty too.

NOTES

5. *Seat 1500:* The *Seat* is the Spanish-made
model of the Italian Fiat. There are two popular models, the small 600 and the more capa-
cious 1500.

10. *kilometraje:* Distance is measured in kilometers. A kilometer is five-eighths of a mile.

11. *litro:* liter, a liquid measure. A little over a
quart.

GRAMMATICAL ITEMS FOR SPECIAL STUDY

I. *a, en cuanto a,* as for, as far as the _____ is
concerned.

Study:

1. En cuanto al alquiler, eso se puede arreglar a
plazos.

2. En cuanto a la gasolina, no gasta mucho.

3. En cuanto a los precios, son económicos.

1. *As far as the rent is concerned, it can be
arranged on terms.*

2. *As for the gasoline, it doesn't use much.*

3. *As for the prices, they are economical.*

II. *Cuando,* when it means "whenever" (i.e., an indefinite or future time), takes the subjunctive.

Study:

1. Cuando lleguen, vamos a decírselo.

2. Usted puede marcharse cuando quiera.

3. Lo haremos cuando venga el cartero.

1. *When they arrive, we're going to tell them (it).*

2. *You can go whenever you wish.*

3. *We'll do it when the mailman comes.*

III. *Por* means "per" in the sense of "rate."

Study:

1. ¿Cuánto cobra usted por sus cuadros?

2. ¿Cuántos kilómetros hace por hora?

3. El veinte por ciento de los problemas es imposible.

1. *How much do you ask for your paintings?*

2. *How many kilometers does it make per hour?*

3. *Twenty per cent of the problems are impossible.*

IV. *Para que* + subjunctive: in order that, so that.

Study:

1. Se lo compro para que se ponga contenta.

2. Se lo digo para que lo sepa.

3. Hay que ayudarles para que terminen pronto.

1. *I'll buy it for her so that she'll be happy.*

2. *I'll tell you so (that) you'll know.*

3. *One must help them so (that) they'll finish soon.*

DRILLS AND EXERCISES

I. Substitute each of the words or expressions in parentheses for the italicized word or expression in the model sentence. Write each new sentence and say it aloud.

   A. En cuanto al *alquiler*, podemos arreglarlo. (precio, problema, viaje, hotel, coche)

   B. Lo podemos hacer cuando vengan *los invitados*. (los señores Andrade, los estudiantes, nuestros amigos, María y José)

   C. No sé cuanto cobran por *hora*. (día, semana, mes, clase, cada viajeró)

   D. Voy a dárselo para que lo *tengan*. (estudien, lean, aprendan, envíen, envuelvan)

   E. Hablaremos de eso cuando usted lo haya *terminado*. (visto, leído, mandado, comprado, arreglado)

   F. En cuanto a *Juan*, puede pagar cuando quiera. (tu amigo, María, su peluquero, nuestro profesor, la empleada)

II. Change these sentences to the present tense. Write the complete sentence and translate. Answers will be found at the back of the book.

   1. Se lo pediremos cuando lleguen.

   2. Me cobraron trescientas pesetas por hora.

   3. Ellos me lo darán para que lo estudie.

   4. No habrá fiesta mañana.

   5. Juan lo compró para dármelo.

III. Translate the following sentences into Spanish, then say them aloud. Answers will be found at the back of the book.

   1. I recommend that you pick up the car at the factory.

2. As for the money, I'll give it to him when he comes.

3. When they arrive, John will tell them.

4. Mary may leave whenever she wishes.

5. They'll include a luggage rack.

6. How much does the gasoline cost per liter?

7. Take as many pamphlets as you want.

8. When you have chosen the model you want, go to the factory.

9. There are no taxes on factory prices, are there?

10. Do you want to meet a great friend of mine?

QUIZ

From among the three choices given, choose the one which correctly renders the English given at the beginning of each sentence. Write the complete sentence, and translate.

1. *(As for)* _____ la gasolina, hay suficiente.
   - (a) Como por
   - (b) Cuanto
   - (c) En cuanto a

2. *(they arrive)* Cuando _____ vamos a darles el regalo.
   - (a) llegan
   - (b) lleguen
   - (c) llegaron

3. *(whenever you want)* Usted puede hacerlo _____.
   - (a) cuando quieres
   - (b) cuando quiera
   - (c) como quiere

4. *(per hour)* Hace ciento viente kilómetros
_____.
   (a) por hora
   (b) por la hora
   (c) para hora

5. *(he'll know)* Voy a decirle el número a Juan,
para que lo _____.
   (a) sabe
   (b) sepa
   (c) sabrá

6. *(tell it to them)* Hay que _____ para que
vengan pronto.
   (a) decírleslo
   (b) les lo decir
   (c) decírselo

7. *(so that)* Escríbale los detalles _____ lo
comprenda bien.
   (a) para que
   (b) para
   (c) porque

8. *(study)* Hay que anunciarles el examen para que
_____.
   (a) estudian
   (b) estudien
   (c) estudiaron

9. *(read)* Dásela a María para que la _____.
   (a) lee
   (b) lea
   (c) leera

10. *(whenever they are)* Yo siempre les trato bien
_____ aqui.
   (a) cuandoquiera sean
   (b) cuando estén
   (c) cuando sean

Answers at back of book.

LESSON 54

EN LA ESTACION DE SERVICIO
AT THE SERVICE STATION

1. Empleado: **¿En qué le puedo servir, señor?**
   What can I do for you, sir?

2. Carlos: **No sé exactamente. Hay algo que no funciona bien. Al apretar el arranque, oigo unos ruidos bastante raros en el motor. Me tienen preocupado.**
   I don't know exactly. There's something that's not working well. When I press the starter, I hear some rather strange noises in the motor. It has me worried.

3. Empleado: **¿No será que el tanque está vacío? ¿Lo ha mirado usted?**
   Can it be that the tank is empty? Did you check it?

4. Carlos: **Creo que aún me quedan algunos litros. De todas maneras, quiero ponerle más. Debe estar casi vacío.**
   I think that there are some liters left. Anyway I want to put more in. It must be almost empty.

5. Empleado: **¿Cuántos litros quiere usted? ¿Se lo lleno?**
   How many liters do you want? Shall I fill it up?

6. Carlos: **Sí, llénelo, por favor. Y hágame el favor de llenar este bote° también, por si acaso. Vamos a hacer un viaje bastante largo.**
   Yes, fill it up, please. And please fill this can too, just in case. We're going to take a rather long trip.

7. Empleado: **Es buena idea. A veces no se encuentran gasolineras.°**

It's a good idea. Sometimes you don't find gas stations.

8. Carlos: **¿Quiere mirar los neumáticos? A ver si necesitan aire.**

Will you check the tires? To see if they need air.

9. Empleado: **Con mucho gusto. Pero, ¿qué es eso? Parece que tiene un pinchazo éste de adelante.**

Of course! But what's that? It looks as if this front tire has a puncture.

10. Carlos: **¿Qué dice? No puede ser. Son nuevos.**

What are you saying? It can't be. They're new.

11. Empleado: **Habrá sido un clavo, o algo parecido. ¿No ha notado usted nada? ¿Ningún movimiento?**

It must have been a nail, or something similar. Didn't you notice anything? No movement?

12. Carlos: **Hace un momento, en la carretera, noté que parecía patinar un poco.**

A little while ago, on the highway, I noticed that it seemed to skid a little.

13. Empleado: **Fue eso entonces. Voy a cambiárselo.**

That was it, then. I'm going to change it for you.

14. Carlos: **Hay un neumático de repuesto allí atrás.**

There's a spare tire back there.

15. Empleado: **Bien. Cambiaré el neumático pinchado y luego lo voy a reparar.**

Good. I'll change the flat tire and then I'm going to repair it.

16. Carlos; **Estupendo. Nos hace falta uno de repuesto.**
Terrific. We need a spare.

17. Empleado: **Como hacen un viaje tan largo, hay que ver si están en buenas condiciones las bujías y el acumulador, si le parece.**
Since you're making a long trip, we must see if the spark plugs and the battery are in good shape, if you want.

18. Carlos: **Por favor. Y échele un poco de agua al radiador. Se estaba calentando el motor hace poco.**
Please. And put a little water in the radiator. The motor was heating up a little while ago.

19. Empleado: **Muy bien, señor. ¿Quiere usted que lo engrase, o que le cambie el aceite?**
Very well, sir. Do you want me to do a lubrication job or change the oil?

20. Carlos: **¡Alto allá! Acabo de comprar este coche.**
Hold it there! I just bought this car.

21. Empleado: **¿Es nuevo, dice usted? Veo varias cosas que necesitan atención de todas maneras.**
It's new, you say? I see several things that need attention anyway.

22. Carlos: **Me habrán vendido un cacharro.°**
They must have sold me a piece of junk.

23. Empleado: **De ningún modo, señor. Estas cosas ocurren siempre con los coches nuevos. Más vale repararlos en seguida.**

Not at all, sir. These things always happen
with a new car. It's better to take care of them
right away.

24. Carlos: **Tiene razón. ¿Tendré que dejarlo en
el garaje?**
You're right. Will I have to leave it in the
garage?

25. Empleado: **Tres horas, por lo menos, si
quiere que lo deje en buenas condiciones.**
Three hours, at least, if you want me to put it
in good shape.

26. Carlos: **Pero necesito el coche sin falta este
fin de semana.**
But I need the car without fail for this weekend.

27. Empleado: **No se preocupe. Estoy seguro que
no hay que pedir piezas nuevas.**
Don't worry, sir. I'm sure it won't be necessary to order any new parts.

28. Carlos: **Haga solamente lo necesario.**
Do only what's necessary.

29. Empleado: **Bien. Si usted quiere volver a las
cinco, todo estará listo.**
Good. If you want to come back at five
o'clock, everything will be ready.

30. Carlos: **De acuerdo. Hasta las cinco, entonces.**
O.K. Until five o'clock, then.

31. Empleado: **Siempre hacemos todo lo que
podemos para dar satisfacción a los clientes.**
We always do whatever we can to please our
customers.

32. Carlos: **Estoy seguro que me lo dejará usted en óptimas condiciones.**
I'm sure you'll put it in the best shape for me.

NOTES

6. *bote:* Here used as "can" or "container," this word is more commonly used for "boat." The words for "can" in Latin America are *lata* and *depósito*.

7. *gasolinera:* In most Latin-American countries the term for "gas station" is *estación de gasolina*.

12. *patinar:* lit., "to skate," but it is often used to describe a motion such as skidding or slipping.

22. *cacharro:* lit., "an earthenware pot." Used often as a synonym for a worthless object.

GRAMMATICAL ITEMS FOR SPECIAL STUDY

I. A. *unos, unas:* some

Study:

1. Oigo unos ruidos muy raros.

2. Hay unas tiendas muy buenas en esta calle.

1. *I hear some very strange noises.*

2. *There are some very good stores on this street.*

B. *algún:* some—singular and plural forms

Study:

1. Algún día vamos a visitarlo.

2. Algunos amigos vinieron ayer.

3. Algunas personas no lo creen.

4. Se lo ha dicho alguna chica.

5. Alguna señora lo ha dejado aquí.

1. *Some day we're going to visit it.*

2. *Some friends came yesterday.*

3. *Some people don't believe it.*

4. *Some girl told him that.*

5. *Some woman left it here.*

II. **ninguno** in negative sentences

1. No diría eso ningún amigo. *(or)* Ningún amigo diría eso.

2. No quedaba ninguna mesa libre en el restaurante.

3. No tengo ningún prejuicio.

4. ¿Tiene usted alguna novela interesante? No tengo ninguna.

5. ¿Ha visto usted una parada de autobús por aquí? No, no he visto ninguna.

1. *No friend would say that.*

2. *There wasn't a free table in the restaurant.*

3. *I don't have any prejudice.*

4. *Do you have any interesting novel? No, I don't have any.*

5. *Have you seen a bus stop along here? No, I haven't seen any.*

III. **unos cuantos:** some, an indefinite amount

Study:

1. ¿Le gustan a usted estos dulces? Sí, deme unos cuantos por favor.

2. ¿Le quedan algunas pesetas? Sí, aun me quedan unas cuantas.

1. *Do you like these candies? Yes, give me some, please.*

2. *Do you have any pesetas left? Yes, I still have some left.*

IV. *lo* + adjective = abstract noun

Study:

1. Lo difícil es hacerlo bien.

2. Lo malo del caso es que no se comprenden.

3. Lo bueno es que vienen todos.

4. Lo extraño es que ha llovido.

1. *The difficult thing (part) is to do it well.*

2. *The bad thing (part) of the matter is that they don't understand each other.*

3. *The good part is that they're all coming.*

4. *The strange thing is that it rained.*

Note: The adjectives may be in the comparative form.

Lo más difícil	*the most difficult thing*
Lo mejor	*the best thing (part)*
Lo más extraño	*the strangest thing*

DRILLS AND EXERCISES

I. Substitute the words or expressions in parentheses for the italicized word or expression in the model sentence. Write each new sentence and say it aloud.

A. Me mandaron unos *cuadros*. (retratos, libros, sellos, folletos, lápices)

B. ¿Tiene usted algunas *pesetas*? (novelas, amigas, casas, noticias, entradas, copas)

C. No he visto ninguna *película* interesante. (comedia, ciudad, tienda, pintura, obra)

D. Juan ha comprado unos cuantos *dulces*. (libros, planos, pañuelos, sobres, sellos)

E. *Lo bueno* es comprenderlo bien. (Lo mejor, Lo interesante, Lo fácil, Lo difícil, Lo imposible)

F. ¿Quiere usted mandarme unas *revistas*? (cartas, noticias, tarjetas, fotos, direcciones)

II. Change these sentences to the negative. Write the complete sentence and translate. Answers are in the back of the book.

1. Me quedan algunas pesetas.

2. ¿Quiere usted algunos periódicos?

3. Ellos tienen algunas dificultades.

4. Queríamos comprar algunas revistas.

5. Me dieron unos cuantos papeles.

III. Translate the following sentences into Spanish, then say them aloud. Answers will be found at the back of the book.

1. I think I left a few letters there.

2. He heard some strange noises.

3. Put a little water in the radiator.

4. I just bought some stamps.

5. Do you want to come back at five?

6. Do only what is necessary (the necessary thing).

7. We'll do everything we can.

8. The good thing is that we arrived early.

9. I'm sure you'll like the car.

10. The bad part of the matter is that they don't understand us.

QUIZ

From among the three choices given, choose the one which correctly renders the English given at the beginning of each sentence. Write the complete sentence, and translate.

1. *(some)* Les voy a enviar _____ programas del concierto.
   (a) unas
   (b) algunas
   (c) unos

2. *(any)* No me ha dado _____ dinero.
   (a) ninguno
   (b) algún
   (c) ningún

3. *(any)* Me gustan las novelas románticas. Tiene usted _____?
   (a) algunas
   (b) ninguna
   (c) ningunas

4. *(some)* Voy a decírselo _____ día.
   (a) alguna
   (b) algún
   (c) algo

5. *(the impossible part)* Eso precisamente es _____ del caso.
   (a) lo imposible
   (b) los imposibles
   (c) imposible

6. *(none)* No se lo ha dicho a _____ de sus amigos.
   - (a) alguno
   - (b) ninguno
   - (c) ninguna

7. *(some)* Querían vender _____ vestidos.
   - (a) algunas
   - (b) unos cuantos
   - (c) unas

8. *(the best thing)* Me gustó la comedia. Los primeras escenas fueron _____ de la obra.
   - (a) la mejor
   - (b) lo mejor
   - (c) los mejores

9. *(any)* ¿Le ha dado _____ dinero?
   - (a) alguno
   - (b) algún
   - (c) ningún

10. *(the most difficult part)* Les he explicado _____.
    - (a) lo difícil
    - (b) lo más dificil
    - (c) los difíciles

Answers at back of book.

LESSON 55

LA ADUANA
CUSTOMS

A. *Al acercarse a la frontera Francesa*
Approaching the French border

1. Juana: **Mira, ¡qué cantidad de coches haciendo cola° delante de la Aduana!**

Look. What a bunch of cars lined up before the customs station!

2. Carlos: **Lo esperaba. ¡Hay tantos turistas que pasan por Port Bou° desde la Costa Brava!**
   I expected it. There are so many tourists who go through Port Bou from the Costa Brava!

3. Juana: **¡Claro! Pero yo creía que los martes sería mejor. Sin duda tendremos una larga espera.**
   Of course! But I thought on Tuesday it would be better. Undoubtedly, we have a long wait.

4. Carlos: **Al contrario. Se dice que aquí pasan con bastante prisa.**
   On the contrary. They say that here they go through rather fast.

5. Juana: **Espero que no nos revisen el equipaje demasiado.**
   I hope they don't look at the luggage too carefully.

6. Carlos: **No creo que sean demasiado estrictos con los turistas. Además no llevamos nada (que declarar).**
   I don't think they're too strict with the tourists. Besides, we don't have anything (to declare).

B. *En la frontera*   At the border

7. Juana: **Ya, estamos en la frontera. Viene el inspector.**
   Here we are at the border. The inspector is coming.

8. Inspector: **Buenos días, señores. ¿Piensan quedarse mucho tiempo en Francia?**
   Good morning. Do you intend to stay very long in France?

9. Carlos: **No, señor. Solamente el fin de se-mana. Vamos a visitar Monte Carlo y Cannes.**
No, sir. Only the weekend. We're going to visit Monte Carlo and Cannes.

10. Inspector: **¿Tienen algo que declarar?**
Do you have anything to declare?

11. Carlos: **Nada, que yo sepa.**
Nothing that I know of.

12. Inspector: **¿Tabaco? ¿Bebidas alcohólicas? ¿Joyas? ¿Perfumes?**
Tobacco? Alcoholic beverages? Jewelry? Perfumes?

13. Carlos: **Lo que llevamos es estrictamente limitado al uso personal. Nada de importancia.**
What we have is strictly limited to personal use. Nothing important.

14. Juana: **No hace falta abrir las maletas, ¿verdad?**
We don't have to open the suitcases, do we?

15. Inspector: **Siento molestarla, señora, pero . . . ¿Quiere usted abrir esa maleta blanca?**
I'm sorry to trouble you, madam, but . . . Will you open that white suitcase?

16. Carlos: **¿Quiere que yo abras las otras?**
Do you want me to open the others?

17. Inspector: **No hace falta. ¿Son nuevos estos vestidos?**
It's not necessary. Are these dresses new?

18. Juana: **¡Ojalá! No, señor, son bastante viejos.**
I wish they were! No, sir, they're rather old.

19. Inspector: **Bien. Me parece que todo está en orden. Puede cerrar la maleta.**
O.K. I think everything's in order. You can close the suitcase.

20. Juana: **Entonces, ¿no tenemos que hacer una declaración ni pagar nada?**
Then we don't have to make out a declaration or pay anything?

21. Inspector: **Eso es, señora. Pero, permítame ver los documentos del coche, y su carnet de conductor.**
That's right, madam. But let me see the papers for the car and your driver's license.

22. Carlos: **Aquí los tiene. Como usted ve, el coche tiene matrícula española. Espero que encuentre todo en orden.**
Here you are. As you see, the car has a Spanish license. I hope you find everything in order.

23. Inspector: **Gracias. Estos están bien. ¿Me permiten ustedes los pasaportes?**
Thank you. These are fine. May I see your passports?

24. Juana: **¿Dónde estarán? Yo creía tenerlos en esta bolsa, pero ahora no los veo en ninguna parte.°**
Where did they go? I thought I had them in this bag but now I don't see them anywhere.

25. Carlos: **Los sacaste hace poco. Estarán en el asiento.**
You took them out a little while ago. They must be on the seat.

26. Juana: **Dile que espere un momento. Deben haberse caído al suelo. ¡Ah! Los encontré. Efectivamente, se habían caído.**

Tell him to wait a minute. They must have fallen on the floor. Ah! I've found them. They *had* fallen.

27. Inspector: **Gracias. Y perdonen la molestia. ¡Qué tengan buen viaje!**
    Thank you. And excuse the trouble. Have a good trip!

28. Carlos: **Gracias. Espero que nos veamos a la vuelta.**
    Thank you. I hope we see each other on the return trip.

29. Juana: **Ha sido mucho más fácil que la última vez, ¿verdad? ¿Te acuerdas? Nos hicieron abrir todas las maletas y perdimos horas. Creo que nos tomaron por criminales.**
    It was much easier than last time, wasn't it? Do you remember? They made us open all the suitcases and we lost (spent) hours. I think they took us for criminals.

30. Carlos: **Me explicaron después que estaban buscando contrabando y que nuestro coche se parecía mucho a uno de los que utilizaba una pandilla de contrabandistas profesionales.**
    They explained to me later that they were looking for contraband and that our car looked very much like one that a band of professional smugglers was using.

31. Juana: **Cada vez que me acuerdo de ello, me pongo nerviosa. No hables de eso, por favor.**
    Every time I remember it, I get nervous. Don't talk about that, please.

32. Carlos: **Está bien, querida. Ya estamos camino de Monte Carlo donde podrás probar suerte en el casino.**
It's all right, dear. Now we're on our way to Monte Carlo, where you can try your luck at the casino.

NOTES

1. *hacer cola:* to get in line, form a line.

2. Port Bou: the small Mediterranean town which is the entrance to France from the Spanish Costa Brava.

11. *Nada, que yo sepa:* Note the subjunctive used with the negative *Nada* as antecedent. The first part of the sentence is understood as, for example, *no tenemos nada...*

24. *no los veo en ninguna parte:* Notice the use of negative *ninguna* after a verb in the negative. The affirmative equivalent would be *alguna:* i.e., *¿Los ve usted en alguna parte?*

GRAMMATICAL ITEMS FOR SPECIAL STUDY

I. Preterite + *hace* + time expression = ago

Study:

1. Los sacaste hace poco.

2. Ellos llegaron hace una semana.

3. Juan salió hace una hora.

1. *You took them out a while ago.*

2. *They arrived a week ago.*

3. *John left an hour ago.*

II. Use **decir** + **que** + subjunctive for indirect commands

Study:

1. Dile que espere.

2. Dígales que vengan en seguida.

3. Dígale a ella que nos lo mande.

1. *Tell him to wait.*

2. *Tell them to come at once.*

3. *Tell her to send it to us.*

III. Adding *-mente* to the feminine form of an adjective to form the adverb

Study:

1. Se lo dije claramente.

2. Le acusaron injustamente.

3. Fue debidamente castigado.

1. *I told it to him clearly.*

2. *They accused him unjustly.*

3. *He was duly punished.*

Note: But adjectives that have only singular and plural forms take the *-mente* ending without any other change. Adjectives with written accents retain them in the adverbial form.

Study:

1. Lo puedes hacer fácilmente.

2. Normalmente, no lo hacemos en esa forma.

3. Posiblemente está aquí todavía.

1. *You can do it easily.*

2. *Normally, we don't do it that way.*

3. *Possibly he's still here.*

IV. Nouns may be formed from adjectives by using the proper form of the article.

Study:

1. La rubia me escribió una carta.

2. No me gustan las morenas.

3. Estos libros no valen nada. Los buenos están allí.

4. Los malos siempre sufren.

5. Me gusta ayudar a los pobres.

1. *The blonde (girl) wrote me a letter.*

2. *I don't like brunettes.*

3. *These books aren't worth anything. The good ones are there.*

4. *The bad always suffer.*

5. *I like to help the poor.*

DRILLS AND EXERCISES

I. Substitute the words or expressions in parentheses for the italicized word or expression in the model sentence. Write each new sentence and say it aloud.

A. Juan y José llegaron hace *una semana.* (una hora, un año, cuatro meses, mucho tiempo, poco)

B. Ellos lo *compraron* hace tres días. (vendieron, escribieron, hicieron, mandaron, recibieron)

C. Dígale a Juana que *venga.* (escriba, llame, entre, trabaje, coma)

D. Ya lo escribí *clara*mente. (mala-, fácil-, difícil-, inútil-, inmediata-)

E. María es la *rubia.* (buena, morena, gorda, tonta, tímida)

F. Los *buenos* son siempre los primeros. (malos, inteligentes, perezosos, imposibles, interesantes)

II. Rewrite these sentences following the example. Write the complete sentence and translate. Answers will be found in the back of the book.

Juan llegó la semana pasada.
Juan llegó hace una semana.

1. Ellos vinieron el año pasado.

2. Ella me escribió el mes pasado.

3. Jorge se casó anteayer.

4. Hoy es el quince de agosto. María se marchó el día dos.

5. Me mandaron el libro el año pasado.

III. Translate the following sentences into Spanish, then say them aloud. Answers will be found at the back of the book.

1. There are so many tourists that go through Port Bou.

2. Are you going to stay in France very long?

3. I thought it would be better on Tuesday.

4. You have to open the suitcases.

5. All the papers are in order.

6. Tell him to wait a minute.

7. I hope we see you on the return trip.

8. It was much easier the last time.

9. I think they took us for criminals.

10. Don't talk about that, please.

QUIZ

From among the three choices given, choose the one which correctly renders the English given at the beginning of each sentence. Write the complete sentence, and translate.

1. *(called)* Juan _____ hace una hora.
   - (a) llama
   - (b) llamó
   - (c) llamaba

2. *(ago)* Nuestros amigos llegaron _____ unas horas.
   - (a) hace
   - (b) hacen
   - (c) hizo

3. *(to wait)* Dígale que _____.
   - (a) espera
   - (b) espere
   - (c) esperar

4. *(easily)* El dice que lo puede hacer _____.
   - (a) fácilmente
   - (b) facilmente
   - (c) facilamente

5. *(did)* Lo _____ Juan hace mucho tiempo.
   - (a) hace
   - (b) hizo
   - (c) haces

6. *(to come)* Dígales _____.
   - (a) venir
   - (b) vienen
   - (c) que vengan

7. *(some days ago)* Los señores Andrade llegaron
   _____.

   - (a) hizo unos días
   - (b) hace unas días
   - (c) hace unos días

8. *(clearly)* El jefe me lo dijo _____.
   - (a) clara
   - (b) claros
   - (c) claramente

9. *(to write)* Dígale a María que _____.
   - (a) escribe
   - (b) escriba
   - (c) escribir

10. *(to declare)* ¿Tienen ustedes algo que
    _____?
    - (a) declarar
    - (b) declare
    - (c) declaran

Answers at back of book.

LESSON 56

EN EL BANCO
AT THE BANK

A. *En la ventanilla de cambio*
   At the foreign-exchange window

  1. Carlos: **¿Pueden cambiarme aquí un cheque
     de viajero?**

Can you cash a traveler's check for me here?

2. Cajero: **Claro que sí. Usted lo tendrá que firmar.**
Of course. You'll have to sign it.

3. Carlos: **¿Qué es el cambio?**
What's the exchange rate?

4. Cajero: **Setenta pesetas por dólar, señor. ¿Quiere enseñarme su pasaporte, por favor?**
Seventy pesetas to the dollar, sir. Will you show me your passport, please?

5. Carlos: **El pasaporte. ¿Por qué?**
My passport. Why?

6. Cajero: **Hay que anotar su nombre, dirección, y el número del pasaporte en este recibo, señor.**
Your name, address and passport number must be entered on this receipt, sir.

7. Carlos: **¡Ah, claro! Aquí lo tiene. Estamos hospedados en el Hotel Emperatriz, aquí en Madrid.**
Of course. Here you are. We're staying at the Hotel Emperatriz, here in Madrid.

8. Cajero: **¿Cómo quiere usted el dinero?**
How do you want the money?

9. Carlos: **Deme cinco billetes de mil, ocho de cien, y doscientas pesetas en monedas, por favor.**
Give me five one thousand peseta notes, eight one hundred, and two hundred pesetas in change, please.

10. Cajero: **Tome usted, señor. Guarde el recibo.**

Here you are, sir. Keep the receipt.

11. Carlos: **Muchas gracias. Para arreglar un
    giro al extranjero, ¿con quién debiera
    hablar, por favor?**
    Thank you very much. To arrange a bank draft
    overseas, with whom should I speak, please?

12. Cajero: **Vea usted al gerente, el señor
    García. Su despacho está allí, directamente
    enfrente.**
    See the manager, Mr. García. His office is
    there, directly opposite.

B. *En el despacho del Señor García*   At Mr. García's office

13. Sr. García: **Buenos días. ¿En qué puedo
    servirle, señor?**
    Good morning. What can I do for you, sir?

14. Carlos: **Quiero mandar unos cuadros a los
    Estados Unidos y quiero que el banco de
    Nueva York pague el importe del embalaje y
    los gastos de flete.**
    I want to send some pictures to the United
    States, and I want the bank in New York to pay
    the cost of packing and shipping.

15. Sr. García: **Entonces, usted necesita tres
    cosas. En primer lugar, permiso de exporta-
    ción; luego un recibo del valor total del
    envío; y finalmente, las declaraciones para
    la aduana. ¿Cómo piensa usted mandar los
    cuadros?**
    Then you need three things. In the first place,
    permission to export; then, a receipt for the
    total value of the shipment; and finally, the
    customs declarations. How do you intend to
    send the pictures?

16. Carlos: **Los quiero mandar por barco. Son bastante pesados y sería demasiado caro por avión.**
I want to send them by boat. They're rather heavy and it would be too expensive by plane.

17. Sr. García: **Lo más fácil sería arreglarlo por intermedio de una agencia que tenga representante en Nueva York, para que ellos puedan ocuparse de los trámites° allá.**
The easiest thing to do would be to arrange it through an agency that has a representative in New York, so that they can handle the business there.

18. Carlos: **¿Es que hay algún agente que pudiera ocuparse de todo el asunto? ¿El embalaje, los papeles, permisos? Todos estos asuntos° son tan complicados.**
Is there any agent who could take care of the whole matter? The packing, the papers, the permits? All these matters are so complicated.

19. Sr. García: **Claro que sí. Vaya usted a ver al señor Gutiérrez de la Compañía Ultramar, en la calle Caballero de Gracia veintisiete. El le solucionará todos los detalles del envío.**
Of course. Go to see Mr. Gutiérrez, of the Ultramar Company, at 27 Caballero de Gracia. He will work out all the details of the shipment for you.

20. Carlos: *¿Me dará un precio global por todos los trámites?*
Will he give me a package price for all the procedures?

21. Sr. García: *Estoy seguro de que él le dará un excelente servicio. Muchos clientes nuestros lo recomiendan.*

I'm sure he'll give you excellent service. Many of our clients recommend him.

22. Carlos: *¿Y pueden ustedes arreglar un giro al banco de Nueva York para cubrir los gastos allá?*
And can you arrange a draft to the bank in New York to cover expenses there?

23. Sr. García: *Sí, señor, con mucho gusto. Tenemos relaciones comerciales con el Nueva York Chemical y es bastante fácil arreglarlo todo.*
Yes, sir, with pleasure. We have commercial connections with the New York Chemical Bank and it's quite easy to take care of everything.

24. Carlos: *Muchísimas gracias. Me ha quitado usted un peso de encima. Me parecía tan difícil al principio que me daban ganas de abandonar la idea del todo. Hoy mismo voy a hablar con el señor Gutiérrez.*
Thank you very much. You've taken a load off my mind. It seemed so difficult to me at first that I felt like giving the idea up completely. I'm going to speak to Mr. Gutiérrez today.

25. Sr. García: *Siempre estamos dispuestos a servirle, señor.*
We're always ready to help you, sir.

26. Carlos: *Estoy muy agradecido por su ayuda. Volveré en cuanto tenga hecho todo lo que se tiene que hacer.*
I'm very grateful for your help. I'll come back as soon as I've done everything that has to be done.

NOTES

17. *trámites, trámite:* a noun which means "proce-
    dure" or "process." Generally used in the
    plural to express the series of steps, or pro-
    ceedings, in a business transaction of any kind.

18. *asunto:* Another word with a rather vague,
    general meaning, referring to "the matter,"
    "the affair" in an abstract way.

GRAMMATICAL ITEMS FOR SPECIAL STUDY

I. The subjunctive is used after verbs or expressions
   of *disbelief, doubt, denial* or *impossibility.*

   Study:

   1. Dudo que Juan esté aquí.
   2. Es imposible que María haga tal cosa.
   3. Niego que sea verdad.
   4. No creo que ellos vengan.

   1. *I doubt that John is here.*
   2. *It's impossible that Mary would do such a thing.*
   3. *I deny that it's true.*
   4. *I don't believe they'll come.*

II. The subjunctive is used in an adjective clause
    when the noun or pronoun referred to is *undeter-
    mined* or *non-existent.*

    Study:

    1. No conozco a nadie que pueda ayudarnos.
    2. No tenemos nada que sea tan interesante.
    3. Voy a buscar una agencia que tenga sucursal en
       Nueva York.

4. ¿Conoce usted a alguien que sepa el precio?

5. No conocen a nadie que tenga este modelo.

6. ¿Dónde puedo encontrar a un guía que hable ruso?

1. *I don't know anyone who can help us.*

2. *We have nothing that is so interesting.*

3. *I'm going to look for an agency that has a branch in New York.*

4. *Do you know anyone who knows the price?*

5. *They don't know anyone who has this model.*

6. *Where can I find a guide who speaks Russian?*

III. Conjunctions referring to *future* or *indeterminate time* take the subjunctive.

Study:

1. Voy a esperar hasta que llegue Juan.

2. Vamos a trabajar mucho mientras estemos aquí.

3. Se lo diré tan pronto como lleguen.

4. En cuanto lo tenga, voy a mandártelo.

1. *I'm going to wait until John arrives.*

2. *We are going to work hard while we're here.*

3. *I'll tell them as soon as they arrive.*

4. *As soon as I have it, I'm going to send it to you.*

IV. The reflexive is used for reciprocal action: one another, each other.

Study:

1. Nos saludamos cada día.

2. Ellos se conocieron en Madrid.

3. No creo que nos veamos otra vez.

4. Siempre se hablan María y Teresa.

1. *We greet each other every day.*

2. *They met each other in Madrid.*

3. *I don't think we'll see each other again.*

4. *Mary and Theresa always talk to each other.*

DRILLS AND EXERCISES

I. Substitute each of the words or expressions in parentheses for the italicized word or expression in the model sentence. Write each new sentence and say it aloud.

A. No creo que ellos lo *sepan*. (compren, vendan, escriban, manden, conozcan)

B. Es imposible que ellos *lleguen* ahora. (hablen, duerman, se levanten, vayan, entren)

C. Busco una casa que sea bastante *grande*. (cómoda, económica, pequeña, bonita, nueva)

D. No conocemos a nadie que hable *ruso*. (italiano, inglés, alemán, griego, árabe)

E. Vamos a esperar hasta que *vengan*. (llamen, lleguen, se levanten, escriban, coman)

F. En cuanto Juan lo *compre*, se lo dirá usted. (vea, venda, reciba, tenga, mande)

II. Change the following sentences to the interrogative. Write the complete sentence and translate. Answers will be found at the back of the book.

1. Juan y José se saludan siempre que se ven.

2. Rafael está buscando una secretaria que hable inglés.

3. Ellos van a esperar hasta que lleguemos.

4. Usted conoce a alguien que trabaja bien.

5. María lo dirá en cuanto lo sepa.

III. Translate the following sentences into Spanish, then say them aloud. Answers will be found at the back of the book.

1. I'm going to look for a book that I like.

2. They don't know anyone who writes poetry.

3. John will wait until we arrive.

4. Do you always see each other in Paris?

5. Will you write to me when you arrive in New York?

6. I doubt that they are here.

7. We don't believe John knows it.

8. John doesn't think Mary will come.

9. He's looking for a bank that has a branch in Madrid.

10. As soon as I buy it, I will show it to you.

QUIZ

From among the three choices given, choose the one which correctly renders the English given at the beginning of each sentence. Write the complete sentence, and translate.

1. (*is*) No creo que María _____ aquí.
   (a) está
   (b) esté
   (c) es

2. (*do*) Es imposible que ellos _____ tal cosa.
   (a) hacen
   (b) hagan
   (c) harán

3. (*can*) No hay ninguno que _____ hacerlo.
   (a) puede
   (b) pueda
   (c) podrá

4. (*has*) Quiero encontrar una casa que _____
   siete habitaciones.
   (a) tiene
   (b) tener
   (c) tenga

5. (*believe*) Es imposible que ella _____ la
   historia.
   (a) cree
   (b) crea
   (c) creerá

6. (*it is*) Niegan que _____ verdad.
   (a) es
   (b) ser
   (c) sea

7. (*speaks*) Tenemos que esperar hasta que Juan
   _____.
   (a) habla
   (b) hable
   (c) hablará

8. (*have*) En cuanto ellos lo _____ se lo
   mandarán a usted.
   (a) tengan
   (b) tienen
   (c) tendrán

9. (*Each other*) _____ vemos todos los días.
   (a) Cada uno
   (b) Nos
   (c) Cada otro

10. (*is*) Busco una bolsa que _____ bastante grande.
    (a) sea
    (b) está
    (c) ser

Answers at back of book.

LESSON 57

EN CORREOS
AT THE POST OFFICE

A. *En la Ventanilla de Sellos*   At the Stamp Window

1. Carlos: **Perdone, señor. Quiero mandar estas tres cartas a los Estados Unidos. ¿Cuál es la tarifa, por favor?**
   Excuse me, sir. I want to send these three letters to the States. What's the rate, please?

2. Empleado: **¿Por avión o por barco?**
   By plane or by ship?

3. Carlos: **Por avión, por favor.**
   Airmail, please.

4. Empleado: **Tengo que pesarlas. Vamos a ver . . . son doce pesetas cada una, señor.**
   I have to weigh them. Let's see . . . they're twelve pesetas each, sir.

5. Carlos: **Quiero mandar ésta urgente° también. ¿Cuánto es?**

I want to send this one special delivery too.
How much is it?

6. Empleado: **Si es para Madrid, son solamente
quince pesetas y será entregada esta tarde.**
If it's for Madrid, it's only fifteen pesetas and
it will be delivered this afternoon.

7. Carlos: **Gracias. Tengo que ver si hay algo
para mí en la lista de correos y mandar un
paquete también. ¿Dónde hay que ir para
mandar paquetes?**
Thank you. I have to see if there's anything for
me in general delivery and to send a package.
Where do you have to go to mail a package?

8. Empleado: **Está en la sección de atrás. Pase
por aquella puerta a la izquierda y la verá
usted. También allí está la lista de correos.**
It's in the rear section. Go through that door on
the left and you'll see it. General Delivery is
there also.

B. *En la Ventanilla de la Lista de Correos*
At the General Delivery Window

9. Carlos: **¿Hay algo para mí? Me llamo Carlos
Andrade y Ramírez.**
Do you have anything for me? My name is
Charles Andrade Ramírez.

10. Empleado: **A ver . . . Sí, señor. Hay varias
postales, una carta certificada, y un paquete
pequeño. Usted tendrá que firmar el recibo
aquí. ¿Me permite su pasaporte?**
Let's see . . . Yes, sir. There are several post-
cards, a registered letter and a small package.
You'll have to sign the receipt here. May I see
your passport?

11. Carlos: **Por supuesto. ¿Dónde hay que firmar?**
Of course. Where must I sign?

12. Empleado: **En esta línea, por favor. Y por el paquete hay que pagar treinta pesetas de aduana.**
On this line, please. And for the package, you'll have to pay thirty pesetas of customs duty.

13. Carlos: **Gracias. ¿Qué será? No esperaba ningún paquete.**
Thank you. What can it be? I wasn't expecting any package.

C. *En la Ventanilla de Telegramas*
At the Telegram Window

14. Carlos: **¿Dónde están los formularios para telegramas?**
Where are the telegram forms?

15. Empleado: **Los encontrará allí en el escritorio, señor. Usted puede escribir el telegrama y traérmelo.**
You'll find them there on the writing desk, sir. You can write the telegram and bring it to me.

16. Carlos: **Es muy fácil. ¡Ya está!° ¿Cuánto es?**
It's very easy. It's finished. How much is it?

17. Empleado: **Permítame contar las palabras. Una, dos, tres, cuatro, cinco...**
Let me count the words. One, two, three, four, five...

18. Carlos: **Pero, ¿cuenta usted las palabras de la dirección también?**
But do you count the words in the address too?

19. Empleado: **Sí, señor. Se cuentan todas.**
Yes, sir. All of them are counted.

20. Carlos: **Tengo que mandar este paquete también. ¿Dónde puedo hacerlo?**
I have to mail this package too. Where can I do it?

21. Empleado: **Para eso hay que ir a aquella ventanilla de enfrente, la número veintiuno.**
For that, you'll have to go to that window opposite, number twenty-one.

D. *En la Ventanilla de Paquetes* At the Package Window

22. Carlos: **Quiero mandar este paquete a los Estados Unidos.**
I want to send this package to the United States.

23. Empleado: **A ver. Lo siento, señor, pero pesa demasiado para ir por correo. Si quiere usted mandarlo, tendrá que hacerlo en la oficina de la RENFE,° en la estación de Atocha.°**
Let's see. I'm sorry, sir, but it weighs too much to go by mail. If you want to send it, you'll have to do it at the offices of RENFE, at the Atocha station.

24. Carlos: **Pero va por barco, ¿no? ¿Por qué hay que ir a la RENFE?**
But it's going by ship, isn't it? Why must I go to the RENFE?

25. Empleado: **Bueno, señor, como usted sabe, tiene que llegar al puerto de embarque. Y para eso, va por tren.**
Well, sir, as you know, it has to get to the port of embarcation, and to do that, it goes by train.

26. Carlos: **Sí, claro. Si no pesara tanto, sería posible mandarlo por correo normal, ¿verdad?**
Yes, of course. If it didn't weigh so much, it would be possible to send it by regular mail, wouldn't it?

27. Empleado: **Desde luego, señor. Si quiere dividirlo en dos paquetes de no más de un kilo cada uno, usted podrá mandarlo desde aquí mismo.**
Certainly, sir. If you want to divide it into two packages of no more than one kilo each, you can send them from right here.

28. Carlos: **No vale la pena. ¡Qué complicación! Bueno, ¿dónde hay que ir?**
It's not worth the trouble. What a complication! Well, where do I have to go?

29. Empleado: **A la estación de Atocha, señor.**
To Atocha Station, sir.

E. *En las Oficinas de la RENFE* At the RENFE Offices

30. Carlos: *Quiero mandar este paquete.*
I want to send this package.

31. Empleado: *Hágame el favor de llenar estas dos declaraciones para la aduana.*
Please fill out these two customs declarations.

32. Carlos: *Me gustaría asegurarlo también.*
I'd like to insure it too.

33. Empleado: *¿Cuál es el valor, señor?*
What's the value, sir?

34. Carlos: *Yo diría unas mil doscientas pesetas.*
I'd say about a thousand two hundred pesetas.

35. Empleado: *Bueno. Pase usted a la caja con esto, y vuelva aquí por el recibo.*
All right. Go to the cashier's with this, and come back here for your receipt.

NOTES

5. *urgente:* lit., "urgent." In Latin America it is more common to say *para entrega inmediata* or *por mensajero especial ("immediate delivery"* or *"by messenger").*

16. *¡Ya está!* In an exclamation of this kind, some idea such as *hecho* ("done," "finished"), or *listo* ("ready"), is understood, as in *¡Ya estoy!* "I'm ready!"

23. *RENFE: la Red Nacional de Ferrocarriles Españoles*—the Spanish National Railroad, almost always referred to by the abbreviation *la RENFE.*
Atocha: One of the large railroad stations of Madrid. Atocha generally serves Andalusia and all points south.

GRAMMATICAL ITEMS FOR SPECIAL STUDY

I. Contrary-to-fact conditions: when "if" introduces a condition contrary-to-fact, the verb is in the *imperfect subjunctive* and the result is expressed by the *conditional.*

Study:

1. Si yo fuera rico, viajaría mucho.

2. Si los señores Andrade estuvieran aquí, podríamos decírselo.

3. Si estuviéramos en Londres ahora, podríamos ver la comedia.

4. Si trabajara más, usted ganaría más dinero.

1. *If I were rich, I would travel a lot.*

2. *If Mr. and Mrs. Andrade were here, we could tell them (it).*

3. *If we were in London now, we could see the comedy.*

4. *If you worked harder, you would earn more.*

II. "If" with the *indicative*

When the present tense is used, the indicative always follows "if."

Study:

1. Si puedo encontrarlo, te lo daré.

2. Si ellos me lo dicen, lo creo.

3. Si llueve, no salgo.

4. Si ella llega a tiempo, podemos ir.

1. *If I can find it, I'll give it to you.*

2. *If they tell me (it), I'll believe it.*

3. *If it rains, I'm not going out.*

4. *If she arrives on time, we can go.*

III. "Let's" expressed by *vamos a + the infinitive* or by the *first person plural of the present subjunctive*

Study:

1. Vamos a hablar del viaje.
   Hablemos del viaje.

2. Vamos a acostarnos temprano esta noche.
   Acostémonos temprano esta noche.

3. Vamos a salir en seguida.
   Salgamos en seguida.

4. Vamos a comprarlo.
   Comprémoslo.

5. Vamos a levantarnos a las siete.
   Levantémonos a las siete.

1. *Let's talk about the trip.*

2. *Let's go to bed early tonight.*

3. *Let's leave at once.*

4. *Let's buy it.*

5. *Let's get up at seven o'clock.*

Note: When the reflexive *-nos* is added, the final *s* of
the verb form is dropped.

Levantémonos.	*Let's get up.*
Sentémonos.	*Let's sit down.*

ss is reduced to *s:*

Comprémossselo becomes *comprémoselo.*
Let's buy it for him.

IV. In the negative "Let's not," the pronoun is not
   attached to the verb.

   Study:

1. No lo compremos.

2. No nos levantemos.

3. No se lo compremos.

1. *Let's not buy it.*

2. *Let's not get up.*

3. *Let's not buy it for him.*

DRILLS AND EXERCISES

I. Substitute each of the words or expressions in parentheses for the italicized word or expression in the model sentence. Write each new sentence and say it aloud.

   A. Si Juan fuera *rico,* lo podría hacer. (norteamericano, dentista, médico, profesor, millonario)
   B. Si tuviéramos *el libro,* lo (la) podríamos leer. (el diccionario, la revista, el periódico, la novela, la carta)
   C. Si veo a *Juan,* se lo digo. (María, los señores Andrade, tu amigo, los estudiantes, mi hermano)
   D. Si llegan *hoy,* yo voy a verlos. (mañana, la semana que viene, el martes, esta mañana, pronto)
   E. Compremos *las entradas.* (el libro, los periódicos, la revista, el billete, los guantes)
   F. Levantémonos *pronto.* (a las ocho, más tarde, en seguida, ahora, después)

II. Rewrite these sentences following the example. Write the complete sentence and translate. Answers will be found at the back of the book.

   Example:

   Vamos a decírselo.
   Digámoselo.

   1. Vamos a acostarnos.

   2. Vamos a comprarlo.

   3. No vamos a decirlo.

   4. Vamos a llegar a tiempo.

   5. Vamos a estudiarlo.

III. Translate the following sentences into Spanish, then say them aloud. Answers will be found at the back of the book.

1. If John were here, I would give him the book.

2. If they had the time, they would go to Barcelona.

3. If Mary were in Paris, she would buy the dress.

4. If it rains, we won't go to the theater.

5. If they see us, we'll talk to them.

6. If you had your car, we would arrive on time.

7. Let's go to the store.

8. Let's not get up early tomorrow.

9. Let's look for the book next week.

10. Let's not give it (the book) to John.

QUIZ

From among the three choices given, choose the one which correctly renders the English given at the beginning of each sentence. Write the complete sentence, and translate.

1. (*were*) Si yo _____ usted, no lo haría.
   (a) fuí
   (b) fuera
   (c) estuve

2. (*worked*) Juan ganaría mucho más si _____ más.
   (a) trabaja
   (b) trabajó
   (c) trabajara

3. (*were*) Yo se lo daría a los señores Andrade si
   _____ aquí.
   (a) estuvieron
   (b) estuvieran
   (c) estan

4. (*read*) Si ellos _____ el periódico sabrían
   lo que ha pasado.
   (a) leen
   (b) lean
   (c) leyeran

5. (*Let's get up*) _____ temprano mañana.
   (a) Vamos a levantar
   (b) Levantémonos
   (c) Levantémosnos

6. (*Let's not read*) _____ el periódico esta
   mañana.
   (a) No leemos
   (b) No leamos
   (c) No leeremos

7. (*arrive*) No les decimos nada si _____
   tarde.
   (a) lleguen
   (b) llegan
   (c) llegaran

8. (*rains*) No queremos ir al campo si _____.
   (a) llueva
   (b) lloverá
   (c) llueve

9. (*Let's talk*) _____ de lo que tenemos que
   hacer.
   (a) Hablamos
   (b) Hablemos
   (c) Hablaremos

10. *(Let me)* _____ contar las palabras.
   (a) Permítame
   (b) Permitamos
   (c) Me permitamos

Answers at back of book.

LESSON 58

LA ROPA
CLOTHING

A. *La lavandería y la tintorería*
   The laundry and the dry cleaners

1. Empleada: **Buenos días, señora Andrade. Veo que usted tiene muchas cosas para lavar.**
   Good morning, Mrs. Andrade. I see you have a lot of things to wash.

2. Juana: **Buenos días, señora. Sí, tengo una lista bastante larga. Para empezar, estas cinco camisas de mi marido.**
   Good morning. Yes, I have rather a long list. To begin with, these five shirts of my husband.

3. Empleada: **¿Las quiere almidonadas?**
   Does he want them starched?

4. Juana: **Solamente el cuello y los puños, por favor.**
   Only the collar and cuffs, please.

5. Empleada: **Muy bien. Me parece que a él no le gusta demasiado almidón, ¿verdad?**
   Very well. It seems to me that he doesn't like too much starch, right?

6. Juana: **Eso es. Este botón se ha caído.
¿Puede usted coserlo?**
That's right. This button fell off. Can you sew
it on?

7. Empleada: **Claro que sí, señora. Yo siempre
miro si están todos los botones. ¿Eso es
todo?**
Of course, madam. I always look to see if all
the buttons are on. Is that all?

8. Juana: **No. Aquí hay unas camisetas, unos
pijamas,° una combinación, varios calzon-
cillos, pañuelos y calcetines. Usted lo lava
todo a mano, ¿verdad?**
No. Here there are some undershirts, some
pajamas, a slip, several shorts, socks and handkerchiefs. You wash everything by hand, don't
you?

9. Empleada: **Claro. Aquí lo hago todo yo. Y se
lava mejor que a máquina. Todo sale más
blanco y más suave. Lo quiere todo plan-
chado, ¿verdad?**
Of course. I do everything here. And it's
washed better than by machine. Everything
comes out whiter and softer. You want everything ironed, don't you?

10. Juana: **Sí, por favor. ¿Estará pasado
mañana?°**
Yes, please. Will it be ready the day after
tomorrow?

11. Empleada: **Lo puede recoger usted mañana
por la tarde, si quiere.**
You can pick it up tomorrow afternoon, if you
wish.

B. *La tintorería*   The dry cleaners

12. Juana: **Señora, me gustaría hacer lavar en seco estos guantes y este vestido de seda. ¿Puede usted recomendarme una buena tintorería?**
Madam, I'd like to have these gloves and this silk dress dry cleaned. Can you recommend a good dry cleaners?

13. Portera: **Hay una aquí mismo en la esquina de General Goded y la Castellana. Dicen que trabajan bien. Creo que es mejor que la de más arriba. Si no es mejor, por lo menos es tan buena como la otra, y es más rápida. No sé si será más cara pero...**
There's one right here at the corner of General Goded and the Castellana. They say that they work well. I think it's better than the one farther up—or if not better, at least as good as the other one, and it's faster. I don't know if it's also more expensive but...

14. Juana: **Bueno, gracias, señora. ¿Vendrán a buscarlo?**
Fine, thank you, madam. Will they come to pick it up?

15. Portera: **Sí, señora. Usted puede llamar, y mandarán un chico a buscarlo. Si quiere dejarlo todo conmigo, yo me ocuparé de ello.° Usted tiene prisa.**
Yes, madam. You can call, and they will send a boy to pick it up. If you want to leave everything with me, I'll take care of it. You're in a hurry.

C. *En la sastrería*   At the tailor shop

16. Carlos: **Me gustaría un traje. El señor Ramírez me lo recomendó a usted.**

I would like a suit. Mr. Ramirez recommended you.

17. Sastre: **Muy bien, señor. El señor Ramírez es muy buen cliente. ¿Quiere mirar estas telas? Aquí tiene usted algunas muy finas. Lana, alpaca, y varias mezclas de fibras sintéticas.**
Tailor: Very good, sir. Mr. Ramirez is a very good customer. Do you want to look at these fabrics? Here you have some very fine ones. Wool, alpaca, and several mixtures of synthetic fibers.

18. Carlos: **Prefiero lana. Esta parece de muy buena calidad. ¿La recomienda usted?**
I prefer wool. This seems to be very good quality. Do you recommend it?

19. Sastre: **Desde luego. Es buenísima. ¿Le gusta a usted este gales?° Es nuevo.**
Certainly. It's very good. Do you like this Prince of Wales pattern? It's new.

20. Carlos: **Sí. Este gales gris me gusta mucho. Me parece más práctico un color oscuro.**
Yes. I like this gray Prince of Wales very much. A dark color seems more practical to me.

21. Sastre: **Claro que sí. Es práctico y elegante a la vez.**
Of course. It's practical and elegant at the same time.

22. Carlos: **Bien. Quiero ver también ese libro de varios modelos para escoger un estilo.**
Well. I would also like to see that pattern book to choose a style.

23. Sastre: **Ahora, a ver las medidas. ¿Quiere quitarse la chaqueta?** (*Tomando las medidas*) **A ver... la cintura, las espaldas, las mangas. ¿Quiere usted la americana° un poco entallada? Es el estilo que se usa más hoy en día.**
Now, let's see the measurements. Will you take off your jacket? (*taking the measurements*) Let's see... the waist, the shoulders, the sleeves. Do you want the coat cut in a little at the waist? It's the style that's worn most nowadays.

24. Carlos: **Creo que sí. Y hágame los pantalones sin basta, por favor.**
I think so. And make the trousers without cuffs, please.

25. Sastre: **Bien. ¿Quiere usted este estilo** (*señalando un dibujo*) **con chaqueta de tres botones, con abertura a ambos lados?**
Fine. Do you want this style (*pointing at a sketch*) with a three-button jacket, with side vents?

26. Carlos: **Me parece que sí. ¿Cuándo puedo volver para la prueba?**
Yes, I think so. When can I come back for the fitting?

27. Sastre: **La primera prueba... A ver... ¿Le va bien el sábado por la mañana?**
The first fitting... Let's see... Is Saturday morning all right with you?

28. Carlos: **Perfectamente. ¿Cuántas pruebas se necesitan?**
Perfect. How many fittings are needed?

29. Sastre: **Creo que lo podemos hacer con tres. Ya veremos.**
I think we can do it with three. We'll see.

D. *Con la modista°*   With the dressmaker

30. Juana: *Me gusta muchísimo el traje que usted me ha hecho, pero hay unos pequeños cambios que hacen falta.*
I like the suit you made for me very much, but there are some little changes that are needed.

31. Modista: *Pero, señora, me parece que le va perfectamente bien. ¿Qué es lo que quiere?*
Dressmaker: But, madam, I think it's perfect on you. What is it you want?

32. Juana: *La falda es demasiado larga para la nueva moda.*
The skirt is too long for the new fashions.

33. Modista: *Las llevan muy cortas ahora, señora, pero no hay que exagerar. A ver, ¿quiere usted ponerse la falda?*
They're wearing them very short now, madam, but we mustn't exaggerate. Let's see. Will you put the skirt on?

34. Juana: *¿No ve que es demasiado larga? La moda de esta temporada . . .*
Don't you see that it's too long? The fashion this season . . .

35. Modista: *Yo podría hacerla más corta si usted quiere. A mí me gusta tal como está.*
I could shorten it if you like. *I* like it just the way it is.

36. Juana: *¿Un centímetro?*
Half an inch?

37. Modista: *O dos. Usted manda, señora. ¿La chaqueta le va bien?*

Or an inch. You're the boss, madam. Does the jacket suit you?

38. Juana: *Sí. Al principio me parecía un poco apretada pero, no, ahora me gusta.*
Yes. At first, it seemed a little tight, but, no, now I like it.

39. Modista: *Bueno, señora. Deje la falda y yo se la arreglo tal como usted quiere. Puede venir a buscarla mañana. O ¿prefiere que se la mande?*
Fine, madam. Leave the skirt and I will fix it just as you wish. You can come to get it tomorrow. Or do you prefer that I send it to you?

40. Juana: *No, gracias. Vendré a probármela otra vez.*
No, thank you. I'll come to try it on again.

NOTES

8. *unos pijamas:* Notice that *pijamas* is masculine, as are other nouns ending in *ma,* for example, *el programa, el dilema,* etc.

10. *¿Estará pasado mañana?:* In this kind of sentence a word such as "finished," "ready" or "done" is understood.

15. *de ello:* neuter pronoun referring to the whole act of taking care of the matter.

19. *Gales:* Wales, used to refer to what is generally called glen-plaid in English.

23. *la americana:* In Spain, the suitcoat is generally called *la americana.* In other parts of the Spanish-speaking world, it is called *el saco* or *la chaqueta.*

Title D. *la modista:* a dressmaker. *La costurera* is a seamstress who makes alterations, but in many Latin American countries this word is used as a synonym for *modista.*

GRAMMATICAL ITEMS FOR SPECIAL STUDY

I. The comparative and superlative with *más* (more) or *menos* (less) used with *nouns, verbs, adjectives,* or *adverbs.*

Study:

1. No puedo andar más.

2. Tengo más tiempo.

3. Juan está menos cansado.

4. Este libro es más interesante.

5. Ellos hablan más fuerte.

6. Ella vendrá más tarde.

1. *I can't walk (any) more.*

2. *I have more time.*

3. *John is less tired.*

4. *This book is more interesting.*

5. *They speak louder.*

6. *She will come later.*

II. Comparatives not formed with *más* or *menos:*

mejor = better, best
peor = worse, worst
mayor = older, oldest; greater, greatest; bigger, biggest
menor = younger, youngest; smaller, smallest; lesser, least

Study:

1. Mis hermanos escriben mejor.

2. Este libro es mejor.

3. Es la mejor novela.

4. Yo soy el hermano menor.

5. El es mi hermano mayor.

1. *My brothers write better.*

2. *This book is better.*

3. *It's the best novel.*

4. *I'm the younger (youngest) brother.*

5. *He is my older (oldest) brother.*

Note: **más grande** and **más pequeño** are used when physical size is emphasized.

III. To distinguish adequately between comparative and superlative in Spanish, the article and a following prepositional phrase or adjective clause may be added.

Study:

1. El es mejor que usted.
   El es el mejor del mundo.

2. Ella es más bonita que Juana.
   Ella es la más bonita de la ciudad.

3. Esta lección es más difícil.
   Es la lección más difícil del libro.

4. Roberto es más fuerte que Juan.
   Roberto es el más fuerte del equipo.

5. Este libro es más interesante.
   Es el libro más interesante que jamás he leído.

6. Ella es más inteligente.
   Ella es más inteligente que nadie.

1. *He's better than you.*
   He's the best in the world.

2. *She's prettier than Jane.*
   She's the prettiest in the city.

3. *This lesson is more difficult.*
   It's the most difficult lesson in the book.

4. *Robert is stronger than John.*
   Robert is the strongest on the team.

5. *This book is more interesting.*
   It's the most interesting book that I've ever read.

6. *She's more intelligent.*
   She's more intelligent than anyone.

IV. "Than" is translated by *de,* with numbers or degrees in comparisons.

Study:

1. Hay más de veinte alumnos.

2. El tiene más de cuarenta dólares.

3. Ellos vieron más de cien aviones.

1. *There are more than twenty students.*

2. *He has more than forty dollars.*

3. *They saw more than a hundred airplanes.*

Note: In the negative, *que* is used before numbers to mean "no more than," or "only."

No tengo más que veinte dólares.
I have only twenty dollars.

DRILLS AND EXERCISES

I. Substitute the word or expression in parentheses for the italicized word or expression in the model sentence. Write each new sentence and say it aloud.

 A. Roberto es más *fuerte* que tú. (ambicioso, inteligente, pobre, rico, lento)

 B. Ellos tienen el restaurante más *típico* de Madrid. (caro, económico, bonito, divertido, antiguo)

 C. Lo siento. No puedo *andar* más. (estudiar, hablar, escribir, mandar, pedir)

 D. Mi hermano menor *canta* mejor que yo. (baila, escribe, juega, lee, contesta)

 E. Es el coche más *moderno* del mundo. (caro, peligroso, rápido, bonito, pequeño)

 F. Ellos me dieron más de cuarenta *libros*. (dólares, números, folletos, sellos, nombres)

II. Rewrite these sentences in the negative. Write the complete sentence and translate. Answers will be found in the back of the book.

 1. Tengo más de tres hermanos.

 2. Me cobraron más de cien pesetas.

 3. Hay más de cinco profesores.

 4. Compraron más de cinco maletas.

 5. Murieron más de veinte soldados.

III. Translate the following sentences into Spanish, then say them aloud. Answers will be found at the back of the book.

 1. They have a better car.

 2. We are older than they.

 3. This dress is more expensive.

4. This soap washes whiter.

5. The cloth that I bought is softer.

6. Jane is the prettiest girl in the class.

7. He is my youngest son.

8. It's the best magazine in the world.

9. I can't write (any) more.

10. He is more intelligent than his older brother.

QUIZ

From among the three choices given, choose the one which correctly renders the English given at the beginning of each sentence. Write the complete sentence, and translate.

1. *(any more)* No quiero estudiar _____.
   (a) alguna más
   (b) más
   (c) algo más

2. *(stronger)* Juan es mucho _____ que José.
   (a) mas fuerte
   (b) más fuerte
   (c) fuerte

3. *(bigger)* Este edificio es bastante _____.
   (a) grande
   (b) más
   (c) más grande

4. *(biggest)* Es el edificio _____ de la ciudad.
   (a) menos grande
   (b) más grande
   (c) mas grande

5. *(than)* No creo que tenga más _____ veinte pesetas.
    (a) que
    (b) de
    (c) de los

6. *(than)* No me dieron más _____ treinta dólares.
    (a) de
    (b) que
    (c) de las

7. *(easier than)* Esta lección es _____ la otra.
    (a) más fácil de
    (b) menos fácil
    (c) más fácil que

8. *(than her sister)* Ella es más inteligente _____.
    (a) de su hermana
    (b) que su hermana
    (c) su hermana

9. *(louder)* El profesor les dijo que hablaran _____.
    (a) alto
    (b) fuerte
    (c) más fuerte

10. *(younger)* Es mi hermana _____.
    (a) menor
    (b) más menor
    (c) la menor

Answers at back of book.

LESSON 59

EL DENTISTA, EL MEDICO,
Y EL FARMACEUTICO

THE DENTIST, THE DOCTOR,
AND THE PHARMACIST

A. *El dentista*   The dentist

1. Dentista: **Buenos días. ¿En qué puedo servirle, señora?**
Good morning. What can I do for you, madam?

2. Juana: **Tengo un diente que me duele mucho.
No lo entiendo, porque nunca me duelen. Es
un dolor punzante.**
I have a tooth that is hurting me very much. I
don't understand it because they never ache. It's
a very sharp pain.

3. Dentista: **A verlo, señora. ¿Quiere sentarse?
Ahora, ¿qué es lo que le pasa?**
Let's see, madam. Would you like to sit down?
Now, what is the matter?

4. Juana: **La encía está un poco hinchada y hasta
sangra a veces.**
The gum is a little swollen and it even bleeds at
times.

5. Dentista: **Más vale tomarle una radiografía.
Eche usted la cabeza un poco para atrás. Y
abra la boca, por favor.**
Better take an X ray. Tilt your head back a little.
And open your mouth, please.

6. Juana: **¿Tardará usted mucho?**
Will you take very long?

7. Dentista: **No. Las radiografías estarán en seguida. Mientras tanto, déjeme examinarle el diente. ¿Cuál es?**
No. The X rays will be ready right away. Meanwhile, let me examine the tooth. Which one is it?

8. Juana: **¡Ay! Me hace usted daño.**
Ouch! You're hurting me.

9. Dentista: **¿Quiere una inyección?**
Do you want an injection?

10. Juana: **Sí, por favor. No aguanto el dolor.**
Yes, please. I can't stand this pain.

11. Dentista: **Ya veo lo que es. Es una muela aquí a la izquierda. No me parece muy serio el asunto.**
Now I see what it is. It's a molar on the left. It doesn't look very serious.

12. Juana: **Menos mal. Espero que no tenga usted que sacármela.**
Good. I hope you don't have to pull it.

13. Dentista: **Vamos a ver la radiografía. Me parece bastante sano el diente. No, no hay que sacarlo.**
Let's look at the X ray. The tooth looks pretty healthy to me. No, it won't have to come out.

14. Juana: **¿Me lo puede arreglar, entonces?**
You can fix it for me, then?

15. Dentista: **Será cosa de unos minutos y no sentirá nada, señora. No se preocupe.**
It will be a matter of a few minutes and you won't feel anything, madam. Don't worry.

B. *La visita del médico*   The doctor's visit

17. Carlos: **Juana, no estoy nada bien. Tengo dolores por todo el cuerpo. Me duele la cabeza, tengo el estómago mal, me duele la garganta.**
I'm not well at all, Jane. I have pains all over my body. My head aches, my stomach is upset, my throat is sore.

18. Juana: **Desde luego, tienes mal aspecto. Voy a llamar al médico. Teresa me recomendó el suyo. A ver si puede venir. Mientras tanto, acuéstate.** *(Llama)*
You surely don't look well. I'm going to call the doctor. Theresa recommended hers. I'm going to see if he can come. Meanwhile, go to bed. *(She calls.)*

19. Médico: *(Más tarde)* **A ver, señor, ¿qué le pasa? Abra la boca, por favor. Tosa... usted tiene fiebre y la garganta está bastante irritada.**
(Later) Let's see, sir. What's wrong with you? Open your mouth, please. Cough . . . You have a fever and your throat is quite irritated.

20. Juana: **¿Qué hay que hacer?**
What must we do?

21. Médico: **Su marido tendrá que guardar cama° dos o tres días, señora, hasta que le pase la fiebre.**
Your husband will have to stay in bed two or three days, madam, until the fever goes away.

22. Juana: **¿Puede comer de todo?**
Can he eat everything?

23. Médico: **No, señora. Sopas o caldos. Bastante líquido. Zumos de frutas, cosas parecidas, y debe tomar estas píldoras que le voy a recetar. Dele una cada cuatro horas hasta que le baje la temperatura. Si no mejora esta noche, vuelva a llamarme.**

No, madam. Soups or broths. A lot of liquids. Fruit juices, similar things, and he ought to take these pills that I'm going to prescribe. Give him one every four hours until his temperature goes down. If he's not better by tonight, call me again.

24. Juana: **¡Qué lástima! Ahora tenemos que aplazar el viaje al sur.**

What a shame! Now we have to postpone the trip south.

25. Médico: **Ya lo creo. No debiera levantarse de la cama. Tendrá que descansar.**

I certainly think so. He shouldn't get out of bed. He'll have to rest.

26. Juana: *(La mañana siguiente)* **¿Cómo te sientes ahora, querido? ¿Has dormido bien?**

(The following day) How do you feel now, dear? Did you sleep well?

27. Carlos: **Mucho mejor, gracias. Me parece que no tengo tanta fiebre como antes. Y no me duele tanto la garganta.**

Much better, thank you. I don't think I have as much fever as before. And my throat isn't so sore.

28. Juana: **Me alegro, querido. Aquí está el periódico de hoy, si lo quieres leer. Voy a bajar a la farmacia. Vuelvo en seguida.**

I'm glad, dear. Here's today's paper if you want to read it. I'm going to go down to the pharmacy. I'll come right back.

C. *En la farmacia*   At the pharmacy

29. Juana: **Por favor, ¿quiere prepararme esta receta del doctor Menéndez? Ojalá no tarde mucho. Tengo prisa.**
Please, will you prepare this prescription of Dr. Menéndez? I hope it doesn't take too long. I'm in a hurry.

30. Farmacéutico: **No se preocupe, señora. Estará dentro de un momento. ¿Quiere alguna otra cosa?**
Druggist: Don't worry, madam. It will be ready in a moment. Do you want anything else?

31. Juana: **Ah, sí. Por poco se me olvida.°** **¿Tiene usted una buena crema de noche para la piel seca?**
Oh, yes. I almost forgot. Do you have a good night cream for dry skin?

32. Farmacéutico: **Esta crema está preparada en nuestros laboratorios y muchas señoras la han probado y la recomiendan.**
This cream is prepared in our laboratories, and many ladies have tried it and recommend it.

33. Juana: **Voy a probarla también. Y quiero unas hojas de afeitar y un tubo de crema dentífrica.**
I'm going to try it too. And I want some razor blades and a tube of toothpaste.

NOTES

21. *guardar cama:* to stay in bed.

31. *Por poco se me olvida:* Notice the present tense for an idea that is usually expressed by the past tense in English. "I almost forgot." *Por poco* is used in this manner quite frequently. *Por poco se me cae el plato.* ("I almost dropped the plate.") *Por poco se pierde Juan.* ("John almost got lost.")

GRAMMATICAL ITEMS FOR SPECIAL STUDY

I. *el mismo que:* the same as

Study:

1. Rafael tiene el mismo disco que yo.

2. Ellos estudian los mismos libros que nosotros.

3. Teresa lleva la misma blusa que ayer.

4. Todos tienen las mismas preocupaciones que él.

1. *Raphael has the same record as I.*

2. *They are studying the same books as we are.*

3. *Theresa is wearing the same blouse as yesterday.*

4. *They all have the same worries as he does.*

II. To make the possessive pronoun, use *the proper form of the article.*

Study:

1. Juan dice que este coche es mejor que el suyo.

2. Aquí está tu pluma. ¿Dónde está la mía?

3. La clase de Rafael empieza a las cuatro. ¿Cuándo empieza la nuestra?

4. Los zapatos de María son nuevos. Me gustan tanto como los tuyos.

5. Préstame tu libro, por favor. He perdido el mío.

6. ¿Las maletas? Las mías están aquí.

7. ¿Los abrigos? El mío está allí y éste es el tuyo.

8. ¿El de Juan? Dile que el suyo está aquí también.

1. *John says this car is better than his.*

2. *Here's your pen. Where's mine?*

3. *Ralph's class begins at four o'clock. When does ours begin?*

4. *Mary's shoes are new. I like them as well as yours.*

5. *Lend me your book, please. I lost mine.*

6. *The suitcases? Mine are here.*

7. *The coats? Mine is there and this one is yours.*

8. *John's? Tell him that his is here too.*

III. You can use *poco, mucho, otro, alguno, ninguno* as nouns.

Study:

1. ¿Flores? Me quedan muy pocas.

2. ¿Botones? ¿Quiere usted muchos?

3. Sí, quiero algunos grandes.

4. No tengo ninguno.

5. ¿Tiene usted otro más barato?

6. ¿Máquina de escribir? Tengo una portátil.

1. *Flowers? I have very few left.*

2. *Buttons? Do you want many?*

3. *Yes, I want some big ones.*

4. *I don't have any.*

5. *Do you have another cheaper one?*

6. *Typewriter? I have a portable one.*

DRILLS AND EXERCISES

I. Substitute the words or expressions in parentheses for the italicized word or expression in the model sentence. Write each new sentence and say it aloud.

A. Margarita ha comprado el mismo *modelo* que yo. (coche, abrigo, sombrero, vestido, traje)

B. Ella siempre compra los mismos *discos* que su amiga. (zapatos, guantes, libros, cuadernos, cigarillos)

C. Creo que esta *casa* es más bonita que la mía. (blusa, máquina, lámpara, mesa, revista)

D. ¿Cuadros? Tenemos *unos* más bonitos. (algunos, pocos, muchos, otros)

E. ¿Máquina de coser? ¿Quiere usted ver una *portátil?* (nueva, barata, bonita, práctica, moderna, alemana)

F. No veo mis *discos* pero aquí están los tuyos. (libros, lápices, papeles, cuadernos, guantes)

II. Change these sentences to the present tense. Write the complete sentence and translate. Answers will be found in the back of the book.

1. Ellos siempre mandaron los mismos periódicos.

2. El compró la misma crema de afeitar que Juan.

3. Tú recibiste el mismo premio que yo.

4. Cuando mi padre recibió su máquina (de escribir) nueva, me dió la vieja.

5. Juan no escuchó el mismo programa que yo.

III. Translate the following sentences into Spanish, then say them aloud. Answers will be found at the back of the book.

1. I like your car but mine is better.

2. We bought the same record as Mary.

3. John always goes to the same school as his brother.

4. When he lost his book, I gave him mine.

5. They bought tickets in the same row as ours.

6. John and I went to the same theater as you.

7. I had my umbrella but John lost his.

8. I bought some candy. Do you want some?

9. Will you give me a few pesetas?

10. Where are yours (pesetas)?

QUIZ

From among the three choices given, choose the one which correctly renders the English given at the beginning of each sentence. Write the complete sentence, and translate.

1. *(the same)* Estos discos son _____ que tengo yo.
   (a) los mismos
   (b) la misma
   (c) mismos

2. *(mine)* Me gusta este coche más que _____.
   (a) la mía
   (b) el mío
   (c) míos

3. *(yours)* Esta es mi pluma. ¿Dónde está
   _____?
   (a) el tuyo
   (b) los tuyos
   (c) la tuya

4. *(ours)* Me gusta esta casa. _____ es más
   pequeña.
   (a) La nuestra
   (b) Las nuestra
   (c) El nuestro

5. *(his)* Me pidió el libro porque había perdido
   _____.
   (a) la suya
   (b) lo suyo
   (c) el suyo

6. *(few)* Puedes llevar estos lápices aunque me.
   quedan muy _____.
   (a) pocas
   (b) pocos
   (c) unos pocos

7. *(some)* Veo que hay muchas revistas. Voy a
   comprar _____.
   (a) alguno
   (b) algunas
   (c) algunos

8. *(the same)* Tengo _____ preocupaciones
   que tú.
   (a) el mismo
   (b) los mismos
   (c) las mismas

9. *(yours)* Aquí están mis maletas. ¿Dónde están
   _____?
   (a) el tuyo
   (b) las tuyas
   (c) la tuya

10. *(hers)* Tu sombrero es muy bonito y me gusta
_____ también.
   (a) la suya
   (b) el suyo
   (c) las suyas

Answers at back of book.

LESSON 60

LOS CULTOS RELIGIOSOS
RELIGIOUS CULTS

A. *Servicios religiosos*   Religious services

1. Carlos: **¿Hay una iglesia protestante cerca del hotel? Queremos asistir el domingo.**
   Is there a Protestant church near the hotel? We want to attend on Sunday.

2. Conserje: **En Madrid hay una iglesia (creo que es la de San Jorge, en la calle Claudio Cuello) donde van los de las colonias inglesa y norteamericana.**
   Concierge: There's a church in Madrid (I think it's Saint George's on Claudio Cuello Street) where (the members of) the British and North American colonies go.

3. Carlos: **¿A qué hora empiezan los servicios?**
   What time do services begin?

4. Conserje: **No estoy seguro. Pero creo que a las once. Si quiere usted, yo averiguaré, y se lo digo.**
   I'm not sure. But I think at eleven o'clock. If you wish, I'll find out and tell you.

5. Carlos: **Gracias. Usted es muy amable. ¿Podemos ir andando? Si sigue este tiempo, sería agradable ir a pie.**
Thank you. You're very kind. Can we walk? If this weather continues, it will be pleasant to walk.

6. Conserje: **Sí. Está en la esquina de Claudio Cuello y María de Molina. Son unas seis u ocho° cuadras.**
Yes. It's at the corner of Claudio Cuello and María de Molina. It's six or eight blocks.

7. Carlos: **¿Son en inglés o en español los servicios?**
Are the services in English or in Spanish?

8. Conserje: **En San Jorge, me parece que es en inglés. Si quiere más informes, aquí tiene usted una lista de las iglesias de Madrid.**
At St. George's, I think it's in English. If you want more information, here's a list of the churches in Madrid.

9. Carlos: **Me gustaría ir a una misa católica en la catedral, también. ¿Qué te parece, Juana?**
I'd like to go to a Catholic mass in the cathedral, too. What do you think, Jane?

10. Juana: **A mí, me encantaría. La música me gusta tanto. Y la catedral es impresionante.**
I'd like to very much. I like the music so much. And the cathedral is impressive.

11. Conserje: **Hay misas los domingos desde las siete de la mañana. Pueden ustedes escoger la hora que prefieran.**
There are masses on Sunday from seven o'clock in the morning. You can choose the hour you prefer.

12. Juana: **Me gustaría oir la misa° en la catedral de Toledo. Podríamos ir allá, ¿verdad, Carlos?**

   I'd like to hear mass in the cathedral of Toledo. We could go there, couldn't we, Charles?

13. Carlos: **Si tú quieres, claro que podríamos. Tardaremos solamente una hora en llegar y luego podríamos pasar el resto de la tarde allí.**

   If you want to, of course we could. It only takes an hour to get there and then we could spend the rest of the afternoon there.

14. Juana: **Sería estupendo si tuviéramos° el coche.**

   It would be great if we had the car.

15. Carlos: **Voy a llamar al mecánico a ver si lo puedo buscar esta tarde.**

   I'll call the mechanic to see if I can get it this afternoon.

16. Juana: **¡Magnífico! Espero que el coche esté arreglado ya. Si no, nos quedamos en Madrid.**

   Terrific! I hope the car's ready now. If not, we'll stay in Madrid.

B. *Invitación a una boda*   Invitation to a wedding

17. Juana: **Mira, Carlos, hemos recibido una invitación a una boda. Se casa el sobrino de Miguel.**

   Look, Charles, we've received an invitation to a wedding. Michael's nephew is getting married.

18. Carlos: **¡Ah, sí! Ahora me acuerdo que habían hablado de eso.**

Oh, yes! Now I remember that they had spoken about that.

19. Juana: *(Leyendo)* **"El señor y la señora González Ballester tienen el placer de anunciar el enlace de su hija María Mercedes con el señor Rafael Herrero y Hernández.**

"Los novios y los padres se complacen en invitarles a la ceremonia religiosa que tendrá lugar en la iglesia de San Gerónimo el día dieciséis de julio."

Voy a llamar a Teresa a ver cómo va vestida. Tengo que pensar en lo que voy a ponerme. ¡Tengo tanto que hacer! Tendré que ir a la peluquería, . . . a ver si aquel vestido azul será apropiado. ¡Me gustan tanto las bodas!

(Reading) "Mr. and Mrs. González Ballester have the pleasure of announcing the wedding of their daughter Mary Mercedes to Mr. Raphael Herrero y Hernández.

"The bride, the groom and their parents take pleasure in inviting you to (attend) the religious ceremony which will take place at Saint Geronimo's church on July sixteenth."

I'm going to call Theresa to see what she's wearing. I have to think about what I'll wear. I have so much to do! I'll have to go to the beauty parlor, . . . let's see if that blue dress is appropriate. I like weddings so much!

20. Carlos: **Las mujeres sois todas iguales. Con tal de tener una ocasión para vestirse y lucir algo nuevo, ya estáis contentas. A mí, me aburren un poco las bodas.**

You women are all alike. As long as you have an occasion to dress and show off something new, you're happy. Weddings bore me a little.

21. **Juana:** *(al teléfono) ¿Teresa? ¡Ah, hola, querida! Mira, acabo de recibir la invitación a la boda de Rafael. Me encanta la idea de ir. ¿Conozco a la novia?... Ah, sí. Me acuerdo de ella. Estaba con él en el baile de los Torres, ¿verdad?... ¡Sí, sí! Es ella. Es una chica monísima y de muy buena familia se ve. ¡Qué bien! ¿Qué vas a llevar?... ¿El de encaje azul claro? Ah, sí, es precioso. No sé qué ponerme. No tengo tiempo para mandarme hacer un traje nuevo.... Bueno, ya lo pensaré. Podemos ir juntas, ¿verdad?... Bueno, ya volveré a llamar para citarnos en algún sitio. Adiós, adiós, querida.*

    (on the telephone) Theresa? Ah, hello, dear! Look, I've just received the invitation to Raphael's wedding. I can't wait to go. Do I know the bride?... Oh, yes! I remember her. She was with him at the Torres' ball, wasn't she?... Yes, yes! That's she. She's an adorable girl and obviously from a very good family. How nice! What are you going to wear?... The light blue lace one? Oh, yes, it's lovely. I don't know what to wear. I don't have time to have a new suit made.... O.K., I'll think about it. We can go together, can't we? O.K., I'll call you back to decide on a meeting place. Good-bye, good-bye, dear.

22. **Carlos:** *¿Ellos van también? Me alegro. Así por lo menos ya conocemos a alguien. ¿A qué hora nos vemos?*

    Are they going too? I'm glad. That way at least we know someone already. What time are we meeting?

23. **Juana:** *No hemos hablado de eso. Tenemos tiempo para eso. Ahora tengo que pensar en lo que me pondré. ¡No tengo nada que ponerme!*

We haven't spoken about that. There's still time for that. Now I have to think about what I'll wear. I have nothing to wear!

24. Carlos: *¿Qué? ¿Por qué no puedes llevar aquel vestido de seda que acabas de comprarte? ¡Te va muy bien!*
What? Why can't you wear that silk dress you just bought yourself? It looks very good on you!

25. Juana: *Pero, es que no tengo sombrero que haga juego. ¡Y zapatos! ¿Qué voy a hacer?*
But I don't have a hat that matches. And shoes! What am I going to do?

26. Carlos: *No veo por qué no puedes llevar aquel sombrero blanco de paja. ¡Es muy bonito!*
I don't see why you can't wear that white straw hat. It's very pretty!

27. Juana: *No para una boda, Carlitos. Necesito algo más elegante. Y tú sabes que no lo tengo.*
Not for a wedding, Charlie. I need something more elegant. And you know very well I don't have it.

28. Carlos: *Bien, querida. Las tiendas están abiertas hasta las siete. Tienes tres horas para buscar un sombrero nuevo.*
O.K., dear. The stores are open until seven. That gives you three hours to look for a new hat.

29. Juana: *¡Eres un sol!° ¿Quieres acompañarme? ¡Ay! Si tuviera más tiempo . . .*
You're a doll! Do you want to come with me? Oh! If I only had more time . . .

30. Carlos: *Te acompaño. Ya sé que mi opinión es muy importante para tí en estos asuntos. De*

todas maneras, no tengo otra cosa más diver-
tida que hacer.

I'll go with you. I *know* that my opinion is very
important to you in these matters. At any rate,
I don't have anything more amusing to do.

NOTES

6. *u ocho:* Notice that *o* ("or") changes to *u*
before a word beginning with *o*.

12. *oír la misa* or *oír misa:* "to hear mass" is
generally used for the idea of attending mass.

14. *si tuviéramos el coche:* "if we had the car."
Notice the use of imperfect subjunctive in a
contrary to fact condition. This might best be
expressed in English by such a phrase as "if
we only had the car."

29. *¡Eres un sol!:* lit., "You are a sun!" Is the
Spanish equivalent to "You are an angel" or
"You are great."

GRAMMATICAL ITEMS FOR SPECIAL STUDY

I. The *past participle* used as a *noun:*
Study:

1. El invitado fué muy simpático.

2. Los heridos fueron muchos.

3. Los más avanzados llegaron.

4. El Valle de los Caídos es impresionante.

5. La más informada nos habló del asunto.

6. Juan es el menos preparado para el trabajo.

7. El preferido fue un hombre mayor.

8. La casada no habló.

9. El más conocido era Don Juan Satrústegui.

1. *The guest ("invited one"—masc.) was very likeable.*

2. *The wounded were many.*

3. *The farthest advanced arrived.*

4. *The Valley of the Fallen is impressive.*

5. *The most informed (one) spoke to us about the matter.*

6. *John is the one least prepared for the job.*

7. *The preferred one was an older man.*

8. *The married one didn't speak.*

9. *The best known one was Don Juan Satrústegui.*

II. Indirect commands: **Que él lo haga.** Let (have) him do it.

Study:

1. Que ellos lo compren.

2. Que él lo diga.

3. Que ella lo mande.

1. *Have them buy it.*

2. *Let him say it.*

3. *Have her send it.*

Note: In these indirect commands, the subject, if expressed, may precede or follow the verb form.

1. Que lo diga Juan.

2. Que lo hagan ellos.

1. *Let John say it.*

2. *Have them do it.*

III. Sequence of tenses with subjunctive. *Past and imperfect subjunctive:*

Study:

1. Me dijo que estudiara la lección.

2. Querían que él lo hiciera.

3. Fue imposible que ellos llegaran tan temprano.

4. Esperaban que Juan lo dijera.

5. Pidió que nosotros mandáramos los paquetes.

6. Era necesario que ustedes lo leyeran.

7. El jefe sentía que ella tuviera que marcharse.

8. Ella se alegró de que no oyéramos las noticias.

1. *He told me to study the lesson.*

2. *They wanted him to do it.*

3. *It was impossible for them to arrive so early.*

4. *They hoped that John would say it.*

5. *He asked us to send the packages.*

6. *It was necessary for you to read it.*

7. *The boss was sorry that she had to leave.*

8. *She was happy that we didn't hear the news.*

IV. *Ojalá*—would that + *imperfect subjunctive*

Study:

1. Ojalá que estuvieran aquí.

2. Ojalá que lo encontrara usted.

3. Ojalá que ella lo supiera.

1. *If only [I wish that] they were here!*

2. *If only [I wish that] you would find it!*

3. *If only [I wish that] she knew it!*

Note: **Ojalá** may be used alone in an exclamation.

1. ¿Que yo soy muy rico? ¡Ojalá!

2. ¿Se casó ella? ¡Ojalá!

1. *Am I very rich? Would that I were! ("I wish I were!")*

2. *Did she get married? I wish she had!*

DRILLS AND EXERCISES

I. Substitute the words or expressions in parentheses for the italicized words or expressions in the model sentence. Write each new sentence and say it aloud.

A. *El desconocido* llegó muy tarde. (La casada, El conocido, La acusada, El herido, La más querida)

B. Que él lo *haga.* (diga, compre, mande, escriba, lea)

C. Ojalá que ellos lo *supieran.* (vendieran, vieran, sintieran, dudaran, dijeran)

D. Era imposible que yo *llegara* a las seis y treinta. (saliera, viniera, me levantara, hablara, llamara)

E. Era *difícil* que ellos me creyeran. (imposible, increíble, necesario, fantástico, probable)

F. El jefe *dijo* que mandáramos las cartas en seguida. (rogó, mandó, pidió, se alegró de, sintió)

II. Change these sentences to the past tense. Write the complete sentence and translate. Answers will be found at the back of the book.

1. Es posible que vengan Juan y José.

2. Lo dice para que lo sepamos.

3. Espero que lo hagan inmediatamente.

4. Dudo que Juan lo oiga.

5. María siente que ellos lo crean.

III. Translate the following sentences into Spanish, then say them aloud. Answers will be found at the back of the book.

1. I'm sorry he's here.

2. He was sorry that I did it.

3. Would that he were here!

4. Let them do it!

5. The best informed (one) spoke to us.

6. They said it so that he would know (it).

7. It's impossible for them to believe it.

8. He doubted that we knew it.

9. They wanted us to buy the book.

10. The boss told me to do it.

QUIZ

From among the three choices given, choose the one which correctly renders the English given at the beginning of each sentence. Write the complete sentence, and translate.

1. *(the best informed girl)* Me gustaría hablar con
   _____.

   (a) el más informado
   (b) la más informada
   (c) las más informadas

2. *(the wounded)* Tenían que ayudar _____.
   (a) los heridos
   (b) herido
   (c) a los heridos

3. *(Have)* _____ él lo escriba.
   (a) Tenga
   (b) Que
   (c) Dígale

4. *(sell)* Fué imposible que ellos _____ el
   coche.
   (a) vendiera
   (b) vendieron
   (c) vendieran

5. *(couldn't)* Sentía que Juan _____ venir.
   (a) no puede
   (b) no podrá
   (c) no pudiera

6. *(go)* Quería que ellos _____ al cine.
   (a) van
   (b) fueran
   (c) fueron

7. *(do)* Que lo _____ Juan.
   (a) haga
   (b) hace
   (c) hagan

8. *(the preferred man)* De todos los empleados,
   Rafael es _____.
   (a) el preferido
   (b) lo preferido
   (c) la preferida

9. *(say)* Querían que el jefe lo _____.
   (a) dice
   (b) dijera
   (c) dijo

10. *(I wish I were)* Dicen que soy muy inteligente.
   ¡_____!
   (a) Quiero estar
   (b) Quería
   (c) Ojalá

Answers at back of book.

SUMMARY OF SPANISH GRAMMAR

1. THE ALPHABET

Letter	Name	Letter	Name	Letter	Name
a	a	j	jota	r	ere
b	be	k	ka	rr	erre
c	c	l	ele	s	ese
ch	che	ll	elle	t	te
d	de	m	eme	u	u
e	e	n	ene	v	ve
f	efe	ñ	eñe	w	doble ve
g	ge	o	o	x	equis
h	hache	p	pe	y	i griega
i	i	q	cu	z	zeta

2. PRONUNCIATION

SIMPLE VOWELS

a as in *ah* or *father*.
e as in *day*.
i as in *machine*.
o as in *open*.
u as in *rule*.

VOWEL COMBINATIONS

{ ai / ay }	*ai* in *aisle*.	ie	*ye* in *yes*.
		io	*yo* in *yoke*.
au	*ou* in *out*.	ua	*wah*.
{ ei / ey }	*áy-ee*.	ou	*wo* in *woe*.
eu	*áy-oo*.	iu	*you*.
{ oi / oy }	*oy* in *boy*.	{ ui / uy }	*óo-ee*.
ia	*ya* in *yard*.		

CONSONANTS

Notice the following points:

b, v   have the same sound. After a pause and after *m* or *n*, both are like *b* in *boy*. When the sound occurs between vowels you bring the upper and lower lips together and blow between them, the way you do when blowing dust from something.[1]

c   before *o, a,* and *u,* and before consonants, is like *c* in *cut.*

c   before *e* and *i* is pronounced in Spain like *th* in *thin.* In Spanish America it is pronounced like *s* in *see.*

ch   as in *church.*

d   after a pause or *n* and *l,* like *d.* When it occurs between vowels, like *th* in *that.*

g   before *a, o,* and *u,* and before consonants, after a pause, and after *n,* like *g* in *go.*

g   before *e* and *i* is a strong rasping *h* (the sound you make when you clear your throat).

h   is not pronounced.

j   is like *g* before *e* and *i* (see above).

ll   is pronounced in Spain like *lli* in *million;* in many countries of Latin America like *y* in *yes.*

ñ   is like *ni* in *onion* or *ny* in *canyon.*

qu   is like *k.*

r   is pronounced by tapping the tip of the tongue against the gum ridge back of the upper teeth.

rr   is trilled several times.

[1]Many Spanish speakers make the same difference between *b* and *v* that we do in English. They pronounce *b* whenever a *b* appears in the spelling and a *v* whenever a *v* appears in the spelling.

s	as in *see*.
x	before a consonant like *s;* between vowels like *x (ks)* in *extra*. Sometimes, however, it is like the *x (gs)* in *examine*.
y	when it begins a word or syllable, like *y* in *yes*.
y	when it serves as a vowel, like *i*.
z	is pronounced the same as the Spanich *c* before *e* and *i* (see above).

3. STRESS

1. Stress the last syllable if the word ends in a consonant other than *n* or *s*.

   ciudad   city

2. Stress the next to the last syllable if the word ends in a vowel or *n* or *s*.

   amigo   friend
   hablan   they speak

3. Otherwise stress the syllable that has the accent (').

   inglés   English
   teléfono   telephone

4. PUNCTUATION

There are several differences between Spanish and English. Notice:

1. Exclamation and question marks precede as well as follow the sentence:

   ¿Adónde va usted?   Where are you going?
   ¡Hombre! ¿Adónde   Man! Where are you
   va Ud.?   going?
   ¡Venga!   Come!
   ¡Qué hermoso día!   What a beautiful day!

2. The question mark is placed before the question part of the sentence:

Juan, ¿a dónde vas?	John, where are you going?
Usted conoce al Sr. Díaz, ¿no es verdad?	You know Mr. Díaz, don't you?

3. Dashes are often used where we use quotation marks:

Muchas gracias—dijo.	"Thanks a lot," he said.
Esta mañana—dijo—, fui a la ciudad.	"This morning," he said, "I went downtown."
—¿Cómo está usted?	"How are you?"
—Muy bien, gracias.	"Very well, thank you."

4. Capitals are not used as frequently as in English. They are only used at the beginning of sentences and with proper nouns. *Yo* "I," adjectives of nationality, the days of the week and the months are not capitalized:

Somos americanos.	We're Americans.
El no es francés sino inglés.	He's not French but English.
Vendré el martes o el miércoles.	I'll come Tuesday or Wednesday.
Hoy es el primero de febrero.	Today is the first of February.

5. Suspension points (. . .) are used more frequently than in English to indicate interruption, hesitation, etc.

5. SOME ORTHOGRAPHIC SIGNS

1. The tilde (˜) is used over the letter *n* to indicate the sound of *ni* in *onion* or *ny* in *canyon*.

2. The diaeresis (¨) is used over *u* in the combination *gu* when it is pronounced *gw*.

vergüenza	shame
paragüero	umbrella man; umbrella stand

6. THE DEFINITE ARTICLE

	SINGULAR	PLURAL
Masculine	*el*	*los*
Feminine	*la*	*las*

SINGULAR

el muchacho	the boy
la muchacha	the girl

PLURAL

los muchachos	the boys
las muchachas	the girls

1. *El* is used before a feminine noun beginning with stressed *a* (or *ha*):

el agua	the water
But—	
las aguas	the waters
el hacha	the axe
But—	
las hachas	the axes

2. The neuter article *lo* is used before parts of speech other than nouns when they are used as nouns:

lo malo	what is bad, the bad part of it
lo hecho	what is done
lo dicho	what is said
lo útil	the useful
lo difícil	the difficult
lo posible	the possible
lo necesario	the necessary

3. The definite article is used:

a. with abstract nouns:

La verdad vale más que las riquezas.	Truth is worth more than riches.

b. with nouns referring to a class:

los soldados	soldiers
los generales	generals

c. with names of languages (except immediately after *hablar* or *en*):

Escribo el español.	I write Spanish.
Habla bien el español.	He or she speaks Spanish well.

But—

Dígalo Ud. en inglés.	Say it in English.
Hablo español.	I speak Spanish.

d. in expressions of time:

la una	one o'clock
las dos	two o'clock
las diez	ten o'clock

e. for the days of the week:

Abren los domingos a las dos y media.	They open Sundays at 2:30.
el lunes próximo	next Monday

f. for the year, seasons, etc.

el año 1945	the year 1945
Vino el año pasado.	He came last year.
la primavera	spring
En el invierno hace frío.	It's cold in winter.

g. with certain geographical names:

El Brasil	Brazil
El Canadá	Canada
El Perú	Peru
El Uruguay	Uruguay
El Ecuador	Ecuador
El Japón	Japan

Note: The definite article is used with parts of the body and articles of clothing:

Me duele la cabeza.	My head hurts.
Quítese el abrigo.	Take your coat off.

7. THE INDEFINITE ARTICLE

	SINGULAR	PLURAL
Masculine	*un*	*unos*
Feminine	*una*	*unas*

SINGULAR

un hombre	a man
una mujer	a woman
unos hombres	men, some (a few) men

PLURAL

unas mujeres	women, some (a few) women

1. *Unos (unas)* is often used where we use "some" or "a few" in English:

unos días	a few days

2. The indefinite article is omitted:

   a. before rank, profession, trade, nationality, etc.:

Soy capitán.	I'm a captain.
Soy médico.	I'm a doctor.

Soy abogado.	I'm a lawyer.
Es profesor.	He's a teacher.
Soy norteamericano.	I'm an American.
Ella es española.	She's Spanish.

b. before *ciento* (or *cien*) "hundred," *cierto* "certain," *mil* "thousand":

cien hombres	a hundred men
cierto hombre	a certain man
mil hombres	a thousand men

c. in various idiomatic expressions, such as:

Salió sin sombrero.	He left without a hat.

8. CONTRACTIONS

1. *de + el = del*	of (from) the
del hermano	from (of) the brother
2. *a + el = al*	to the
al padre	to the father

9. THE DAYS OF THE WEEK

The days of the week are masculine and are not capitalized. The article is usually necessary, except after *ser*:

el domingo	Sunday
el lunes	Monday
el martes	Tuesday
el miércoles	Wednesday
el jueves	Thursday
el viernes	Friday
el sábado	Saturday
El domingo es el primer día de la semana.	Sunday is the first day of the week.

| *Van a visitarlos el domingo.* | They're going to pay them a visit on Sunday. |
| *Mañana es sábado.* | Tomorrow is Saturday. |

Notice that "on Sunday," "on Monday," etc., are *el domingo, el lunes*, etc.

10. THE NAMES OF THE MONTHS

The names of the months are masculine and are not capitalized. They are usually used without the definite article:

enero	January
febrero	February
marzo	March
abril	April
mayo	May
junio	June
julio	July
agosto	August
septiembre	September
octubre	October
noviembre	November
diciembre	December

11. THE NAMES OF THE SEASONS

el invierno	winter
la primavera	spring
el verano	summer
el otoño	fall

The names of seasons are usually not capitalized. They are preceded by the definite article but after *de* and *en* the article may or may not be used:

| *Hace frío en (el) invierno.* | It's cold in (the) winter. |
| *Trabajo durante los meses de verano.* | I work during the summer months. |

12. MASCULINE AND FEMININE GENDER

Nouns referring to males are masculine; nouns referring to females are feminine:

el padre	the father	*la madre*	the mother
el hijo	the son	*la hija*	the daughter
el hombre	the man	*la mujer*	the woman
el toro	the bull	*la vaca*	the cow
el gato	the tomcat	*la gata*	the she-cat

The masculine plural of certain nouns stands for both genders:

Los padres	the parents, the father and mother
los reyes	the king and queen
mis hermanos	my brothers and sisters

Masculine nouns and adjectives usually end in -*o*; feminine nouns and adjectives in -*a*.

MASCULINE NOUNS

1. Nouns ending in -*o* are usually masculine:

el cuerpo	the body
el cielo	the sky
el dinero	the money

   Common Exceptions:

la mano	the hand
la radio	the radio

2. Nouns ending in *r, n,* and *l* are generally masculine:

el calor	the heat
el pan	the bread
el sol	the sun

3. Names of trees, days of the week, months, oceans, rivers, mountains, and other parts of speech used as nouns are generally masculine:

el álamo	the poplar
el martes	Tuesday
el Atlántico	The Atlantic Ocean
el Tajo	The Tagus River
los Andes	The Andes
el ser joven	being young, the fact of being young

FEMININE NOUNS

1. Nouns ending in -a (also -dad, -tad, -tud, -ción, -sión, -ez, -umbre, -ie) are usually feminine:

la cabeza	the head
la ciudad	the city
la cantidad	quantity
la libertad	liberty
la virtud	virtue
la condición	the condition
la costumbre	the custom
tensión	tension
madurez	maturity

Common Exceptions:

el día	the day
el mapa	the map
el drama	the drama
el clima	the climate
el problema	the problem
el poeta	the poet

2. Names of cities, towns and fruits are feminine:

Barcelona es muy bonita.	Barcelona is very nice.
la naranja	the orange
la manzana	the apple

Note: Certain nouns differ in meaning depending on whether they take *el* or *la*:

el orden	order (arrangement)
el capital	capital (money)
el cura	priest

But—

la orden	order (command)
la capital	capital (city)
la cura	curé

13. THE PLURAL

1. Nouns ending in an unstressed vowel add -*s*:

el libro   the book   *los libros*   the books

2. Nouns ending in a consonant add -*es*:

el avión   the airplane
los aviones the airplanes

3. Nouns ending in -*z* change the *z* to *c* and then add *es*:

la luz	the light	*las luces*	the lights
el lápiz	the pencil	*los lápices*	the pencils

4. Some nouns are unchanged in the plural:

los martes	Tuesdays
los Martínez	the Martínez family

14. THE POSSESSIVE

English -'s or -s' is translated by *de* "of":

el libro de Juan	John's book ("the book of John")
los libros de los niños	the boys' books ("the books of the boys")

15. ADJECTIVES

1. Singular and Plural

SINGULAR

un muchacho alto	a tall boy
una muchacha alta	a tall girl

PLURAL

dos muchachos altos	two tall boys
dos muchachas altas	two tall girls

Notice that the adjective comes after the noun and is masculine if the noun is masculine, plural if the noun is plural, etc.

2. Feminine Endings

a. If the ending is *-o*, it becomes *-a*:

MASCULINE		FEMININE	
alto	tall	*alta*	tall
rico	rich	*rica*	rich
bajo	low	*baja*	low

b. In other cases there is no change:

MASCULINE	FEMININE	
grande	*grande*	big, large
azul	*azul*	blue
cortés	*cortés*	polite
útil	*útil*	useful
triste	*triste*	sad

Examples:

una cosa útil	a useful thing
una majer triste	a sad woman
una muchacha cortés	a polite girl

c. Adjectives of nationality add -a or change o to a:

MASCULINE	FEMININE	
español	*española*	Spanish
francés	*francesa*	French
inglés	*inglesa*	English
Americano	*Americana*	American

Examples:

una señora inglesa	an English woman
la lengua española	the Spanish language

d. Adjectives ending in -*án*[1] and -*or* add -*a*:

MASCULINE	FEMININE	
holgazán	*holgazana*	lazy
burlón	*burlona*	jesting
preguntón	*preguntona*	inquisitive
encantador	*encantadora*	charming
fascinador	*fascinadora*	fascinating

3. The following adjectives drop the final -*o* when they come before a masculine singular noun:

uno	one
bueno	good
malo	bad
alguno	some one
ninguno	no one
primero	first
tercero	third

Examples:

un buen amigo	a good friend
ningún hombre	no man
el mal tiempo	the bad weather
el primer día	the first day

[1]Notice that the accent is dropped in the feminine.

4. *Grande* becomes *gran* when it comes before a singular noun:

un gran amigo	a great friend
un gran poeta	a great poet
un gran hombre	a great (important) man

But—

un hombre grande	a large (tall) man

5. *Santo* becomes *San* when it comes before a noun (except those beginning in *To-* and *Do-*):

San Juan	Saint John
San Luis	Saint Louis

But—

Santo Tomás	Saint Thomas
Santo Domingo	Saint Dominic

6. *Ciento* becomes *cien* before a noun:

cien dólares	a hundred dollars

16. POSITION OF ADJECTIVES

1. Descriptive adjectives usually follow the noun:

un libro blanco	a white book
una casa blanca	a white house
mi sombrero nuevo	my new hat
dinero español	Spanish money
un hombre inteligente	an intelligent man
huevos frescos	fresh eggs

2. Exceptions are adjectives which describe an inherent quality:

la blanca nieve	the white snow

3. Articles, numerals, possessives and quantitatives usually precede the noun:

un buen muchacho	a good boy
muchas personas	many persons
poca gente	few people
cuatro huevos	four eggs

4. Some descriptive adjectives can come either before or after the noun:

una niña pequeña or *una pequeña niña*	a little girl
un día hermoso or *un hermoso día*	a nice (beautiful) day
una linda muchacha or *una muchacha linda*	a pretty girl

Other common adjectives used this way are *bueno* "good," *malo* "bad" and *bonito* "pretty."

5. A few adjectives have one meaning when they come before a noun and another when they follow:

un hombre pobre	a poor man
¡Pobre hombre!	Poor man!
un hombre grande	a large (tall) man
un gran hombre	a great (important) man
un libro nuevo	a new (recent) book
un nuevo hombre	a different man
cierto hombre	a certain man
una noticia cierta	a true piece of news

17. COMPARISON

1. Regular Comparison
fácil   easy

más fácil	easier
menos fácil	less easy
el más fácil	the easiest
el menos fácil	the least easy

2. Irregular Comparison

bueno	good	*mejor*	better, best
malo	bad	*peor*	worse, worst
mucho	much	*más*	more, most
poco	little	*menos*	less, least
grande	great	{ *mayor* *más grande*	
pequeño	small	{ *menor* *más pequeño*	

Más grande means "larger," "bigger"; *mayor* means "older":

Esta mesa es más grande que aquélla.	This table is larger than that one.
Pedro es mayor que Juan.	Peter is older than John.

Similarly, *más pequeño* means "smaller"; *menor* means "younger."

3. "More (less)... than..." = *más (menos) ... que ...*

El español es más fácil que el inglés.	Spanish is easier than English.
Es más inteligente de lo que parece.	He's more intelligent than he looks.

4. "As... as..." = *tan... como...* or *tanto ... como...*

a. before an adjective or adverb:

Tan fácil como...	As easy as ..
El habla español tan bien como yo.	He speaks Spanish as well as I do.

b. before a noun:

Tiene tanto dinero como Ud.	He has as much money as you.

5. "The more (less)... the more (less)..." = *cuanto más (menos)... tanto más (menos)...*

Cuanto más le trate tanto más le agradará.	The more you get to know him (deal with him) the more you like him.

6. "Most" = *-ísimo*

Es muy útil.	It's very useful.
Es utilísimo.	It's most useful.

The *-isimo* form (called the "absolute superlative") always stands by itself (that is, never modifies another word).

18. PRONOUNS

Pronouns have different forms depending on whether they are:
1. the subject of a verb
2. used after a preposition
3. the object of a verb
4. used as indirect objects
5. used with reflexive verbs

1. Pronouns as the subject of a verb:

SINGULAR

yo	I
tú	you
él	he
ella	she
ello	it
usted	you *(polite)*

PLURAL

nosotros	we *(masc.)*
nosotras	we *(fem.)*
vosotros	you *(masc.)*
vosotras	you *(fem.)*
ellos	they *(masc.)*
ellas	they *(fem.)*
ustedes	you *(polite)*

SINGULAR

(yo) hablo	I speak
(tú) hablas	you speak *(familiar)*
(él) habla	he speaks
(ella) habla	she speaks
(usted) habla	you speak *(polite)*

PLURAL

(nosotros) hablamos	we speak *(masc.)*
(nosotras) hablamos	we speak *(fem.)*
(vosotros) habláis	you speak *(masc.)*
(vosotras) habláis	you speak *(fem.)*
(ellos) hablan	they speak *(masc.)*
(ellas) hablan	they speak *(fem.)*
(ustedes) hablan	you speak *(polite)*

The personal pronouns *yo*, *tú*, etc., are not ordinarily used. "I speak" is just *hablo*, "we speak" *hablamos*, etc. They are used for emphasis or clearness (*usted habla* "you speak" and *él habla* "he speaks").

2. Pronouns used after prepositions:

para mí	for me
para tí	for you *(fam.)*
para él	for him
para ella	for her
para usted	for you *(polite)*

para nosotros	for us *(masc.)*
para nosotras	for us *(fem.)*
para vosotros	for you *(masc.)*
para vosotras	for you *(fem.)*
para ellos	for them *(masc.)*
para ellas	for them *(fem.)*
para ustedes	for you *(polite)*

Notice that the form of the pronoun used after a preposition is the same as the form of the pronoun used before a verb, except for *mí* "me" and *tí* "you" *(fam.)*.

There is a special form for "with me," "with you" and "with him": *conmigo* "with me," *contigo* "with you" and *consigo* "with him."

3. Pronouns as direct objects:

me	me
te	you *(fam.)*
le	him, you *(polite)*
la	her
lo	it
nos	us
os	you
los	them, you *(polite)*
las	them *(fem.)*

4. Pronouns as indirect objects:

me	to me
te	to you *(fam.)*
le	to him, her, you *(polite)*
nos	to us
os	to you
les	to them *(masc. and fem.)*
	to you *(masc. and fem.) (polite)*

Le as indirect object means "to him," "to her," "to you" (usted), and *les* means "to them," "to you" (ustedes). The preposition *a* and the prepositional forms *él, ella, usted* and *ellos, ellas, ustedes* are often added for clearness.

SHORT FORM

$$le\ doy = \begin{cases} \text{I give to him} \\ \text{I give to her} \\ \text{I give to you} \end{cases}$$

$$les\ doy = \begin{cases} \text{I give to them } (masc.) \\ \text{I give to them } (fem.) \\ \text{I give to you} \end{cases}$$

FULL FORM

le doy a él	I give (to) him
le doy a ella	I give (to) her
le doy a usted	I give (to) you
les doy a ellos	I give (to) them
les doy a ellas	I give (to) them
les doy a ustedes	I give (to) you

This double construction is used even when the object is a noun:

Le escribí a María ayer.	I wrote to Mary yesterday.

5. Reflexive pronouns:

Reflexive pronouns are used when a person (or thing) does something to himself, herself (or itself): e.g. "I wash myself."

me	myself
te	yourself *(fam.)*
se	himself, herself, yourself *(polite)*
nos	ourselves
os	yourselves
se	themselves, yourselves *(polite)*

For examples, see pp. 70 and 71.

19. POSITION OF PRONOUNS

1. When there are both direct and indirect object pronouns in a sentence (*he gives it to me*) the Spanish order is the following:

ENGLISH	SPANISH
1 2	*2 1*
He gives it to me.	*Me lo da.*

1 2	*2 1*
They give it to us.	*Nos lo dan.*

That is, the indirect pronoun precedes the direct. If both begin with *l*, the indirect (*le, les*) becomes *se:*

Se lo diré (instead of *le lo diré*).	I will tell it to him (to her, to you, etc.)

2. When *se* is present it comes before the other conjunctive pronouns. It denotes:
   a. an impersonal action:

Se dice.	It is said.
Se la trató bien.	She was treated well.

   b. a personal object (may or may not be reflexive):

Se lo dice.	He says it to him (her) *or* he says it to himself *or* she says it to herself.

3. If *se* is not present, the first pronoun of the group has the meaning of an indirect object and the second that of a direct object:

Me lo da.	He gives it to me.

4. Object pronouns come before the verb:

Le veo.	I see him.
Se lo da.	He gives it to him.

They come after an infinitive or present participle:

Tenerlo.	To have it.
Dárselo.	To give it to him.
Quiero verle.	I want to see him.
Voy a verle.	I'm going to see him.
Teniéndolo.	Having it.
Diciéndolo.	Saying it.
Estoy mirándole.	I am looking at him.

Object pronouns follow affirmative commands:

Tómalo.	Take it.
Dígamelo Ud.	Tell it to me.

They come before negative commands (these are always in the subjunctive):

No me lo diga Ud.	Don't tell me.

5. *Te* and *os* precede all pronouns except *se:*

Te lo diré.	I will tell it to you.

But—

Se te dijo.	It was told to you.

6. *Le lo, la, les, los,* and *las* take the last place before the verb:

Yo se lo doy.	I give it to him.
El se lo dijo.	He told it to him.

20. CONJUNCTIONS

y	and
o	or
pero	but
mas	but
que	that
pues	since, as
si	if

por que	why
porque	because
ni . . . ni	neither . . . nor

NOTES

1. *y* "and"

Roberto y Juan son hermanos.	Robert and John are brothers.

e is used instead of *y* before a word beginning with *i-* or *hi-*:

María e Isabel son primas.	Mary and Elizabeth are cousins.
Madre e hija.	Mother and daughter.

2. *o* "or"

Cinco o seis pesos.	Five or six pesos.
Voy con mi hermano o con mi hermana.	I'm going with my brother or with my sister.

u is used instead of *o* before a word beginning with *o-* or *ho-*:

Siete u ocho horas.	Seven or eight hours.
Cinco u ocho meses.	Five or eight months.

3. *pero* "but"

Quiero venir pero no puedo.	I want to come but I can't.

4. *mas* "but" is more formal and literary:

Pensé que vendría mas no pudo.	I thought he would come but he wasn't able to.

5. *sino* "but" is used instead of *pero* after a negative statement:

No es francés sino inglés.	He is not French but English.
No viene hoy sino mañana.	He is not coming today but tomorrow.

21. QUESTION WORDS

1. ¿Qué?	What?
¿Qué dice usted?	What are you saying?
2. ¿Por qué?	Why?
¿Por qué dice usted eso?	Why do you say that?
3. ¿Cómo?	How?
¿Cómo se dice en español esto?	How do you say this in Spanish?
¿Cómo se llama usted?	What's your name? ("How do you call yourself?")
4. ¿Cuánto?	How much?
¿Cuánto dinero necesita usted?	How much money do you need?
¿Cuántos libros hay?	How many books are there?
¿Cuánto hay de Madrid a Barcelona?	How far is it from Madrid to Barcelona?
5. ¿Cuál?	What? Which one?
¿Cuál es su nombre?	What's your name?
¿Cuál quiere usted?	Which one do you want?
6. ¿Quién?	Who?
¿Quién vino con usted?	Who came with you?
¿Quién tiene eso?	Who has that?
7. ¿Dónde?	Where?
¿Dónde está su amigo?	Where is your friend?
8. ¿Cuándo?	When?
¿Cuándo se marcha Ud?	When are you going (leaving)?
¿Cuándo ocurrió eso?	When did that happen?

Notice that the question words are written with an accent.

22. ADVERBS

1. Spanish *-mente* corresponds to "*-ly*" in English.
   It is added to the feminine form of the adjective:

exclusivamente   exclusively

   When there are two adverbs, the ending *-mente* is added only to the last one:

clara y concisamente   clearly and concisely

   Adverbs are compared like adjectives.

POSITIVE	*alegremente*	cheerfully
COMPARATIVE SUPERLATIVE	*más alegremente*	more cheerfully, most cheerfully

2. Irregular Comparatives:

POSITIVE		COMPARATIVE	
bien	well	*mejor*	better, best
mal	badly	*peor*	worse, worst
mucho	much	*más*	more, most
poco	little	*menos*	less, least

3. Adverbs as prepositions or conjunctions.
   Many adverbs act as prepositions when *de* is added:

ADVERB:	*después*	afterwards
PREPOSITION:	*después de las cinco*	after five o'clock
ADVERB:	*además*	besides
PREPOSITION:	*además de*	besides

   When *que* is added they act as conjunctions:

después de que venga   after he comes

   Other words which act similarly: *antes* "before"; *cerca* "near"; *delante* "before," "in front of"; *enfrente* "opposite."

4. Adverbs of time:

hoy	today
ayer	yesterday
mañana	tomorrow
temprano	early
tarde	late
a menudo	often
siempre	always
nunca	never
jamás	never
luego	afterwards
aprisa	quickly
despacio	slowly
antes que	before
después	afterwards

5. Adverbs of place:

aquí	here
acá	herc (motion)
ahí	there
allí	there (farther away)
allá	there (motion)
adelante	forward, on
atrás	behind
dentro	inside
arriba	up, above
fuera	outside
abajo	down, below
cerca	near
lejos	far

6. Adverbs of quantity:

muy	very
mucho	much
poco	little
más	more
menos	less

además	besides
cuan	how much
cuanto	how much
tan	so much
tanto	so much
demasiado	too much
apenas	scarcely

7. Adverbs expressing affirmation:

sí	yes
verdaderamente	truly
cierto	certainly
ciertamente	certainly
claro	of course
desde luego	of course
por supuesto	of course

8. Adverbs expressing negation:

no	no, not
nunca	never
jamás	never
nunca jamás	never (more emphatic)
ya no	no more, not now
todavía no	not yet
tampoco	neither, either
no tal	no indeed
ni	nor
ni . . . ni	neither . . . not
ni siquiera	not even

9. Here and There:

Aquí "here" refers to something near the speaker:

| *Tengo aquí los libros.* | I have the books here. |

Ahí "there" refers to something near the person spoken to:

| *¿Qué tiene Ud. ahí?* | What do you have there? |
| *¿Está Ud. ahí?* | Are you there? |

Acá "here" expresses motion toward the speaker:

¡Venga Ud. acá!	Come here!

Allá "there" indicates motion away from the speaker:

¡Vaya Ud. allá!	Go there!
Va allá.	He's going there.

Allí "there" refers to something remote from both:

Vienen de allí.	They come from there.
Viví en Sud América por varios años. ¿Ha estado Ud. allí?	I've lived in South America for several years. Have you ever been there?

23. DIMINUTIVES AND AUGMENTATIVES

The endings *ito (-cito, -ecito)*, *-illo (-cillo, -ecillo)*, *-uelo (-zuelo, -ezuelo)* imply smallness. In addition, *ito* often implies attractiveness or admiration, *-illo* and *-uelo* unattractiveness or depreciation. (They should be used with care.)

chico	boy	*chiquillo*	little boy
señora	lady, Mrs.	*señorita*	young lady, Miss
un poco	a little	*un poquito*	a little bit
pedazo	piece	*pedacito*	a little piece
gato	cat	*gatito*	kitten
papá	papa	*papaíto*	daddy
cuchara	tablespoon	*cucharita*	teaspoon
Venecia	Venice	*Venezuela*	Venezuela ("little Venice")
cigarro	cigar	*cigarrillo*	cigarette
autor	author	*autorcillo*	unimportant author

The ending *-ón (ona)* and *-ote* indicate largeness (often awkwardness and unattractiveness as well):

tonto	foolish, silly fool	*tontón*	big fool
silla	chair	*sillón*	big chair
cuchara	spoon	*cucharón*	a ladle
hombre	man	*hombrón*	he-man

24. DEMONSTRATIVES

1. Demonstrative Adjectives:

MASCULINE	FEMININE	
este	*esta*	this
ese	*esa*	that
aquel	*aquella*	that (farther removed)
estos	*estas*	these
esos	*esas*	those
aquellos	*aquellas*	those (farther removed)

a. Spanish demonstrative adjectives usually precede the nouns they modify and always agree in gender and number:

este muchacho	this boy
aquellos vecinos	those neighbors

b. *Ese* and *aquel* both mean "that." *Aquel* points out a thing removed in space or time from the speaker or from the person spoken to:

Esa señora es muy amable.	This lady is very kind.
Aquel señor que llegó el mes pasado.	That gentleman who arrived last month.

2. Demonstrative Pronouns:

MASCULINE	FEMININE	
éste	*ésta*	this (one)
ése	*ésa*	that (one)
aquél	*aquélla*	that (one)
éstos	*éstas*	these
ésos	*ésas*	those
aquéllos	*aquéllas*	those

NEUTER	
esto	this (one)
eso	that (one)
aquello	that (one)

The same difference exists between the pronouns *ése* and *aquél* as between the adjectives *ese* and *aquel*:

No quería éste sino aquél.	I didn't want this one but the one over there.

Este and *aquél* also mean "the latter" and "the former":

Acaban de llegar el embajador y su secretario.	The ambassador and his secretary just arrived.
Este es joven y aquél es viejo.	The former is old and the latter is young.

Notice that the Spanish order is the opposite of the English: *éste . . . aquél* ("the latter . . . the former").

The neuter demonstrative pronouns *esto, eso* and *aquello* refer to an idea previously stated and not to a specific thing:

Me dijo que aquello fué horrible.	He told me that that was horrible.

25. INDEFINITE ADJECTIVES
AND PRONOUNS

todos	all
tal	such
ni uno	not one
otro	other
alguien	someone
nadie	nobody
algo	something, anything
ninguno	no one, none
alguno	someone
varios	several
nada	nothing
cualquiera	whatever, whoever
quienquiera	whoever

26. NEGATION

1. *No* "not" comes before the verb:

No veo.	I don't see.
El no habla	He isn't speaking.

2. There are two forms for "nothing," "never," "no one," etc.—one with and one without *no:*

No veo nada.	I see nothing.
No voy nunca.	I never go.
No viene nadie.	No one comes.
Or—	
Nada veo.	I see nothing
Nunca voy.	I never go.
Nadie viene.	No one comes.

27. WORD ORDER

1. The usual order is subject—verb—adverb—object:

Juan vió allí a sus amigos.	John saw his friends there.

2. The tendency in Spanish is to put the longer member of the sentence or the emphasized part last:

Me dió una carta.	He gave me a letter.
¿Compró la casa su señor padre?	Did your father buy the house?
Han caído veinte soldados.	Twenty soldiers were killed.

3. As in English, questions sometimes have the same order as statements but with the question intonation (that is, with a rise in pitch at the end):

¿Juan va a ir allí?	John is going to go there?

4. However, the more usual way of asking a question is to put the subject after the verb:

¿Va a ir allí Juan?	Is John going to go there?
¿Viene su amigo?	Is your friend coming?
¿Ha comido Ud.?	Have you eaten?
¿Habla usted español?	Do you speak Spanish?
¿Tiene usted dinero?	Do you have any money?
¿Por qué volvió Ud.?	Why did you return?
¿Ha recibido Juan mi carta?	Did John get my letter?

5. Adjectives come right after *ser:*

¿Es tarde?	Is it late?
¿Es bueno?	Is it good?
¿Es difícil la prueba?	Is the test difficult?
¿Es fácil el problema?	Is the problem easy?

28. THE TENSES OF THE VERB

Spanish verbs are divided into three classes ("conjugations") according to their infinitives:

Class I —*hablar*
Class II —*comer*
Class III—*vivir*

1. The Present:

I	II	III
-o	*-o*	*-o*
-as	*-es*	*-es*
-a	*-e*	*-e*
-amos	*-emos*	*-imos*
-áis	*-éis*	*-ís*
-an	*-en*	*-en*

hablar to speak	*comer* to eat	*vivir* to live
hablo	*como*	*vivo*
hablas	*comes*	*vives*
habla	*come*	*vive*
hablamos	*comemos*	*vivimos*
habláis	*coméis*	*vivís*
hablan	*comen*	*viven*

The following verbs insert *g* in the first person singular of the present indicative:

tener—tengo	I have
venir—vengo	I come
traer—traigo	I bring
poner—pongo	I put
hacer—hago	I do
decir—digo	I say
salir—salgo	I leave

The present can be translated in several ways:

Hablo español.
{ I speak Spanish
{ I am speaking Spanish.
{ I do speak Spanish.

2. The Imperfect:

I	II AND III
-aba	-ía
-abas	-ías
-aba	-ía
-ábamos	-íamos
-abais	-íais
-aban	-ían

a. The imperfect is used:

1. to indicate continued or customary action in the past:

Cuando yo estaba en Madrid, siempre visitaba los teatros.
When I was in Madrid, I always used to visit the theaters.

Le encontraba todos los días.
I used to meet him every day.

2. to indicate what was happening when something else happened:

El escribía cuando ella entró.
He was writing when she entered.

b. Irregular Imperfects:

The following are the only Spanish verbs which are irregular in the imperfect:

ser—era, eras, era, éramos, erais, eran
ir—iba, ibas, iba, íbamos, ibais, iban
ver—veía, veías, veía, veíamos, veíais, veían

3. **The Future:**

The future of regular verbs is formed by adding to the infinitive the ending *-é, -ás, -á, -emos, -éis, -án*:

hablar to speak	*comer* to eat	*vivir* to live
hablaré	*comeré*	*viviré*
hablarás	*comerás*	*vivirás*
hablará	*comerá*	*vivirá*
hablaremos	*comeremos*	*viviremos*
hablaréis	*comeréis*	*viviréis*
hablarán	*comerán*	*vivirán*

The future generally expresses a future action:

Lo compraré.	I'll buy it.
Iré mañana.	I'll go tomorrow.

Sometimes it expresses probability or conjecture:

¿Qué hora será?	What time can it be? What time do you think it must be?
Será la una.	It must be almost one.
Estará comiendo ahora.	He's probably eating now.

4. **The Preterite:**

There are two sets of preterite endings:

1. One set is used with the stem of Conjugation I *(-ar):*

2. The other set is used with the stem of Conjugation II *(-er)* and Conjugation III *(-ir):*

1.	2.
-é	*-í*
-aste	*-iste*
-ó	*-ió*
-amos	*-imos*
-asteis	*-isteis*
-aron	*-ieron*

The preterite expresses an action that began in the past and ended in the past:

El lo dijo.	He said it.
Habló conmigo.	He spoke with me.
Fuí allí.	I went there.
El nos vió.	He saw us.
Escribí una carta.	I wrote a letter.
Llovió todo el día.	It rained all day.
El tren se paró.	The train stopped.
Pasó tres años allí.	He spent three years there.
Lo ví.	I saw him (it).

5. The Present Perfect:

The present perfect is formed by adding the past participle to the present tense of *haber*. It is used to indicate a past action which continues into the present or which ended only recently:

Ha venido con su amigo.	He has come with his friend.
Nos ha escrito.	He has written to us.

6. The Pluperfect:

The pluperfect is formed by adding the past participle to the imperfect of *haber*. It translates the English pluperfect:

Ya habían llegado.	They had already arrived.

7. The Future Perfect:

The future perfect is formed by adding the past participle to the future of *haber*. It translates the English future perfect:

Habrán llegado para entonces.	They will have arrived by then.

Sometimes it indicates probability:

Habrán llegado ayer.	They probably arrived yesterday.

8. The Preterite Perfect[1]:

The preterite perfect, which is rather rare, is formed by adding the past participle to the preterite of *haber*. It is used to indicate that something has occurred immediately before some other action in the past:

Apenas hubo oído eso, se marchó.	No sooner had he heard that than he left.

29. THE SUBJUNCTIVE

The indicative simply makes a statement; the subjunctive indicates a certain attitude towards the statement—uncertainty, desire, emotion, etc. The subjunctive is used in subordinate clauses when the statement is unreal, doubtful, indefinite, subject to some condition or is affected by will, emotion, etc.

1. Forms

a. The subjunctive endings of the second and third conjugations are the same.

b. The present subjunctive is formed by adding the subjunctive endings to the stem of the first person singular, present indicative; the imperfect and future subjunctive, by adding the endings of the stem of the third person plural, preterite.

The subjunctive endings are as follows:

Conjugation I

PRES. SUBJ.:	*-e, -es, -e, -emos, -éis, -en*
IMPERF. SUBJ.:	*-ara, -aras, -ara, -áramos, -arais, -aran*
	Or—
	-ase, -ases, -ase, -ásemos, -aseis, -asen

[1] Also called "past anterior."

FUTURE SUBJ.: *(-are, -ares, -are, -áremos, -areis, -aren)*[1]

Conjugations II and III

PRES. SUBJ.: *-a, -as, -a, -amos, -áis, -an*

IMPERF. SUBJ.: *-iera, -ieras, -iera, -iéramos, -ierais, -ieran*

Or—

-iese, -ieses, -iese, -iésemos, -ieseis, -iesen

FUTURE SUBJ.: *(-iere, -ieres, -iere, -iéremos, -iereis, -ieren)*

EXAMPLES

	I	II	III
INFINITIVE:	*hablar*	*comer*	*vivir*
PRES. SUBJ.:	*hable*	*coma*	*viva*
IMPERF. SUBJ.:	*hablara*	*comiera*	*viviera*
	hablase	*comiese*	*viviese*
FUTURE SUBJ.:	*(hablare*	*comiere*	*viviere)*
	(hablare	*comiere*	*viviere)*

2. Uses

   a. The subjunctive is used with verbs of desire, request, suggestion, permission, approval and disapproval, judgment, opinion, uncertainty, emotion, surprise, fear, denial, etc.:

Quisiera verle.	I'd like to see him.
¡Ojalá que lo haga!	I wish he would do it!
¡Ojalá lo supiera!	I wish I knew it!
Temo que se lo diga él.	I'm afraid he may tell it to him.
No creo que él le haya visto.	I don't believe he's seen him.
Niega que le haya visto.	He denies that he's seen him.
Me sorprende mucho que él no lo haya hecho.	I'm greatly surprised that he hasn't done it.

[1] Forms in parentheses are rare.

Espero que no venga.	I hope he doesn't come.
Me alegro de que Ud. esté aquí.	I'm glad you're here!
Temo que esté enfermo.	I'm afraid he's sick.
Temo que no llegue a tiempo.	I'm afraid he won't (mayn't) come in time.
Duda que lo hagamos.	He doubts that we'll do it.
Dudo que sea verdad.	I doubt that it's true.
Dudo que sea posible.	I doubt whether it's possible.
No creo que lo sepa.	I don't think he knows it.
Se lo digo para que lo sepa.	I'm telling you so you may know it.

    b. The subjunctive is used in commands:

        1. Affirmative or negative commands in the polite form:

¡Abra usted la ventana!	Open the window!
¡No hablen ustedes ahora!	Don't talk now!

        2. Negative commands in the familiar form:

No me digas (tú).	Don't tell me!
No habléis ahora.	Don't talk now!

        3. Suggestions in which the speaker is included:

Leamos.	Let's read!
Entremos.	Let's go in!

        4. Indirect commands (that is, commands in the third person):

Que vaya él.	Let him go.
¡Viva España!	Long live Spain!
¡Que vengan!	Let them come!
¡Que entren!	Let them come in!
¡Que no venga!	Let him not come!

c. The subjunctive is used in conditional sentences which are contrary to fact:

Si estaba allí, yo no le ví.	If he was there, I didn't see him. *(Indicative)*
No iremos si llueve.	If it rains, we won't go. *(Indicative)*

But—

Si fuese él, lo haría.	If I were him (he), I'd do it.
Si fuera mío esto, lo vendería.	If this were mine, I'd sell it.
Si tuviera el dinero, lo compraría.	If I had the money, I'd buy it.
Aunque hubiese tenido dinero no hubiera ido.	Even if I had had the money I wouldn't have gone.
Si lo hubiera sabido, no habría venido.	If I had known it, I wouldn't have come.
Si hubiese estado aquí, habríamos ido.	If he had been here, we would have gone.
Aunque lo hubiese intentado no hubiera podido hacerlo.	Even if I would have tried, I wouldn't have been able to do it.

d. The subjunctive is used after impersonal verbs which do not express certainty:

Es menester que vengan.	It's necessary for them to come.
Es preciso que estén aquí.	It's necessary for them to be here.
Es necesario que Ud. venga.	It's necessary that you come.
Es posible que lo tenga.	It's possible that he has it.
Era lástima que no vinieran.	It was a pity that they didn't come.

e. The subjunctive is used after various conjunctive adverbs:

1. Certain conjunctive adverbs are always followed by the subjunctive because they never introduce statements of accomplished fact:

antes (de) que	before
a condición de	on condition that
aunque	even if
a (fin de) que	in order that
a menos que	unless
como si	as if
con tal (de) que	provided that, providing
dado que	granted that, given . . .
no obstante que	notwithstanding that
supuesto que	supposing that

2. Other conjunctive adverbs may or may not introduce a statement of accomplished fact. When they do, they take the indicative; otherwise the subjunctive:

a menos que	unless
a pesar de que	in spite of, notwithstanding
antes que	before
así que	as soon as
aunque	although, even though
con tal que	provided (that)
cuando	when
de manera que	so that
de modo que	so that
después (de) que	after
en cuanto	as soon as
hasta que	until
luego que	as soon as
mientras que	as long as, while
para que	in order that, so that
siempre que	provided that, whenever
Aunque él no lo quiera, se lo daré.	I'll give it to him even though he may not want it.

Lo compraré aunque me cueste mucho.	I'll buy it even if it costs me a lot.
Se lo digo para que lo sepa.	I'm telling you so that you may know it.
Aunque llueva mañana.	Although it may rain tomorrow.
Se fué sin que lo supiésemos.	He went away without our knowing it.
Iré con Ud. con tal que tenga tiempo.	I'll go with you provided I have time.
En caso que llegue.	In case he arrives.
Compare:	
Iremos aunque llueve.	We'll go even though it's raining.
Iremos aunque llueva.	We'll go even if it rains (even if it should rain).

f. The subjunctive is used when an indefinite antecedent is limited by an adjective (relative) clause:

No hay ningún hombre que entienda esto.	There is no man who understands this.
Busco a alguien que hable español.	I'm looking for someone who speaks Spanish.
No conozco a nadie que pueda hacerlo.	I don't know anyone who can do it (could do it).

g. The subjunctive is used after compounds of *-quiera* "-ever": *quienquiera* "whoever," *dondequiera* "wherever," *cualquier* "whatever," "whichever":

Quienquiera que sea.	Whoever he (it) may be.
El quiere hacer cualquier cosa que ella haga.	He wants to do whatever she does.
El quiere ir dondequiera que ella vaya.	He wants to go wherever she goes.

30. THE CONDITIONAL

1. The present conditional of all verbs is formed by adding to the infinitive the endings of the imperfect indicative of *haber*: *ía, ías, íamos, íais, ían*. It translates the English "would" or "should":

I	II	III
hablar to speak	*comer* to eat	*vivir* to live
hablaría	*comería*	*viviría*
hablarías	*comerías*	*vivirías*
hablaría	*comería*	*viviría*
hablaríamos	*comeríamos*	*viviríamos*
hablaríais	*comeríais*	*viriríais*
hablarían	*comerían*	*vivirían*

Sometimes it expresses probability or conjecture:

Serían las dos cuando él llegó.	It was probably about two o'clock when he arrived.
¿Qué hora sería?	What time could it have been?

2. The perfect conditional is formed by adding the past participle to the conditional of *haber*. It translates the English "would have" or "should have":

Habría hablado.	I would have spoken.
Habría ido	I would have gone.

3. If a sentence contains a clause beginning with *si* "if," the tense of the verb is determined by the tense of the verb in the main clause.

If the main clause has a verb in the:	The "if" clause has a verb in the:
Present	Present
Future	Present
Imperfect	Imperfect
Preterite	Preterite
Conditional	Past Subjunctive (-ra or -se)

Si está aquí, trabaja.	If he is here, he is working.
Si estaba aquí, trabajaba.	If he was here, he was working.
Si está aquí mañana, trabajará.	If he's here tomorrow, he'll be working.
Si estuviera aquí, trabajería.	If he were here, he'd be working.

A main verb indicating a condition contrary to fact may be in the -ra form of the subjunctive.

Si estuviera aquí, trabajara.	If he were here, he'd be working.

31. COMMANDS AND REQUESTS (THE IMPERATIVE)

There are two types of commands, one with tú *(vosotros)* and one with *usted (ustedes)*.

1. Familiar Commands *(Tú)*

    Familiar commands are used with people to whom you would say *tú*. The singular is the same as the third person singular of the present indicative:

¡Habla (tú)!	Speak!
¡Come (tú)!	Eat!
¡Sube (tú)!	Go up!

The plural is always formed by removing the -*r* of the infinitive and adding -*d:*

I

hablar to speak

SINGULAR: *¡Habla (tú)!*   Speak!
PLURAL: *¡Hablad (vosotros, -as)!*   Speak!

II

apprender to learn

SINGULAR: *¡Aprende (tú)!*   Learn!
PLURAL: *¡Aprended (vosotros, -as)!* Learn!

III

escribir to write

PLURAL: *¡Escribe (tú)!*   Write!
SINGULAR: *¡Escribid (vosotros, -as)!*   Write!

Common exceptions in the singular (the plural is always regular):

| | | IMPERATIVE | |
INFINITIVE		SINGULAR	PLURAL
ser	to be	*sé*	*sed*
decir	to say	*dí*	*decid*
ir	to go	*ve*	*id*
hacer	to do	*haz*	*haced*
poner	to put	*pon*	*poned*
tener	to hold	*ten*	*tened*
venir	to come	*ven*	*venid*

Familiar commands in the negative are in the present subjunctive:

SINGULAR

¡No hables!	Don't speak!
¡No me hables!	Don't talk to me!
¡No comas!	Don't eat!

PLURAL

¡No habléis!	Don't speak!
¡No comáis!	Don't eat!

Other Examples:

¡Háblame!	Speak to me!
¡Háblales!	Speak to them!
¡No les hables!	Don't speak to them!
¡Hablad!	Speak!
¡No habléis!	Don't speak!
¡Dame!	Give me!
¡No me des!	Don't give me!
¡Dímelo!	Tell it to me!
¡No me lo digas (tú)!	Don't tell it to me!
¡No me digas (tú) eso!	Don't tell me that!
¡Decídnoslo!	Tell it to us!
¡No nos lo digáis!	Don't tell it to us!
¡No estudiéis demasiado!	Don't study too much!

Notice that the object pronouns follow the affirmative imperative and precede the negative imperative.

2. Polite Commands *(Usted)*

Polite commands are used with people to whom you would say *usted* and are in the subjunctive. To make the subjunctive you change the ending of the third person present indicative to *a* if it is *e*, or to *e* if it is *a*.

INDICATIVE		SUBJUNCTIVE	
Habla.	He speaks.	*Hable Ud.*	Speak!
Come.	He eats.	*Come Ud.*	Eat!

The plural is formed by adding *n* to the singular:

¡Hablen Uds.!	Speak!
¡Coman Uds.!	Eat!
¡Desciendan Uds.!	Go down!

Other Examples:

¡Cómalo (Ud.)!	Eat it!
¡Venga (Ud.) a verme!	Come to see me!
¡Tómelo!	Take it!
¡Dígamelo!	Tell it to me!
¡Escríbame (Ud.) una carta!	Write me a letter!
¡Escríbamelo!	Write it to me!
¡Abra (Ud.) la ventana!	Open the window!

NEGATIVE

¡No hable Ud.!	Don't speak!
¡No lo coma Ud.!	Don't eat it!
¡No me lo diga Ud.!	Don't tell me!
¡No me escriba Ud.!	Don't write to me!
¡No hablen Uds. demasiado!	Don't talk too much!

The pronoun objects follow the affirmative imperative and are attached to it:

¡Léelo (tú)!	Read it!
¡Habladle!	Speak to him!
¡Véndamelo!	Sell it to me!
¡Dígamelo!	Tell it to me!

3. Indirect Commands

Indirect commands are in the subjunctive and are usually preceded by *que:*

¡Que entren!	Let them come in!
¡Qué él lo haga!	Let him do it!
¡Que lo haga Juan!	Let John do it!
¡Que le habla María!	Let Mary talk to him!
¡Que venga!	Let him come!
¡Que vaya él!	Let him go!
¡Que no venga!	Let him not come!
¡Viva España!	Long live Spain!
¡Dios guarde a nuestro país!	God keep our country!

4. "Let's" is expressed by the subjunctive:

¡Hablemos un rato!	Let's talk a while!
¡No hablemos!	Let's not talk!
¡Vayamos!	Let's go!
¡Esperemos!	Let's wait!

5. Imperative of Reflexive Verbs
The final *-d* of the plural is dropped when *-os* is added; that is, *"sentados"* becomes *sentaos:*

FAMILIAR FORM
SINGULAR

¡Siéntate!	Sit down!
¡Despiértate!	Wake up!
¡No te sientes!	Don't sit down!

PLURAL

¡Sentaos!	Sit down!
¡Despertaos!	Wake up!
(despertad + os)	
¡No os sentéis!	Don't sit down!

POLITE FORM
SINGULAR

¡Siéntese Ud.!	Sit down!
¡No se siente Ud.!	Don't sit down!

PLURAL

¡Siéntense Uds.!	Sit down *(pl.)*!
¡No se sienten!	Don't sit down!
¡Sentémonos!	Let's sit down!
(sentemos + nos)	

32. THE PARTICIPLE

1. The present participle (also called the "gerund") of Conjugation I is formed by dropping the *-ar* of the infinitive and adding *-ando;* the present participle of Conjugations II and III is

made by dropping the *-er (-ir)* and adding
-iendo:

	I		II
hablar	to speak	*comer*	to eat
hablando	speaking	*comiendo*	eating

	III
vivir	to live
viviendo	living

Pronoun objects are attached to the present
participle (in such cases the verb has a written
accent):

comprándolos	buying them
vendiéndomelo	selling it to me
dándoselo	giving it to him

The present participle is often used absolutely,
describing some action or state of being of the
subject of the sentence:

| *Durmiendo, no me oyeron.* | Since they were sleeping, they didn't hear me. They didn't hear me because they were sleeping. |
| *Estando cansandos, dormían.* | Being tired, they were sleeping. They were taking a nap because they were tired. |

2. The past participle is formed by adding *-ado* to
the stem of *-ar* verbs (that is, the infinitive
minus *-ar*) and *-ido* to the stem of *-er* and *-ir*
verbs:

	I		II
hablar	to speak	*comer*	to eat
hablado	spoken	*comido*	eaten

III

vivir	to live
vivido	lived

3. Irregular Participles
   The following are some of the commonest verbs
   with irregular present and past participles:

INFINITIVE		IRREGULAR PAST PARTICIPLE	IRREGULAR PRESENT PARTICIPLE
abrir	to open	*abierto*	
caer	to fall	*caído*	*cayendo*
creer	to believe	*creído*	*creyendo*
cubrir	to cover	*cubierto*	
decir	to say	*dicho*	*diciendo*
despedirse	to take leave of		*despidiéndose*
dormir	to sleep		*durmiendo*
escribir	to write	*escrito*	
hacer	to do, make	*hecho*	
ir	to go		*yendo*
leer	to read	*leído*	*leyendo*

INFINITIVE		IRREGULAR PAST PARTICIPLE	IRREGULAR PRESENT PARTICIPLE
morir	to die	*muerto*	*muriendo*
oir	to hear		*oyendo*
pedir	to ask for		*pidiendo*
poder	to be able to		*pudiendo*
poner	to put	*puesto*	
seguir	to follow		*siguiendo*
sentir	to feel		*sintiendo*
traer	to bring	*traído*	*trayendo*
venir	to come		*viniendo*
ver	to see	*visto*	
volver	to return	*vuelto*	

33. PROGRESSIVE TENSES

The Spanish progressive tenses are made up of the forms of *estar* plus the present participle. As in English, they denote a continuing action (that is, they describe the action as going on):

Estoy trabajando aquí.	I'm working here.
Estábamos leyendo un periódico.	We were reading a newspaper.
Estoy divirtiéndome.	I'm having a good time.
Está hablando.	He's speaking.
Estaba esperándome.	He was waiting for me.

34. PASSIVE VOICE

The passive voice is made up of the forms of *ser* plus the past participle:

La carta fué escrita por ella.	The letter was written by her.

The passive is used as in English. Very often, however, Spanish uses the reflexive where English uses the passive (see p. 70):

Aquí se habla inglés.	English is spoken here.

35. TO BE

There are two words in Spanish for "to be": *ser* and *estar*. In general *ser* indicates a permanent state (I'm an American); *estar* a temporary one (I'm tired).

SER	ESTAR	
yo soy	*yo estoy*	I am
tú eres	*tú estás*	you are
usted es	*usted está*	you are

él es	*él está*	he is
ella es	*ella está*	she is
ello es	*ello está*	it is
nosotros somos	*nosotros estamos*	we are
nosotras somos	*nosotras estamos*	we are
vosotros sois	*vosotros estáis*	you are
vosotras sois	*vosotras estáis*	you are
ustedes son	*ustedes están*	you are
ellos son	*ellos están*	they are
ellas son	*ellas están*	they are

SER

1. indicates a permanent condition or state:

Mi hermano es alto.	My brother is tall.

2. is used with a predicate noun, in which case it links two equal things:

El es médico.	He is a doctor.
Es escritor.	He's a writer.
Es español.	He's a Spaniard.

3. is used with an adjective to indicate an inherent quality.

El libro es rojo.	The book is red.
Ella es joven.	She is young.
El hielo es frío.	Ice is cold.
Es inteligente.	He's intelligent.
Es encantadora.	She's charming.

4. is used with pronouns:

Soy yo.	It's I.

5. indicates origin, source or material:

¿De dónde es Ud.?	Where are you from?
Soy de España.	I'm from Spain.
Es de madera.	It's made of wood.
Es de plata.	It's silver.

6. indicates possession:

¿De quién es esto?	Whose is this?
Los libros son del señor Díaz.	The books belong to Mr. Diaz.

7. is used in telling time:

Es la una.	It's one o'clock.
Son las dos.	It's two o'clock.
Son las nueve y diez.	It's ten past nine.

8. is used to indicate cost:

Son a quince centavos la docena.	They are fifteen cents a dozen.
Son a nueve dólares cada uno.	They are nine dollars each.

9. is used in impersonal constructions:

Es tarde.	It's late.
Es temprano.	It's early.
Es necesario.	It's necessary.
Es lástima.	It's a pity.
¿No es verdad?	Isn't it?

ESTAR

1. expresses position or location:

Está allí.	He's over there.
Está en México.	He's in Mexico.
Nueva York está en los Estados Unidos.	New York is in the United States.
Los Andes están en Sud América.	The Andes are in South America.
El Canal está en Panamá.	The Canal is in Panama.
¿Dónde está el libro?	Where's the book?
Está sobre la mesa.	It's on the table.

2. indicates a temporary quality or characteristic:

Ella está contenta.	She's pleased.
Estoy cansado.	I'm tired.
Estoy listo.	I'm ready.
El café está frío.	The coffee's cold.
Está claro.	It's clear.
La ventana está abierta (cerrada).	The window's open (shut).

3. is used to form the present progressive tense:

Están hablando.	They are talking.
Están caminando.	They are walking. They keep (on) walking.

4. is used in the expression "How are you?" etc.:

¿Cómo está Ud.?	How are you?
¿Cómo están ellos?	How are they?

Some adjectives may be used with either *ser* or *estar* with a difference in meaning.

El es malo.	He is bad.
El está malo.	He is sick.
Es pálida.	She has a pale complexion.
Está palida.	She is pale (at this moment).

	With *ser*	With *estar*
bueno	good	well, in good health
listo	clever	ready, prepared
cansado	tiresome	tired

THE FORMS OF THE REGULAR VERBS

A. CONJUGATIONS I, II, III

INDICATIVE AND CONDITIONAL

INFINITIVE	PRES. & PAST PARTICIPLES	PRESENT INDICATIVE	IMPERFECT	PRETERITE	FUTURE	CONDITIONAL	PRESENT PERFECT	PLUPERFECT	PRETERITE PERFECT
I. -ar ending hablar to speak	hablando hablado	hablo hablas habla hablamos habláis hablan	hablaba hablabas hablaba hablábamos hablabais hablaban	hablé hablaste habló hablamos hablasteis hablaron	hablaré hablarás hablará hablaremos hablaréis hablarán	hablaría hablarías hablaría hablaríamos hablaríais hablarían	he has ha + hablado hemos habéis han	había habías había + hablado habíamos habíais habían	hube hubiste hubo + hablado hubimos hubisteis hubieron
II. -er ending comer to eat	comiendo comido	como comes come comemos coméis comen	comía comías comía comíamos comíais comían	comí comiste comió comimos comisteis comieron	comeré comerás comerá comeremos comeréis comerán	comería comerías comería comeríamos comeríais comerían	he has ha + comido hemos habéis han	había habías había + comido habíamos habíais habían	hube hubiste hubo + comido hubimos hubisteis hubieron
III. -ir ending vivir to live	viviendo vivido	vivo vives vive vivimos vivís viven	vivía vivías vivía vivíamos vivíais vivían	viví viviste vivió vivimos vivisteis vivieron	viviré vivirás vivirá viviremos viviréis vivirán	viviría vivirías viviría viviríamos viviríais viviríanhan	he has ha + vivido hemos habéis han	había habías había + vivido habíamos habíais habían	hube hubiste hubo + vivido hubimos hubisteis hubieron

FUTURE PERFECT	CONDITIONAL PERFECT	PRESENT	IMPERFECT (-r-)	IMPERFECT (-s-)	PRESENT PERFECT	PLUPERFECT (-r-)	PLUPERFECT (-s-)	IMPERATIVE
habré	habría	hable	hablara	hablase	haya	hubiera	hubiese	¡Habla (tú)!
habrás	habrías	hables	hablaras	hablases	hayas	hubieras	hubieses	¡Hable (Ud.)!
habrá + hablado	habría + hablado	hable	hablara	hablase	haya + hablado	hubiera + hablado	hubiese + hablado	¡Hablemos (nosotros)!
habremos	habríamos	hablemos	habláramos	hablásemos	hayamos	hubiéramos	hubiésemos	¡Hablad (vosotros)!
habréis	habríais	habléis	hablarais	hablaseis	hayáis	hubierais	hubieseis	¡Hablen (Uds.)!
habrán	habrían	hablen	hablaran	hablasen	hayan	hubieran	hubiesen	
habré	habría	coma	comiera	comiese	haya	hubiera	hubiese	¡Come (tú)!
habrás	habrías	comas	comieras	comieses	hayas	hubieras	hubieses	¡Coma (Ud.)!
habrá + comido	habría + comido	coma	comiera	comiese	haya + comido	hubiera + comido	hubiese + comido	¡Comamos (nosotros)!
habremos	habríamos	comamos	comiéramos	comiésemos	hayamos	hubiéramos	hubiésemos	¡Comed (vosotros)!
habréis	habríais	comáis	comierais	comieseis	hayáis	hubierais	hubieseis	¡Coman (Uds.)!
habrán	habrían	coman	comieran	comiesen	hayan	hubieran	hubiesen	
habré	habría	viva	viviera	viviese	haya	hubiera	hubiese	¡Vive (tú)!
habrás	habrías	vivas	vivieras	vivieses	hayas	hubieras	hubieses	¡Viva (Ud.)!
habrá + vivido	habría + vivido	viva	viviera	viviese	haya + vivido	hubiera + vivido	hubiese + vivido	¡Vivamos (nosotros)!
habremos	habríamos	vivamos	viviéramos	viviésemos	hayamos	hubiéramos	hubiésemos	¡Vivid (vosotros)!
habréis	habríais	viváis	vivierais	vivieseis	hayáis	hubierais	hubieseis	¡Vivan (Uds.)!
habrán	habrían	vivan	vivieran	viviesen	hayan	hubieran	hubiesen	

B. RADICAL CHANGING VERBS

1. Group I: *-ar* and *-er* verbs only

a) Change the *o* to *ue* when stress falls on root (ex: *contar, volver*).
b) Change the *e* to *ie* when stress falls on root (ex: *pensar, perder*).

INFINITIVE*	PRESENT INDICATIVE	PRESENT SUBJUNCTIVE	IMPERATIVE	SIMILARLY CONJUGATED VERBS		
contar(ue) to count	cuento cuentas cuenta contamos contáis cuentan	cuente cuentes cuente contemos contéis cuenten	cuenta contad	acordar acordarse acostarse almorzar apostar aprobar	avergonzar avergonzarse colgar costar encontrar jugar (*u* to *ue*)	probar recordar recordarse sonar soñar volar
volver(ue) to return	vuelvo vuelves vuelve volvemos volvéis vuelven	vuelva vuelvas vuelva volvamos volváis vuelvan	vuelve volved	devolver doler dolerse llover morder mover	oler soler	

pensar(ie) to think	pienso piensas piensa pensamos pensáis piensan	piense pienses piense pensemos penséis piensen	piensa pensad	acertar apretar calentar cerrar confesar despertar	empezar encerrar gobernar plegar quebrar sentarse	temblar tentar
perder(ie) to lose	pierdo pierdes pierde perdemos perdéis pierden	pierda pierdas pierda perdamos perdáis pierdan	pierde perded	ascender atender defender descender encender entender	extender tender	

*In all the other tenses, these verbs are conjugated like all other regular verbs.

287

B. RADICAL CHANGING VERBS

2. Group II: -ir verbs only

a) Change o to ue when stress falls on root (ex: *dormir*).
b) Change o to u when stress falls on ending (ex: *dormir*—present subj. only).
c) Change e to ie when stress falls on root (ex: *sentir*).
d) Change e to i when stress falls on ending (ex: *sentir*—present subj. only).

INFINITIVE*	PRESENT INDICATIVE	PRESENT SUBJUNCTIVE	IMPERATIVE	SIMILARLY CONJUGATED VERBS
dormir to sleep	duermo duermes duerme dormimos dormís duermen	duerma duermas duerma durmamos durmáis duerman	duerme dormid	morir (past parti.: *muerto*)
sentir to feel	siento sientes siente sentimos sentís sienten	sienta sientas sienta sintamos sintáis sientan	siente sentid	advertir herir arrepentirse mentir consentir preferir convertir presentir diferir referir divertir sugerir

*In all the other tenses, these verbs are conjugated like all other regular verbs.

3. Group III: -ir verbs only

Change *e* to *i* when stress falls on root (ex: *pedir*)

INFINITIVE†	PRESENT INDICATIVE	PRESENT SUBJUNCTIVE	PRETERITE INDICATIVE	IMPERFECT SUBJUNCTIVE	IMPERATIVE	SIMILARLY CONJUGATED VERBS	
pedir to ask	pido pides pide pedimos	pida pidas pida pidamos	pedí pediste pidió pedimos	pidiera (-se) pidieras (-ses) pidiera (-se) pidiéramos (-semos)	pide pedid	competir conseguir corregir	expedir reír repetir
	pedís piden	pidáis pidan	pedisteis pidieron	pidierais (-seis) pidieran (-sen)		despedir despedirse elegir	seguir servir vestir

†In all the other tenses, these verbs are conjugated like all other regular verbs.

289

C. REGULAR VERBS
WITH SPELLING CHANGES

1. VERBS ENDING IN -car

Example: buscar to look for

Verbs ending in *-car; c* changes to *qu* when followed by *e.* This occurs in:

1. the first person singular of the preterite
2. all persons of the present subjunctive

PRETERITE INDICATIVE	PRESENT SUBJUNCTIVE
busqué	*busque*
buscaste	*busques*
buscó	*busque*
buscamos	*busquemos*
buscasteis	*busquéis*
buscaron	*busquen*

Verbs conjugated like *buscar:*

acercar	to place near	*sacrificar*	to sacrifice
educar	to educate	*secar*	to dry
explicar	to explain	*significar*	to signify, mean
fabricar	to manufacture	*tocar*	to touch, play
indicar	to indicate		(music)
pecar	to sin	*verificar*	to verify
sacar	to take out		

2. VERBS ENDING IN -gar

Example: *pagar* to pay

Verbs ending in *-gar: g* changes to *gu* when followed by *e.* This occurs in:

1. the first person singular of the preterite indicative

2. all persons of the present subjunctive

PRETERITE INDICATIVE	PRESENT SUBJUNCTIVE
pagué	*pague*
pagaste	*pagues*
pagó	*pague*
pagamos	*paguemos*
pagasteis	*paguéis*
pagaron	*paguen*

Verbs conjugated like *pagar:*

ahogar	to drown	*investigar*	to investigate
apagar	to extinguish	*juzgar*	to judge
arriesgar	to risk	*llegar*	to arrive
cargar	to load	*obligar*	to compel
castigar	to punish	*otorgar*	to grant
congregar	to congregate	*pegar*	to hit
entregar	to deliver	*tragar*	to swallow

3. VERBS ENDING IN -*guar*

Example: averiguar to ascertain, investigate

Verbs ending in -*guar: gu* changes to *gü* when followed by *e*. This occurs in:

1. the first person singular of the preterite indicative

2. all persons of the present subjunctive

PRETERITE INDICATIVE	PRESENT SUBJUNCTIVE
averigüé	*averigüe*
averiguaste	*averigües*
averiguó	*averigüe*
averiguamos	*averigüemos*
averiguasteis	*averigüéis*
averiguaron	*averigüen*

Verbs conjugated like *averiguar:*

aguar	to water, dilute
atestiguar	to attest

4. VERBS ENDING IN -zar

Example: *gozar* to enjoy

Verbs ending in -*zar*: *z* changes to *c* when followed by *e*. This occurs in:

1. the first person singular of the preterite indicative
2. all persons of the present subjunctive

PRETERITE INDICATIVE	PRESENT SUBJUNCTIVE
gocé	*goce*
gozaste	*goces*
gozó	*goce*
gozamos	*gocemos*
gozasteis	*gocéis*
gozaron	*gocen*

Verbs conjugated like *gozar*:

abrazar	to embrace	*organizar*	to organize
alcanzar	to reach	*rechazar*	to reach
cruzar	to cross	*rezar*	to pray
enlazar	to join	*utilizar*	to utilize

5. VERBS ENDING IN -ger

Example: *coger* to catch

Verbs ending in -*ger*: *g* changes to *j* when followed by *o* or *a*. This occurs in:

1. the first person singular of the present indicative
2. all persons of the present subjunctive

PRESENT INDICATIVE	PRESENT SUBJUNCTIVE
cojo	*coja*
coges	*cojas*
coge	*coja*
cogemos	*cojamos*
cogéis	*cojáis*
cogen	*cojan*

Verbs conjugated like *coger:*

acoger	to welcome	*proteger*	to protect
escoger	to choose, select	*recoger*	to gather

6. VERBS ENDING IN -*gir*

Example: *dirigir* to direct

Verbs ending in -*gir: g* changes to *j* when followed by *o* or *a*. This occurs in:

1. the first person singular of the present indicative
2. all persons of the present subjunctive

dirijo	*dirija*
diriges	*dirijas*
dirige	*dirija*
dirigimos	*dirijamos*
dirigís	*dirijáis*
dirigen	*dirijan*

Verbs conjugated like *dirigir:*

afligir	to afflict	*rugir*	to roar
erigir	to erect	*surgir*	to come forth
exigir	to demand		

7. VERBS ENDING IN-*guir*

Example: *distinguir* to distinguish

Verbs ending in -*guir: gu* changes to *g* when followed by *o* or *a*. This occurs in:

1. the first person singular of the present indicative
2. all persons of the present subjunctive

PRESENT INDICATIVE	PRESENT SUBJUNCTIVE
distingo	*distinga*
distingues	*distingas*
distingue	*distinga*

distinguimos	*distingamos*
distinguís	*distingáis*
distinguen	*distingan*

Verbs conjugated like *distinguir*:

conseguir	to get, obtain	*perseguir*	to persecute
extinguir	to extinguish	*seguir*	to follow

8. VERBS ENDING IN -cer, -cir

(Preceded by a vowel)

Examples: *conocer* to know   *lucir* to shine

Some verbs ending in *-cer, -cir,* preceded by a vowel, change *c* to *zc* before *o* or *a*. This occurs in:

1. the first person singular of the present indicative
2. all persons of the present subjunctive

conozco	*conozca*	*luzco*	*luzca*
conoces	*conozcas*	*luces*	*luzcas*
conoce	*conozca*	*luce*	*luzca*
conocemos	*conozcamos*	*lucimos*	*luzcamos*
conocéis	*conozcáis*	*lucís*	*luzcáis*
conocen	*conozcan*	*lucen*	*luzcan*

Verbs conjugated like *conocer*:

aborrecer	to hate	*desaparecer*	to disappear
acaecer	to happen	*desobedecer*	to disobey
acontecer	to happen	*desvanecer*	to vanish
agradecer	to be grateful	*embellecer*	to embellish
amanecer	to dawn	*envejecer*	to grow old
anochecer	to grow dark	*fallecer*	to die
aparecer	to appear	*favorecer*	to favor
carecer	to lack	*merecer*	to merit
compadecer	to pity	*nacer*	to be born
complacer	to please	*obedecer*	to obey
conducir	to conduict	*ofrecer*	to offer
crecer	to grow	*oscurecer*	to grow dark

padecer	to suffer	*placer*	to please
parecer	to seem	*reconocer*	to recognize
permanecer	to last	*traducir*	to translate
pertenecer	to belong to		

9. VERBS ENDING IN -*cer*
(Preceded by a Consonant)

Example: *vencer* to conquer

Verbs ending in -*cér*, preceded by a consonant: *c* changes to *z* when followed by *e* or *a*. This occurs in:

1. the first person singular of the present indicative
2. all persons of the present subjunctive

PRESENT INDICATIVE	PRESENT SUBJUNCTIVE
venzo	*venza*
vences	*venzas*
vence	*venza*
vencemos	*venzamos*
vencéis	*venzáis*
vencen	*venzan*

Verbs conjugated like *vencer:*

convencer to convince   *ejecer* to exercise

10. VERBS ENDING IN -*uir*
(But not -*guir* and -*quir*)

Example: *construir* to build

Verbs ending in -*uir*, except those ending in -*guir* or *quir*, add *y* to the stem of the verb before *a, e, o*. This occurs in:

1. all persons of the present indicative (except the first and second familiar persons plural)
2. all persons of the present and imperfect subjunctive
3. the imperative singular *(tú)*
4. third singular and plural of the preterite

PRESENT INDICATIVE	PRESENT SUBJUNCTIVE
construyo	*construya*
construyes	*construyas*
construye	*construya*
construimos	*construyamos*
construís	*construyáis*
construyen	*construyan*

(*i* between two other vowels changes to *y*)

PRETERITE INDICATIVE	IMPERFECT SUBJUNCTIVE
construí	*construyera (se)*
construiste	*construyeras (ses)*
construyó	*construyera (se)*
construimos	*construyéramos (semos)*
construisteis	*construyerais (seis)*
construyeron	*construyeran (sen)*

IMPERATIVE

construye
construid

Verbs conjugated like *construir:*

atribuir	to attribute	*huir*	to flee
constituir	to constitute	*influir*	to influence
contribuir	to contribute	*instruir*	to instruct
destituir	to deprive	*reconstruir*	to rebuild
destruir	to destroy	*restituir*	to restore
distribuir	to distribute	*substituir*	to substitute
excluir	to exclude		

11. VERBS LIKE *Creer*

Creer to believe

In verbs whose stem ends in *e*, the *i* of the regular endings beginning with *-ie, ió*, becomes *y*. This occurs in:

1. the present participle *creyendo*.

2. the third person singular and plural of the preterite indicative

3. both forms of the imperfect subjunctive

PRETERITE INDICATIVE	IMPERFECT SUBJUNCTIVE
creí	*creyera (se)*
creíste	*creyeras (ses)*
creyó	*creyera (se)*
creímos	*creyéramos (semos)*
creísteis	*creyerais (seis)*
creyeron	*creyeran (sen)*

Verbs conjugated like creer:

caer	to fall (irregular)	*leer*	to read
construir	to build	*poseer*	to possess

12. VERBS LIKE *Reír*

Reír to laugh

In verbs whose stem ends in *i*, the *i* of the regular endings, *-ie*, *-ió*, is dropped to avoid two *i*'s. This occurs in:

1. the present participle *riendo*

2. the third person singular and plural of the preterite indicative

3. all persons of both forms of the imperfect subjunctive

PRETERITE INDICATIVE	IMPERFECT SUBJUNCTIVE
reí	*riera (se)*
reiste	*rieras (ses)*
rió	*riera (se)*

reímos	*riéramos (semos)*
reísteis	*rierais (seis)*
rieron	*rieran*

Verbs conjugated like *reír; sonreír* to smile.

13. VERBS ENDING IN -*ller*, -*llir*, -*ñer*, -*ñir*

Example: *tañer* to toll

Present Participle: *tañendo*

PRETERITE INDICATIVE	IMPERFECT SUBJUNCTIVE
tañí	*tañera (se)*
tañiste	*tañeras (ses)*
tañó	*tañera (se)*
tañimos	*tañéramos (semos)*
tañisteis	*tañerais (seis)*
tañeron	*tañeran (sen)*

In verbs whose stem ends in *ll* or *ñ*, the *i* of the regular endings beginning with -*ie*, -*ió* is dropped. This occurs in:

1. the present participle
2. the third person singular and plural of the preterite indicative
3. all persons of both forms of the imperfect subjunctive

Verbs conjugated like *tañer:*

bullir	to boil	*gruñir*	to growl

14. VERBS ENDING IN -*iar*, -*uar*

Examples: *enviar* to send *continuar* to continue

PRES. IND.	PRES. SUBJ.	PRES. IND.	PRES. SUBJ.
envío	*envíe*	*continúo*	*continúe*
envías	*envíes*	*continúas*	*continúes*
envía	*envíe*	*continúa*	*continúe*

enviamos	*enviemos*	*continuamos*	*continuemos*
enviáis	*enviéis*	*continuáis*	*continuéis*
envían	*envíen*	*continúan*	*continúen*

IMPERATIVE

envía	*continúa*
enviad	*continuad*

Some verbs ending in *-iar* or *-uar* take a written accent over the *i* or the *u* of the stem. There is no definite rule.

1. in all persons of the present indicative (except the first plural and second plural familiar).
2. in all persons of the present subjunctive (except the first plural and the second plural familiar).
3. in the singular of the imperative *(tú)*.

Verbs conjugated like *enviar:*

confiar	to trust	*desconfiar*	to distrust
criar	to bring up	*fiar*	to give credit
desafiar	to challenge	*guiar*	to guide

Verbs conjugated like *continuar:*

actuar	to act	*evaluar*	to evaluate
efectuar	to carry out	*perpetuar*	to perpetuate

THE FORMS OF THE IRREGULAR VERBS*

INFINITIVE, PRESENT AND PAST PARTICIPLES	PRESENT INDICATIVE	PRESENT SUBJUNCTIVE	IMPERFECT	PRETERITE	FUTURE	CONDITIONAL	IMPERATIVE
andar "to walk" andando andado	ando andas anda andamos andáis andan	ande andes ande andemos andéis anden	andaba andabas andaba andábamos andabais andaban	anduve anduviste anduvo anduvimos anduvisteis anduvieron	andaré andarás andará andaremos andaréis andarán	andaría andarías andaría andaríamos andaríais andarían	anda andad
caber "to fit," "to be contained in" cabiendo cabido	quepo cabes abe cabemos cabéis caben	quepa quepas quepa quepamos quepáis quepan	cabía cabías cabía cabíamos cabíais cabían	cupe cupiste cupo cupimos cupisteis cupieron	cabré cabrás cabrá cabremos cabréis cabrán	cabría cabrías cabría cabríamos cabríais cabrían	cabe cabed
caer "to fall" cayendo caído	caigo caes cae caemos caéis caen	caiga caigas caiga caigamos caigáis caigan	caía caías caía caíamos caíais caían	caí caíste cayó caímos caísteis cayeron	caeré caerás caerá caeremos caeréis caerán	caería caerías caería caeríamos caeríais caerían	cae caed
conducir "to lead," "to drive" conduciendo conducido	conduzco conduces conduce conducimos conducís conducen	conduzca conduzcas conduzca conduzcamos conduzcáis conduzcan	conducía conducías conducía conducíamos conducíais conducían	conduje condujiste condujo condujimos condujisteis condujeron	conduciré conducirás conducirá conduciremos conduciréis conducirán	conduciría conducirías conduciría conduciríamos conduciríais conducirían	conduce conducid

300

dar "to give" dando dado	Pres. Ind.	Pres. Subj.	Imperfect	Preterite	Future	Conditional	Imperative
	doy	dé	daba	di	daré	daría	da
	das	des	dabas	diste	darás	darías	dad
	da	dé	daba	dió	dará	daría	
	damos	demos	dábamos	dimos	daremos	daríamos	
	dais	déis	dabais	disteis	daréis	daríais	
	dan	den	daban	dieron	darán	darían	
decir "to say," "to tell" diciendo dicho	digo	diga	decía	dije	diré	diría	di
	dices	digas	decías	dijiste	dirás	dirías	decid
	dice	diga	decía	dijo	dirá	diría	
	decimos	digamos	decíamos	dijimos	diremos	diríamos	
	decís	digáis	decíais	dijisteis	diréis	diríais	
	dicen	digan	decían	dijeron	dirán	dirían	
estar "to be" estando estado	estoy	esté	estaba	estuve	estaré	estaría	está
	estás	estés	estabas	estuviste	estarás	estarías	estad
	está	esté	estaba	estuvo	estará	estaría	
	estamos	estemos	estábamos	estuvimos	estaremos	estaríamos	
	estáis	estéis	estabais	estuvisteis	estaréis	estaríais	
	están	estén	estaban	estuvieron	estarán	estarían	
haber "to have" (auxiliary) habiendo habido	he	haya	había	hube	habré	habría	
	has	hayas	habías	hubiste	habrás	habrías	
	ha	haya	había	hubo	habrá	habría	
	hemos	hayamos	habíamos	hubimos	habremos	habríamos	
	habéis	hayáis	habíais	hubisteis	habréis	habríais	
	han	hayan	habían	hubieron	habrán	habrían	

*To form compound tenses, use the appropriate form of *haber* together with the past participle of the irregular verb.

THE FORMS OF THE IRREGULAR VERBS*

INFINITIVE, PRESENT AND PAST PARTICIPLES	PRESENT INDICATIVE	PRESENT SUBJUNCTIVE	IMPERFECT	PRETERITE	FUTURE	CONDITIONAL	IMPERATIVE
hacer "to do," "to make" *haciendo* *hecho*	hago haces hace hacemos hacéis hacen	haga hagas haga hagamos hagáis hagan	hacía hacías hacía hacíamos hacíais hacían	hice hiciste hizo hicimos hicisteis hicieron	haré harás hará haremos haréis harán	haría harías haría haríamos haríais harían	haz haced
ir "to go" *yendo* *ido*	voy vas va vamos vais van	vaya vayas vaya vayamos vayáis vayan	iba ibas iba íbamos ibais iban	fui fuiste fué fuimos fuisteis fueron	iré irás irá iremos iréis irán	iría irías iría iríamos iríais irían	ve id
oír "to hear" *oyendo* *oído*	oigo oyes oye oímos oís oyen	oiga oigas oiga oigamos oigáis oigan	oía oías oía oíamos oíais oían	oí oíste oyó oímos oísteis oyeron	oiré oirás oirá oiremos oiréis oirán	oiría oirías oiría oiríamos oiríais oirían	oye oíd
poder "to be able," "can" *pudiendo* *podido*	puedo puedes puede podemos podéis pueden	pueda puedas pueda podamos podáis puedan	podía podías podía podíamos podíais podían	pude pudiste pudo pudimos pudisteis pudieron	podré podrás podrá podremos podréis podrán	podría podrías podría podríamos podríais podrían	puede poded

	Present	Pres. Subj.	Imperfect	Preterite	Future	Conditional	Imperative
poner "to put," "to place" *poniendo* *puesto*	pongo pones pone ponemos ponéis ponen	ponga pongas ponga pongamos pongáis pongan	ponía ponías ponía poníamos poníais ponían	puse pusiste puso pusimos pusisteis pusieron	pondré pondrás pondrá pondremos pondréis pondrán	pondría pondrías pondría pondríamos pondríais pondrían	pon poned
querer "to want," "to love" *queriendo* *querido*	quiero quieres quiere queremos queréis quieren	quiera quieras quiera queramos queráis quieran	quería querías quería queríamos queríais querían	quise quisiste quiso quisimos quisisteis quisieron	querré querrás querrá querremos querréis querrán	querría querrías querría querríamos querríais querrían	quiere quered
reír "to laugh" *riendo* *reído*	río ríes ríe reímos reís ríen	ría rías ría riamos riáis rían	reía reías reía reíamos reíais reían	reí reíste rió reímos reísteis rieron	reiré reirás reirá reiremos reiréis reirán	reiría reirías reiría reiríamos reiríais reirían	ríe reíd
saber "to know" *sabiendo* *sabido*	sé sabes sabe sabemos sabéis saben	sepa sepas sepa sepamos sepáis sepan	sabía sabías sabía sabíamos sabíais sabían	supe supiste supo supimos supisteis supieron	sabré sabrás sabrá sabremos sabréis sabrán	sabría sabrías sabría sabríamos sabríais sabrían	sabe sabed

THE FORMS OF THE IRREGULAR VERBS*

INFINITIVE, PRESENT AND PAST PARTICIPLES	PRESENT INDICATIVE	PRESENT SUBJUNCTIVE	IMPERFECT	PRETERITE	FUTURE	CONDITIONAL	IMPERATIVE
salir "to go out," "to leave" *saliendo* *salido*	salgo sales sale salimos salís salen	salga salgas salga salgamos salgáis salgan	salía salías salía salíamos salíais salían	salí saliste salió salimos salisteis salieron	saldré saldrás saldrá saldremos saldréis saldrán	saldría saldrías saldría saldríamos saldríais saldrían	sal salid
ser "to be" *siendo* *sido*	soy eres es somos sois son	sea seas sea seamos seáis sean	era eras era éramos erais eran	same as preterite of *ir.*	seré serás será seremos seréis serán	sería serías sería seríamos seríais serían	sé sed
tener "to have" *teniendo* *tenido*	tengo tienes tiene tenemos tenéis tienen	tenga tengas tenga tengamos tengáis tengan	tenía tenías tenía teníamos teníais tenían	tuve tuviste tuvo tuvimos tuvisteis tuvieron	tendré tendrás tendrá tendremos tendréis tendrán	tendría tendrías tendría tendríamos tendríais tendrían	ten tened

	Present	Present Subjunctive	Imperfect	Preterite	Future	Conditional	Imperative
traer "to bring" *trayendo* *traído*	traigo traes trae traemos traéis traen	traiga traigas traiga traigamos traigáis traigan	traía traías traía traíamos traíais traían	traje trajiste trajo trajimos trajisteis trajeron	traeré traerás traerá traeremos traeréis traerán	traería traerías traería traeríamos traeríais traerían	trae traed
valer "to be worth" *valiendo* *valido*	valgo vales vale valemos valéis valen	valga valgas valga valgamos valgáis valgan	valía valías valía valíamos valíais valían	valí valiste valió valimos valisteis valieron	valdré valdrás valdrá valdremos valdréis valdrán	valdría valdrías valdría valdríamos valdríais valdrían	val valed
venir "to come" *viniendo* *venido*	vengo vienes viene venimos venís vienen	venga vengas venga vengamos vengáis vengan	venía venías venía veníamos veníais venían	vine viniste vino vinimos vinisteis vinieron	vendré vendrás vendrá vendremos vendréis vendrán	vendría vendrías vendría vendríamos vendríais vendrían	ven venid
ver "to see" *viendo* *visto*	veo ves ve vemos veis ven	vea veas vea veamos veáis vean	veía veías veía veíamos veíais veían	vi viste vió vimos visteis vieron	veré verás verá veremos veréis verán	vería verías vería veríamos veríais verían	ve ved

ANSWERS
TO DRILLS AND EXERCISES
AND QUIZZES

ANSWERS
LESSON 41

Drills and Exercises

II. 1. Acabamos de llegar.
We have just arrived.

2. Los niños tienen ganas de comer.
The children want to eat.

3. Ustedes pueden hacerlo
You can do it.

4. Las muchachas están contentas de verlos.
The girls are happy to see them.

5. Lo podemos hacer ahora.
We can do it now.

III. 1. El acaba de entrar.
2. Ella acaba de comer.
3. Tenemos ganas de ir al cine.
4. Tengo ganas de bailar.
5. Puedo hacerlo ahora.
6. Podemos verle mañana.
7. Ellos podrán ir allá.
8. Estoy contento de verle a usted.
9. Estamos sorprendidos de oirlo.
10. Están contentos de saberlo.

Quiz

1. ¿Quién habla?
Who's speaking?

2. ¡Qué gusto!
What a pleasure!

3. ¡Qué manera más agradable de empezar el día!
What an agreeable way to begin the day!

4. Espero que hayan hecho buen viaje.
I hope that you have had a good trip.

5. Vimos a Miguel en el Café Gijón.
   We saw Michael at the Café Gijón.

6. Estabamos aquí todo el día.
   We were here all day.

7. Hay muchos monumentos en Madrid.
   There are many monuments in Madrid.

8. ¿Quiere usted sentarse aquí?
   Do you want to sit down here?

9. El señor tiene tanto dinero.
   The man has so much money.

10. Acabamos de llegar.
    We have just arrived.

LESSON 42

Drills and Exercises

II. 1. Ellos saben bailar.
   They know how to dance.

2. Ustedes conocerán a los señores Perez.
   You must know Mr. and Mrs. Perez.

3. Hay unas clases por la tarde.
   There are some classes in the afternoon.

4. Me hacen falta unas pesetas.
   I need some pesetas.

5. ¿Quiénes son los medicos?
   Who are the doctors?

III. 1. ¿Sabe usted el número?
   2. Ellos saben bailar.
   3. Había muchos desfiles.
   4. ¿Cuál de estos libros quiere usted?
   5. ¿Quiénes son esos hombres en la esquina?

6. ¿Qué necesita usted? ¿Qué le hace falta a usted?
7. ¿Saben la dirección?
8. ¿Quién conoce a María?
9. Les hacen falta muchas clases. Necesitan muchas clases.
10. Nos hace falta más tiempo. Necesitamos más tiempo.

Quiz

1. Estoy seguro que ellos conocen a María.
   I'm sure they know Mary.

2. Me dijeron que ellos sabían el titulo del libro.
   They told me that they knew the title of the book.

3. Me hace falta un libro nuevo.
   I need a new book.

4. Hay una revista muy buena que sale el lunes.
   There is a very good magazine which comes out on Monday.

5. No me dijo cuál de estas novelas es mejor.
   He didn't tell me which one of these novels is better.

6. En este lado hay muchos periódicos extranjeros.
   On this side there are many foreign newspapers.

7. Es interesante esta revista alemana.
   This German magazine is interesting.

8. Este librito debe ser lo que quieren ustedes.
   This little book must be what you want.

9. Ellos tienen ganas de ir a la fiesta.
   They feel like going to the party.

10. Este libro le da a usted muchos informes.
    This book gives you a great deal of information.

LESSON 43

Drills and Exercises

II. 1. No me lo diga.
   Don't say it to me.

2. No te vayas.
   Don't go away.

3. No se lo ponga.
   Don't put it on.

4. No te lo quites.
   Don't take it off.

5. No me lo compres.
   Don't buy it for me.

III. 1. Trabajo más que Juan.
   2. Viajarán más de tres horas hoy.
   3. Tenemos más de diez páginas que leer.
   4. Van a comprar un coche neuvo.
   5. Va a descansar mañana.
   6. Ibamos a vender la casa.
   7. ¿Quiere usted ver al médico?
   8. Quiere darme el libro.
   9. No se lo mande (a él).
   10. Ellos no quieren marcharse.

Quiz

1. Usted encontrará el listín allí.
   You will find the telephone book there.

2. Tenemos más dinero que ellos.
   We have more money than they do.

3. Quieren mandarle el libro.
   They want to send the book to him.

4. Tenía que entrar en la cabina.
   He had to go into the cabin.

5. Dígale que estoy en Madrid.
   Tell him that I am in Madrid.

6. Puedo poner una conferencia con Madrid.
   I can make a long-distance call to Madrid.

7. ¿Sabe usted el número?
   Do you know the number?

8. No se lo diga.
   Don't tell it to him.

9. Mándenoslo usted mañana.
   Send it to us tomorrow.

10. Ellos quieren mandarlos en seguida.
    They want to send them at once.

LESSON 44

Drills and Exercises

II. 1. Ellos tienen que verlo mañana.
   They have to see it (or him) tomorrow.

   2. Nosotros tendremos que levantarnos temprano.
   We will have to get up early.

3. Ellas están lavando los platos.
   They are washing the dishes.

4. Vosotros tenéis que leer las novelas.
   You have to read the novels.

5. Ustedes me dieron treinta pesetas por los libros.
   You gave me thirty peśetas for the books.

III. 1. Juan compró el coche para su esposa.
   2. Pagaron treinta pesetas por los billetes.
   3. Tenemos que marcharnos en seguida.
   4. Están escribiendo cartas ahora.
   5. ¿Cuánto quiere usted por el traje?
   6. Tiene que pasar por el parque para llegar al
      museo.
   7. Le dieron doscientas pesetas para pagar el
      viaje.
   8. Estaban esuchando la radio cuando llegué.
   9. Para ver bien, hay que estar en la primera fila.
   10. Miguel tiene que comprar un libro nuevo.

Quiz

1. Juan cree que tenemos que ir al banco.
   John thinks that we have to go to the bank.

2. Paca pagó el billete.
   Paco paid for the ticket.

3. Hace cuarenta kilómetros por hora.
   It does forty kilometers per hour.

4. Los vimos andando por la calle.
   We saw them walking along the street.

5. Nosotros estabamos sentados en la terraza.
   We were sitting on the terrace.

6. Juan está leyendo el periódico.
   John is reading the newspaper.

7. Esta propina es para el camarero.
   This tip is for the waiter.

8. Ella tiene que comprar el traje.
   She has to buy the suit.

9. No sé lo que quieren.
   I don't know what they want.

10. Ellos van a los mismos sitios que nosotros.
    They are going to the same places we are.

LESSON 45

Drills and Exercises

II. 1. Usted no se acuerda de María.
   You don't remember Mary.

2. Hace una semana que Juan no está aquí.
   John hasn't been here for a week.

3. Teresa no tiene que llamar al médico.
   Theresa doesn't have to call the doctor.

4. No se come bien en este restaurante.
   The food isn't any good in this restaurant.

5. Ellos no se acuerdan del viaje.
   They don't remember the trip.

III. 1. Hace un mes que están aquí.
   2. Tiene que llamar al médico.
   3. Me acuerdo muy bien de usted.
   4. Hace dos horas que duermo.
   5. Se come bien en este restaurante.
   6. No veo a María.
   7. Podemos sentarnos a descansar un rato.
   8. Tenemos ganas de andar.
   9. Tiene que volver a la derecha.
   10. Vamos a visitar el museo.

Quiz

1. Estoy aquí hace dos años.
   I have been here for two years.

2. Ellos viven en Madrid hace tres meses.
   They have been living in Madrid for three months.

3. ¿Hace cuánto tiempo que está usted aquí?
   How long have you been here?

4. Aquí se habla ruso.
   Russian is spoken here.

5. Se encuentran muchos anuncios en el periódico.
   One finds many ads in the newspaper.

6. Creo que ellos se acuerdan de la fecha.
   I think that they remember the date.

7. Esta es una fiesta en la que se conoce a mucha gente simpática.
   This is a party at which one meets many nice people.

8. ¿Conoce usted a mi amigo?
   Do you know my friend?

9. Hace tres años que están en Nueva York.
   They have been in New York for three years.

10. Hace una hora que espero.
    I have been waiting for an hour.

LESSON 46

Drills and Exercises

II. 1. Ella va a comprárselo.
   She is going to buy it for him.

   2. Ellos quieren mandárselo (a él).
   They want to send it to him.

   3. Nosotros podemos regalárselos (a ella).
   We can give them to her.

   4. Tu prefieres pedírselo.
   You prefer to ask him for it.

   5. Tenéis que enviárselo (a ellos).
   You have to send it to them.

III. 1. Quieren dármelo.
   2. Usted tendrá que pedírselo a él.
   3. Queremos mandárselo a ellos.
   4. Tendrá que ponérselo.
   5. Nos gusta viajar por España.
   6. Aquí los tiene usted. Aquí están.
   7. Te gusta el helado.
   8. Voy a buscárselo.
   9. ¿Quiere usted llevar el paquete?
   10. Podemos mandárselo, si quiere.

Quiz

   1. Aquí los tiene usted.
   Here they are.

   2. Quiere dármelos ahora.
   He wants to give them to me now.

   3. Dámelo.
   Give it to me.

4. Los tenemos de todas clases.
   We have them in all styles.

5. Aquí lo tiene usted.
   Here it is.

6. Voy a buscarle el paquete.
   I am going to look for the package for you.

7. Quiero comprar un vestido de seda.
   I want to buy a silk dress.

8. ¿Es demasiado caro? Creo que lo es.
   Is it too expensive? I think it is.

9. Aquí lo tiene usted.
   Here it is. (Here you are.)

10. ¿Quiere usted mandármelas?
    Do you want to send them to me?

LESSON 47

Drills and Exercises

II. 1. Se lo digo al volver.
   I will tell it to you when you return.

2. Juan me lo da.
   John gives it to me.

3. Usted tiene razón.
   You are right.

4. Vengo por la mañana.
   I am coming in the morning.

5. Ellos pueden dártelo.
   They can give it to you.

III. 1. ¿Dónde estarán los billetes?
   2. Habrán ido a casa.

3. Al entrar, él nos saludó. El nos saludó al entrar.
4. Usted puede pagarlo al salir.
5. Creo que él tiene razón.
6. Se lo doy a usted mañana.
7. ¡Qué guapo estás!
8. Le hace falta un corte de pelo.
9. Estás más bonita que nunca.
10. ¿Le gusta el color?

Quiz

1. Será difícil.
   It must be difficult.

2. Usted puede dármelo al salir.
   You can give it to me when you leave.

3. Creo que siempre tienes razón.
   I think you are always right.

4. ¿Quién será?
   Who can it be?

5. La señora está aquí al lado en la peluquería.
   The lady is right next door in the beauty shop.

6. Creo que voy mañana.
   I think that I'm going tomorrow.

7. Claro que usted empezó una hora antes que yo.
   Of course you began an hour before I did.

8. Le gusta tener razón siempre.
   You always like to be right.

9. Nos saludamos al llegar al hotel.
   We say hello upon arriving at the hotel.

10. Hay algo más.
    There is something else.

LESSON 48

Drills and Exercises

II. 1. Nosotros somos actores.
       We are actors.

    2. Ellos están en los Estados Unidos.
       They are in the United States.

    3. Ustedes son de México.
       You are from Mexico.

    4. Vosotros estáis cansados.
       You are tired.

    5. Ellas están en la sala.
       They are in the living room.

III. 1. ¿A qué hora empieza la función?
     2. ¡Qué gusto de verle otra vez!
     3. Acabo de comprar este vestido.
     4. Es una comedia muy divertida.
     5. Vi una película el miércoles pasado.
     6. No me acuerdo del título.
     7. Va a volver a empezar. Va a empezar otra
        vez.
     8. Un amigo mío fue a ver la comedia.
     9. Le gustó a ella.
    10. Vamos a entrar en seguida.

Quiz

    1. ¡Qué hermosa es la vida!
       How beautiful life is!

    2. Usted lo encuentra siempre.
       You always find it.

    3. Ellos dicen que pueden ir mañana.
       They say that they can go tomorrow.

4. ¡Qué día mas agradable!
   What a pleasant day!

5. Parece que él es un hombre muy importante.
   It seems that he is a very important man.

6. Yo lo entiendo todo.
   I understand it all.

7. Juana les cuenta una historia todos los días.
   Jane tells them a story every day.

8. ¿Dónde estará el libro?
   Where can the book be?

9. El hermano de Juan era el héroc.
   John's brother was the hero.

10. ¡Qué placer me da verles aquí!
    What a pleasure it gives me to see you here!

LESSON 49

Drills and Exercises

II. 1. No escribo nunca a nadie.
   I don't write anything to anyone.

   2. No me escribe nadie.
      No one writes to me.

   3. No compramos nunca nada.
      We never buy anything.

   4. Juan y José no van nunca a ninguna parte.
      John and Joe never go anywhere.

   5. No he visto nunca a tanta gente en el museo.
      I've never seen so many people in the museum.

III. 1. Hay tanta gente aquí.
   2. Lo explicó tan claramente que lo comprendí todo.
   3. Nunca he estado tan ocupado.
   4. Usted estará cansado. Usted debe estar cansado.
   5. Juan y María deben estudiar más.
   6. No quiero verla nunca. Nunca quiero verla.
   7. ¡Qué alargadas parecen todas las figuras!
   8. Tenemos que hacer un viaje a Toledo.
   9. ¿Cuándo podemos hacerlo?
   10. Quiero ver la famosa pintura.

Quiz

1. Es tan difícil comprenderlo.
   It's so difficult to understand it.

2. No le veo nunca.
   I don't ever see him.

3. Creo todo lo que me dice Juan.
   I believe everything that John tells me.

4. Juan ha comprado todos los libros que quería.
   John bought all the books that he wanted.

5. ¡Roberto tiene tanto tiempo libre!
   Robert has so much free time!

6. No quiero nada ahora.
   I don't want anything now.

7. Me parece que yo debo levantarme ahora.
   It seems to me that I ought to get up now.

8. No he tenido nunca tantos problemas.
   I haven't ever had so many problems.

9. No le debo nada.
   I don't owe you anything.

10. Nunca ha leído libros tan difíciles.
    He has never read such difficult books.

LESSON 50

Drills and Exercises

II. 1. No pienso nunca en el viaje.
       I don't ever think about the trip.

2. No vamos al museo el lunes.
   We are not going to the museum on Monday.

3. No le gusta comprar todo lo que ve.
   He doesn't like to buy everything he sees.

4. Los niños no comieron todo el helado.
   The children didn't eat all the ice cream.

5. No es difícil comprenderlo.
   It's not difficult to understand it.

III. 1. Nos han hablado tanto del museo.
2. Se dice que es más divertido el domingo.
3. Podemos acompañarte mañana.
4. Hay que saber regatear.
5. No debes dar la impresión de ser rico.
6. Se conoce todo el trabajo de aquella fábrica por el estilo.
7. Se lo puedo dejar todo a muy buen precio.
8. Eso depende de lo que quiere decir.
9. Todos los cuadros son caros.
10. Debe tenerlos envueltos ahora.

Quiz

1. Le veo todos los martes.
   I see him every Tuesday.

2. He pasado toda la tarde en la piscina.
   I spent all afternoon in the swimming pool.

3. Juan estaba leyendo todo el día.
   John was reading all day.

4. Voy a verle el domingo.
   I am going to see him on Sunday.

5. Usted cree todo lo que él le dice.
   You believe everything that he says.

6. Normalmente voy a visitarle todos los sábados.
   Normally I go to visit him every Saturday.

7. El miércoles, vamos a ir de compras.
   On Wednesday, we are going to go shopping.

8. Nunca pienso en ella ahora.
   I never think about her now.

9. Siempre oigo todas las noticias por radio.
   I always hear all the news on the radio.

10. Yo no estaba pensando en comprarlo.
    I wasn't thinking of buying it.

LESSON 51

Drills and Exercises

II. 1. Lo compras para él.
   You are buying it for him.

2. Los señores Andrade hacen el viaje conmigo.
   Mr. and Mrs. Andrade are making the trip with me.

3. No le veo jamás contigo.
   I never see him with you.

4. Ellos me lo regalan a mí.
   They are giving it to me.

5. El cuadro es para usted.
   The picture is for you.

III. 1. Prefiero comprar aquella máquina en la otra tienda.
   2. Debemos comprar por lo menos dos rollos de película en color.
   3. Podemos sacar unas fotos maravillosas de aquel parque.
   4. ¿Le gusta la vista con aquel edificio en el fondo?
   5. Quieren sacar una foto de usted.
   6. No se olvide de quitar la tapa de los lentes.
   7. Tenemos que hacer copias para nuestros amigos.
   8. Querían ir a aquel museo el domingo.
   9. Tenemos que comprar más película en blanco y negro.
   10. ¡Cree usted que le guste aquel traje?

Quiz

1. Van a ir conmigo.
   They are going to go with me.

2. Déselo a él.
   Give it to him.

3. No me gustan aquellas lámparas. Dame dos de éstas.
   I don't like those lamps. Give me two of these.

4. La novela que más me gusta es ésa que tienes en la mano.
   The novel that I like best is that one that you have in your hand.

5. Esta alfombra es muy bonita pero recuerdas aquélla que vimos ayer.

This carpet is very pretty, but you remember that one that we saw yesterday.

6. Dicen que hay que estudiar mucho.
   They say that one must study a great deal.

7. Tenemos que llevar todos estos papeles a casa.
   We have to take all of these papers home.

8. La historia es muy interesante. Pablo no me contó todo eso.
   The story is very interesting. Paul didn't tell me all that.

9. Hay muchas cosas que leer.
   There are many things to read.

10. Juan no me explicó todo el problema.
    John didn't explain the whole problem to me.

LESSON 52

Drills and Exercises

II. 1. Ellos no quieren ningún coche.
   They don't want any car.

2. Ellas no han comprado ningún regalo.
   They didn't buy any gift.

3. Esperamos que Juan llegue a tiempo.
   We hope that John arrives on time.

4. Ellas quieren que Teresa estudie esta noche.
   They want Theresa to study tonight.

5. Preferimos que usted se vaya.
   We prefer that you go away.

III. 1. Quieren que veamos la película.
   2. Deseamos que tengan un buen viaje.

3. Juan quiere que usted compre película de color.
4. No hay dinero en esta chaqueta.
5. Se dice que es un gran hotel.
6. (El) Era un gran poeta.
7. No me dé usted un libro cualquiera.
8. ¿Quiere usted que ellos lo hagan?
9. (El) Era un gran amigo.
10. Temo que no pueda irse ahora.

Quiz

1. Me alegro de que haga tan buen tiempo.
   I am happy that it is such nice weather.

2. ¿Ha terminado usted el primer capítulo?
   Have you finished the first chapter?

3. Espero que nos veamos algun día.
   I hope that we see each other some day.

4. Juan no tiene ningún dinero.
   John doesn't have any money.

5. Es un hombre muy bueno.
   He's a very good man.

6. No me dé usted un libro cualquiera.
   Don't give me just any book.

7. Es una gran idea.
   It's a great idea.

8. Espero que te gusten las habitaciones.
   I hope that you like the rooms.

9. Prefieren que nosotros lo hagamos ahora.
   They prefer that we do it now.

10. Juan quiere que vayamos.
    John wants us to go.

LESSON 53

Drills and Exercises

II. 1. Se lo pedimos cuando lleguen.
    We are going to ask them for it when they arrive.

   2. Me cobran trescientas pesetas por hora.
    They are charging me 300 pesetas per hour.

   3. Ellos me lo dan para que lo estudie.
    They are giving it to me so that I will study it.

   4. No hay fiesta mañana.
    There is no fiesta tomorrow.

   5. Juan lo compra para dármelo.
    John is buying it to give it to me.

III. 1. Le recomiendo que vaya a buscar el coche a la fábrica.
   2. En cuanto al dinero, se lo daré (a él) cuando venga.
   3. Cuando lleguen, Juan se lo dirá.
   4. María puede marcharse cuando quiera.
   5. Incluirán un porta-equipajes.
   6. ¿Cuánto cuesta la gasolina por litro?
   7. Llévese todos los folletos que quiera.
   8. Cuando haya escogido el modelo que quiere, vaya a la fábrica.
   9. No hay impuestos sobre los precios de fábrica, ¿verdad?
   10. ¿Quiere usted conocer a un gran amigo mío?

Quiz

   1. En cuanto a la gasolina, hay suficiente.
    As for the gasoline, there is enough.

2. Cuando lleguen, vamos a darles el regalo.
   When they arrive, we are going to give them
   the gift.

3. Usted puede hacerlo cuando quiera.
   You can do it whenever you want.

4. Hace ciento veinte kilómetros por hora.
   It does 120 kilometers per hour.

5. Voy a decirle el número a Juan, para que lo
   sepa.
   I am going to tell the number to John so that
   he'll know it.

6. Hay que decírselo para que vengan pronto.
   One must tell it to them so that they will come
   at once.

7. Escríbale los detalles para que lo comprenda
   bien.
   Write him the details so that he will understand
   it well.

8. Hay que anunciarles el examen para que estu
   dien.
   One must announce the examination to them so
   they will study.

9. Dásela a María para que la lea.
   Give it to Mary so she will read it.

10. Yo siempre les trato bien cuando estén aquí.
    I always treat them well whenever they are
    here.

LESSON 54

Drills and Exercises

II. 1. No me quedan ningunas pesetas.

I don't have any pesetas left.

2. ¿No quiere usted algunos periódicos?
Don't you want some newspapers?

3. Ellos no tienen ningunas dificultades.
They don't have any difficulties.

4. No queríamos comprar ningunas revistas.
We didn't want to buy any magazines.

5. No me dieron ningunos papeles.
They didn't give me any papers.

III. 1. Creo que dejé unas cuantas cartas allí.
   2. El oyó unos ruidos raros.
   3. Eche un poco de agua en el radiador.
   4. Acabo de comprar algunos sellos (postales).
   5. ¿Quiere usted volver a las cinco?
   6. Haga usted sólo lo necesario.
   7. Haremos todo lo que podamos.
   8. Lo bueno es que llegamos temprano.
   9. Estoy seguro que le gustará el coche.
  10. Lo malo del asunto es que ellos no nos comprenden.

Quiz

1. Les voy a enviar unos programas del concierto.
I am going to send them some programs of the concert.

2. No me ha dado ningún dinero.
He didn't give me any money.

3. Me gustan las novelas románticas. ¿Tiene usted algunas?
I like romantic novels. Do you have any?

4. Voy a decírselo algún día.
I am going to tell it to him someday.

5. Eso precisamente es lo imposible del caso.
   That is precisely the impossible part of the matter.

6. No se lo ha dicho a ninguno de sus amigos.
   He didn't tell it to any of his friends.

7. Querían vender unos cuantos vestidos.
   They wanted to sell some dresses.

8. Me gustó la comedia. Las primeras escenas fueron lo mejor de la obra.
   I liked the comedy. The first scenes were the best (thing) in the play.

9. ¿Le ha dado algún dinero?
   Did you give him any money?

10. Les he explicado lo más difícil.
    I have explained to them the most difficult part.

LESSON 55

Drills and Exercises

II. 1. Ellos vinieron hace un año.
    They came a year ago.

2. Ella me escribió hace un mes.
   She wrote me a month ago.

3. Jorge se casó hace dos días.
   George got married two days ago.

4. Hoy es el quince de agosto. María se marchó hace trece días.
   Today is the fifteenth of August. Mary left thirteen days ago.

5. Me mandaron el libro hace un año.
   They sent me the book a year ago.

III. 1. Hay tantos turistas que pasan por Port Bou.
2. ¿Van a quedarse en Francia mucho tiempo?
3. Creía que sería mejor el martes.
4. Hay que abrir las maletas.
5. Todos los papeles están en orden.
6. Dígale que espere un momento.
7. Espero verle en el viaje de vuelta.
8. Fue mucho más fácil la última vez.
9. Creo que nos tomaron por criminales.
10. No hable usted de eso, por favor.

Quiz

1. Juan llamó hace una hora.
   John called an hour ago.

2. Nuestros amigos llegaron hace unas horas.
   Our friends arrived a few hours ago.

3. Dígale que espere.
   Tell him to wait.

4. El dice que lo puede hacer fácilmente.
   He says that he can do it easily.

5. Lo hizo Juan hace mucho tiempo.
   John did it a long time ago.

6. Dígales que vengan.
   Tell them to come.

7. Los señores Andrade llegaron hace unos días.
   Mr. and Mrs. Andrade arrived a few days ago.

8. El jefe me lo dijo claramente.
   The boss told it to me clearly.

9. Dígale a María que escriba.
   Tell Mary to write.

10. ¿Tienen ustedes algo que declarar?
Do you have anything to declare?

LESSON 56

Drills and Exercises

II. 1. ¿Se saludan Juan y José siempre que se vean?
Do John and Joseph say hello whenever they see each other?

2. ¿Está buscando Rafeal una secretaria que hable inglés?
Is Raphael looking for a secretary who speaks English?

3. ¿Van ellos a esperar hasta que lleguemos?
Are they going to wait until we arrive?

4. ¿Conoce usted a alguien que trabaje bien?
Do you know anyone who works well?

5. ¿Lo dirá María en cuanto lo sepa?
Will Mary say it as soon as she knows it?

III. 1. Voy a buscar un libro que me guste.
2. No conocen a nadie que escriba poesía.
3. Juan esperará hasta que lleguemos.
4. ¿Se ven siempre ustedes en París?
5. ¿Me escribirá usted cuando llegue a Nueva York?
6. Dudo que estén aquí.
7. No creemos que Juan lo sepa.
8. Juan no cree que María venga.
9. El busca un banco que tenga sucursal en Madrid.
10. En cuanto lo compre, se lo enseñaré.

Quiz

1. No creo que María esté aquí.
   I don't think Mary is here.

2. Es imposible que ellos hagan tal cosa.
   It's impossible for them to do such a thing.

3. No hay ninguno que pueda hacerlo.
   There is no one who can do it.

4. Quiero encontrar una casa que tenga siete habitaciones.
   I want to find a house that has seven rooms.

5. Es imposible que ella crea la historia.
   It's impossible for her to believe the story.

6. Niegan que sea verdad.
   They deny that it's true.

7. Tenemos que esperar hasta que Juan hable.
   We have to wait until John speaks.

8. En cuanto ellos lo tengan, se lo mandarán a usted.
   As soon as they have it, they will send it to you.

9. Nos vemos todos los días.
   We see each other every day.

10. Busco una bolsa que sea bastante grande.
    I am looking for a purse that is large enough.

LESSON 57

Drills and Exercises

II. 1. Acostémonos.
   Let's go to bed.

2. Comprémoslo.
   Let's buy it.

3. No lo dígamos.
   Let's not say it.

4. Lleguemos a tiempo.
   Let's arrive on time.

5. Estudiémoslo.
   Let's study it.

III. 1. Si Juan estuviera aquí, le daría el libro.
   2. Si ellos tuvieran tiempo, irían a Barcelona.
   3. Si María estuviera en París, compraría el vestido.
   4. Si llueve, no iremos al teatro.
   5. Si ellos nos ven, les hablaremos.
   6. Si usted turiera el coche, llegaríamos a tiempo.
   7. Vamos a ir a la tienda.
   8. No nos levantemos temprano mañana.
   9. Busquemos el libro la semana que viene.
   10. No se lo demos a Juan.

Quiz

1. Si yo fuera usted, no lo haría.
   If I were you I wouldn't do it.

2. Juan ganaría mucho más si trabajara más.
   John would earn a lot more if he worked harder.

3. Yo se lo daría a los señores Andrade si estuvieran aqui.
   I would give it to Mr. and Mrs. Andrade if they were here.

4. Si ellos leyeran el periódico, sabrían lo que ha pasado.

If they read the newspaper, they would know what has happened.

5. Levantémonos temprano mañana.
Let's get up early tomorrow.

6. No leamos el periódico esta mañana.
Let's not read the newspaper this morning.

7. No les decimos nada si llegan tarde.
We won't say anything to them if they arrive late.

8. No queremos ir al campo si llueve.
We don't want to go to the country if it rains.

9. Hablemos de lo que tenemos que hacer.
Let's talk about what we have to do.

10. Permítame contar las palabras.
Let me count the words.

LESSON 58

Drills and Exercises

II. 1. No tengo más que tres hermanos.
I have only three brothers.

2. No me cobraron más que cien pesetas.
They charged me only 100 pesetas.

3. No hay más que cinco profesores.
There are only five professors.

4. No compraron más que cinco maletas.
They only bought five suitcases.

5. No murieron más que veinte soldados.
Only twenty soldiers died.

III. 1. Tienen un coche mejor.

2. Somos mayores que ellos.
3. Este vestido es más caro.
4. Este jabón lava más blanco.
5. La tela que compré es más suave.
6. Juana es la muchacha más bonita de la clase.
7. El es mi hijo menor.
8. Es la mejor revista del mundo.
9. No puedo escribir más.
10. El es más inteligente que su hermano mayor.

Quiz

1. No quiero estudiar más.
   I don't want to study anymore.

2. Juan es mucho más fuerte que José.
   John is much stronger than Joe.

3. Este edificio es bastante más grande.
   This building is quite a bit bigger.

4. Es el edificio más grande de la ciudad.
   It's the biggest building in the city.

5. No creo que tenga más de veinte pesetas.
   I don't think I have more than twenty pesetas.

6. No me dieron más que treinta dolares.
   They didn't give me more than thirty dollars.

7. Esta lección es más fácil que la otra.
   This lesson is easier than the other one.

8. Ella es más inteligente que su hermana.
   She is more intelligent than her sister.

9. El profesor les dijo que hablaran más fuerte.
   The professor told them that they should speak more loudly.

10. Es mi hermana menor.
    She is my younger sister.

LESSON 59

Drills and Exercises

II. 1. Ellos siempre mandan los mismos periódicos.
They always send the same newspapers.

2. El compra la misma crema de afeitar que Juan.
He buys the same shaving cream as John.

3. Tú recibes el mismo premio que yo.
You receive the same prize as I do.

4. Cuando mi padre recibe su máquina (de escribir) nueva, me da la vieja.
When my father receives a new typewriter, he gives me the old one.

5. Juan no escucha el mismo programa que yo.
John isn't listening to the same program as I am.

III. 1. Me gusta tu coche pero el mío es mejor.
2. Compramos el mismo disco que María.
3. Juan siempre va a la misma escuela que su hermano.
4. Cuando perdió su libro le dí el mío.
5. Compraron entradas en la misma fila que las nuestras.
6. Juan y yo fuimos al mismo teatro que tú.
7. Yo tenía mi paraguas pero Juan perdió el suyo.
8. Compré unos dulces. ¿Quieres algunos?
9. ¿Quiere usted darme algunas pesetas?
10. ¿Dónde están las suyas?

Quiz

1. Estos discos son los mismos que tengo yo.
These records are the same ones that I have.

2. Me gusta este coche más que el mío.
   I like this car better than mine.

3. Esta es mi pluma. ¿Dónde está la tuya?
   This is my pen. Where is yours?

4. Me gusta esta casa. La nuestra es más pequeña.
   I like this house. Ours is smaller.

5. Me pidió el libro porque había perdido el suyo.
   He asked me for the book because he had lost his.

6. Puedes llevar estos lápices aunque me quedan muy pocos.
   You can take these pencils, although I have very few left.

7. Veo que hay muchas revistas. Voy a comprar algunas.
   I see that there are many magazines. I am going to buy some.

8. Tengo las mismas preocupaciones que tú.
   I have the same worries as you.

9. Aquí están mis maletas. ¿Dónde están las tuyas?
   Here are my suitcases. Where are yours?

10. Tu sombrero es muy bonito y me gusta el suyo también.
    Your hat is very pretty, and I like hers too.

LESSON 60

Drills and Exercises

II. 1. Era posible que vinieran Juan y José.
   It was possible that John and Joe came.

2. Lo dijo para que lo supiéramos.

He said it so that we would know it.

3. Esperaba que lo hicieran inmediatamente.
   I hoped that they would do it immediately.

4. Dudaba que Juan lo oyera.
   I doubted that John heard it.

5. María sentía que ellos lo creyeran.
   Mary was sorry that they believed it.

III. 1. Siento que él esté aquí.
   2. El sintió que yo lo hiciera.
   3. ¡Ojalá él estuviera aquí!
   4. ¡Que lo hagan ellos!
   5. El más informado nos habló.
   6. Lo dijeron para que él lo supiera.
   7. Es imposible que ellos lo crean.
   8. El dudaba que lo supiéramos.
   9. Ellos querían que compráramos el libro.
   10. El jefe me dijo que lo hiciera. (El jefe me
       mandó hacerlo.)

Quiz

1. Me gustaría hablar con la más informada.
   I would like to talk to the best-informed girl.

2. Tenían que ayudar a los heridos.
   They had to help the wounded.

3. Que él lo escriba.
   Have him write it.

4. Fué imposible que ellos vendieran el coche.
   It was impossible for them to sell the car.

5. Sentía que Juan no pudiera venir.
   I was sorry that John couldn't come.

6. Quería que ellos fueran al cine.
   I wanted them to go to the movies.

7. Que lo haga Juan.
   Let John do it.

8. De todos los empleados, Rafael es el preferido.
   Of all the employees, Raphael is the preferred man.

9. Querían que el jefe lo dijera.
   They wanted the boss to say it.

10. Dicen que soy muy inteligente. ¡Ojala!
    They say that I am very intelligent. I hope so!